# BE AN EFFECTIVE
# COMMUNICATOR—NOW

Whether you want to advance in your career, improve your grades in school, or just enjoy the wealth of words in the English language, *The New American Three-Step Vocabulary Builder* is an invaluable tool. Covering topics ranging from basic terms of finance to common foreign words to names of people and places, this guide offers an easy-to-use program to help you build your vocabulary and pronounce words correctly. In just minutes a day, you will gain a better understanding of the origins and development of the most diverse words in the English language. There's no better time than right now to start becoming a more effective speaker, reader, and writer—and there's no better guide than *The New American Three-Step Vocabulary Builder*.

**MARY DE VRIES** is a specialist in communication and word usage. She is the author of 50 books, many of which deal with vocabulary development and other aspects of language skills. Formerly a college instructor, she also taught writing and communication skills to organizational clients for many years. She has written *How to Run a Meeting, The New American Dictionary of Abbreviations, The New Roberts Rules of Order,* and *The New Handbook of Letter Writing,* all available in Signet editions from Penguin Putnam.

# THE
# NEW AMERICAN
# THREE-STEP
# VOCABULARY
# BUILDER

---

*How to Supercharge
Your Vocabulary in
Just Minutes a Day*

# Mary A. De Vries

A SIGNET BOOK

SIGNET
Published by the Penguin Group
Penguin Putnam Inc., 375 Hudson Street,
New York, New York 10014, U.S.A.
Penguin Books Ltd, 27 Wrights Lane,
London W8 5TZ, England
Penguin Books Australia Ltd, Ringwood,
Victoria, Australia
Penguin Books Canada Ltd, 10 Alcorn Avenue,
Toronto, Ontario, Canada M4V 3B2
Penguin Books (N.Z.) Ltd, 182–190 Wairau Road,
Auckland 10, New Zealand

Penguin Books Ltd, Registered Offices:
Harmondsworth, Middlesex, England

First published by Signet, an imprint of Dutton Signet,
a member of Penguin Putnam Inc.

First Printing, March, 1998
10  9  8  7  6  5  4  3  2  1

 REGISTERED TRADEMARK—MARCA REGISTRADA

Printed in the United States of America

# Contents

# 1. Discover the Power of Words

*For most of us, a treasure of words is far more practical and useful than a treasure of jewels that glitter.*

This is a book about our endless hunger for one of the greatest treasures in the civilized world—words. These jewels of modern society tease and tempt us to acquire more and more of them. When he have plenty of them, we feel protected, confident, and prepared to face life's challenges. When we have too few of them, we feel naked, insecure, and fearful of failure.

Yes, words really do have that much power over us. But they also *give* us power. It's a fair exchange. But you already know that, don't you? Otherwise, you wouldn't be looking for a way to improve and expand your vocabulary. Like many of us, you don't seriously believe that your vocabulary is adequate to take you to the end of your days on earth.

The reasons for wanting to have a more powerful vocabulary may differ. But regardless of the reason, most of us share a strong desire to have a large stock of words. We want to have access to the benefits and opportunities that a superior vocabulary offers.

Some people who want to pump up their word power may have their eyes on a promotion or salary increase. They realize how important it is to communicate skillfully with their bosses, coworkers, and clients or customers. Others may have their eyes on public relations, political, or other opportunities where words and their delivery are crucial to success. Still others may have their eyes on a writing career or other position that requires the extensive word supply and enhanced verbal skills of a wordsmith.

Some of us, however, may simply want to be better informed. We want to be able to participate more effectively and enjoyably in our social and home lives. We don't want to be show-offs. But we wouldn't mind being able to impress others with our dynamic vocabulary. Especially, we'd like to be able to find the words we need to make our points clearly, forcefully, and convincingly. We'd also like to avoid the embarrassment of using words incorrectly and the frustration of not being able to find the right word when we most need it.

## Building a Powerful Vocabulary

*The New American Three-Step Vocabulary Builder* was developed to offer an interesting and enjoyable path to a bigger and better vocabulary. Consisting of 51 exercises, it's a three-steps-per-exercise program designed to supercharge your vocabulary in just minutes a day.

Each of the vocabulary-building chapters follows the same general plan. New words to be learned are always introduced in groups of ten, usually with ten new words per exercise. Most exercises consist of three easy steps to follow in learning the ten words.

Step 1.    Define the word
Step 2.    Double-check the meaning
Step 3.    Reinforce your understanding

Usually, when the ten words in an exercise are first introduced, the pronunciation of each one is given in parentheses immediately after the word. Most of the time, at least one of the three steps in an exercise involves writing out the word. This gives you an opportunity to practice spelling the word, which reinforces the learning process. The aim in each case is to ensure that before you leave an exercise, you've had a chance to pronounce the word, learn its definition, and write and spell it.

Because of the way the program is designed, you can decide how much time you want to spend each day. For example, each of the three steps in an exercise requires an *average* of three minutes. Because of the difference in complexity of some topics, certain steps require less time, and others take more time.

If you're really rushed, you may decide to do only one step. Otherwise, you may want to do all three steps and complete the exercise. You may even decide to do more than one exercise. Except in chapters involving technical subjects, the three steps of an exercise can usually be completed in ten minutes or less. However, you may find that you like to work faster. Or you may prefer a slower pace to be certain that you're absorbing everything. It's up to you.

Fourteen chapters have exercises, with two to six exercises per chapter. Chapter 2 has no exercises but, rather, consists of some *preliminary* tests. These tests are designed to preview the upcoming exercises and check your current vocabulary level. They'll give you a chance to grade yourself and find out where you stand *before* you begin the exercises.

Chapters 3 through 16 are the main vocabulary-building chapters, with a variety of verbal workouts. The words in these chapters cover a wide range of topics and include new words, old words, unusual words, foreign words, and both specialized and non-specialized words.

A section called "Bonus Words" follows the exercises in Chapters 3 through 16. It consists of additional words not given in the preceding exercises and their meanings—a final chance for you to stockpile extra terms concerning the subject of the chapter.

Chapter 17 consists of a series of *final* tests, reviewing the various topics and the words that you learned throughout the book. In it you can grade yourself and find out how much you've retained from the previous chapters.

A variety of tests are used in the book. They include fill-in-the-blank, matching, multiple-choice, and true-false tests. They're not given in any particular order. At any time we may switch from a fill-in to a true-false test or from a multiple-choice to a matching or other type of test. But regardless, each test will have ten items or questions, and most will have an answer section at the end.

Each of the fourteen vocabulary-building chapters ends with a review test. This test draws on all words learned up to that point in the book. After the answer section it has a place where you can write the number of correct and incorrect answers that you give in the test and compute your score. Since there are always ten questions in a review test, you can easily judge how well you're doing.

For example, if you have five out of ten correct answers, your score is 50 percent. If you have eight out of ten correct answers, your score is 80 percent. Most of us would obviously like to score better than

50 percent (average) and as close to 100 percent as possible (more about scores in Chapter 2).

The words, pronunciations, exercises, tests, and other items were all evaluated by a teacher and word specialist, Alice Hubbard, in Newbury Park, California. She additionally timed and scored all of the tests from beginning to end. Also, the exercises, bonus words, and various tests have all been tried out on others. The test takers found that most tests with words about nonspecialized topics, such as words that describe, take one to two minutes each. Review tests, however, sometimes take two to three minutes longer.

The tests in the chapters on specialized topics, such as law or health, may take several minutes longer than those on nonspecialized topics. The tests in Chapter 11 deal with the process of forming new words by adding prefixes and suffixes to existing words. Because these tests involve more steps than usual, they also may take a few minutes longer than the regular tests.

In our trial run, the longest time taken on any test was six minutes. The shortest time was less than a minute.

In addition to test taking, pronunciation is of special interest to many people. Later in this chapter you'll find a guide to pronunciation that will answer your questions about that subject. Be sure to read this material before you begin the exercises.

Another area of concern involves the definitions. Many of you may be nervously wondering if they're going to be hard or easy to learn. If you hate long, complex descriptions, you'll be happy to discover that each word is defined as briefly as possible.

Have you heard of the military's *KISS principle*? It means "*K*eep *i*t *s*imple, *s*tupid." In vocabulary building, it's easier to remember a short, simple definition than a long, complex one. Therefore, most of the time we give only one brief definition of each word. However, if you look in a dictionary, you may find a half dozen or more meanings for a particular word. Thus, it's important to keep in mind that the definition of a word we selected for this book may not be the only definition.

We also define a word in just one part of speech, such as in its noun form (parts of speech for the words are identified and explained in the chapters). But if you check a dictionary, you may find that the word can also be used as a verb, adjective, or some other part of speech. If you want to find out about such matters or, generally, explore a word in greater depth, refer to a dictionary. Use one that provides additional meanings, different parts of speech for each word, and other information, such as pronunciations and word origins.

The index at the end of this book lists every word defined in the exercises, bonus sections, or somewhere clsc, such as in the introductory chapter discussions. The page number given after each word is the place where the word is first introduced in the book.

## Word Origins and Vocabulary Building

To some people the study of language and the origins of words is endlessly fascinating. At the least, most of us understand that it can be very helpful in vocabulary-building exercises to know where the words in our language originated and how our language came to be what it is today. Sometimes, it is essential to know this in order to understand aspects of vocabulary building such as pronunciation and word forming or combining of parts.

Before you begin your vocabulary-building exercises, take time to look in a dictionary or other book that lists the origins of words. If nothing else, think about the huge number of English words that can be traced to other times, other places, and other languages. English is indisputably an *international* language. It's not surprising, therefore, that many people worldwide consider it one of the richest and most colorful of all languages anywhere on earth.

## The Beginning of the English Language

Have you ever wondered where all the words in the English language came from? Like the American people, the English language has its origins in many other countries around the world. The United States is as much a melting pot of languages as it is of people and cultures.

The fact that *most* of our words aren't really native to English is one of many interesting revelations to come from a study of the history of the English language. Another interesting fact concerns the difference in attitudes that other countries have toward word borrowing. Some of the countries from which we borrowed words, such as France, have taken a very different position from us. They've tried to maintain a certain language purity, keeping out foreign words. Not so in America. We've eagerly sought and accepted a rich infusion of words from French, Latin, and a multitude of other languages. In Chapter 9 we'll have more to say about our use of foreign words.

*Etymology.* Some dictionaries provide additional information about the origins of words. They give the *etymology,* or history, of a word, tracing its development from the earliest known times. In such dictionaries, for example, if you look up the word *book,* you'll find that it comes from the Old English word *boc* (pronounced *bohk*).

Dictionaries that have such information usually list it after stating the entry head and pronunciation. The facts are commonly given in abbreviated form, using letters such as *MF* (Middle French), *OE* (Old English), *L* (Latin), and *GK* (Greek). Refer to the guide in the front of each dictionary to find out how such information is presented. If you want to know even more about word origins than a dictionary offers, look for books especially devoted to this subject. Many such guides are available.

*Word Roots.* Some teachers believe that the best way to remember a word is to understand its *root:* the main element of a word or the principal component of meaning. Guides describing roots from other languages, such as *oct(o)* (Latin: "eight"), are also available. Once you know what the root *oct(o)* means, you're on the way to figuring out the meanings of words such as *octopus* (a sea creature with eight arms), *octosyllable* (a word having eight syllables, or units), and *octogenarian* (a person whose age is in the eighties).

Some guides provide lists of roots from Greek, Latin, or other sources, as well as combining forms: another word or part that can be combined with a root to create a complete word. Chapter 11, for example, talks about letters that can be added to the beginning (prefix) or end (suffix) of a root to form a new word.

*From Old English to Modern English.* New English words are probably being coined as you read this. They're being created in schools and companies all across the country. But some of the already existing words are anything but new. They may even have originated in some form in the far distant past of humankind.

Early humans didn't leave a written record of *words* to tell us about their vocabularies. So we don't know exactly how far beyond grunts and groans their vocabularies went. But we do know that they communicated; even animals "talk" to each other.

However, if you had to point to a *precise* place on a globe where the first seeds of American English were planted, where would you point? Most people would point to England. But some language experts believe that a distant forerunner of English first appeared somewhere else. They speculate that it first became known thousands of years before the birth of Christ, perhaps somewhere in the Near East of biblical times.

When focusing on more precise, and more recent, dates, places, and events for the beginning of English, historians note one thing in particular: the arrival of three Germanic tribes—the Angles, Saxons, and Jutes—in England nearly five hundred years after the birth of Christ. It was after that time that several varieties, or dialects, of English emerged.

*Old English (about 740 to 1066).* The English language began with the speech of Germanic tribespeople. These visitors and settlers came to the British Isles in the fifth century after the birth of Christ. As a result, the Old English vocabulary was initially almost totally Germanic. Later in the Anglo-Saxon period, however, it included Latin and Scandinavian (Norse) words. This expansion came with the influence of Christianity and the arrival of Scandinavian soldiers and settlers in England.

*Middle English (about 1066 to 1476).* After the Norman Conquest of 1066, the French language of the

Norman conquerors also had a huge impact on the English of that period. Soon, Old English words were being replaced by the French words. For several hundred years thereafter, French was the official language of the British Isles. However, most of the population continued to speak a form of English.

*Early Modern English (about 1476 to 1776).* The strong influence of Latin and French continued throughout the Early Modern period. But in time other languages, such as Italian, Dutch, Greek, Japanese, and Chinese, also made a contribution. By the end of the period, in fact, English had become a notably diverse language. But the most significant development of Early Modern times was the establishment of a standard form of written English.

*Modern English (about 1776 to the present).* Although for Americans the center of the English language was London at the beginning of this period, that would change in time. Other changes were also forthcoming. The rate of word borrowing from other languages was decreasing, and English was being spread throughout the world at an astonishing rate. Today, in fact, there are several hundred million people worldwide who use English as their first language.

In more recent times American English has been recognized as a variety of English apart from British English. This has occurred as Americans have been coining their own words and using a distinct style of pronunciation.

In general, English today is a giant linguistic umbrella. It encompasses all the American regional and other varieties of English—including the northern, southern, midland (roughly, New Jersey to Illinois), and black varieties—as well as the British and other nonnative varieties.

## Language-Classification System

To make it easier to study and understand English and the hundreds of other languages in the world, experts have developed a language-classification system. It consists of families, subgroups, branches, major languages, and minor languages. The largest unit, for example, is the family. It includes groups such as the Indo-European, Caucasian, Sino-Tibetan, and Afro-Asian families. English, which fits into the *Indo-European family,* shares its family home with numerous other languages: German, Latin, French, Dutch, Spanish, Greek, Afrikaans, Russian, Nepali, and many others.

The subgroup of the Indo-European family in which English belongs is the *Germanic subgroup.* It has two branches: a Western branch and a Northern (Scandinavian) branch. The Western branch has six major languages—English, German, Yiddish, Dutch, Flemish, and Afrikaans—and two minor languages—Frisian and Luxembourgian. The Northern branch has four major languages—Swedish, Danish, Norwegian, and Icelandic—and one minor language—Faroese.

The Indo-European family has seven other subgroups—Italic, Romance, Celtic, Hellenic, Slavic, Baltic, and Indo-Iranian—and nearly fifty additional languages. Latin, for example, is in the Italic subgroup; French is in the Romance subgroup; and Russian is in the Slavic subgroup. Some dictionaries and other books about languages have large charts showing this worldwide language-classification system in detail.

## Easy Learning Strategies

Most of us find suitable ways to learn a particular subject. Golfers who have trouble with their "form" may watch a videotape that shows them how professionals stand, hold their clubs, swing, putt, and so forth. Studying a golf videotape, therefore, is one type of learning strategy that a golfer might use.

In this book we want to learn the meanings of words as well as their spellings and pronunciations. An audio- or videotape might help with pronunciation. But other strategies are generally more effective for matters such as learning the meanings and spellings of words or for learning about the correct usage.

We'll mention a few common strategies for learning and remembering words, and you can add any others that you know or discover. However, as you think about the various learning techniques and devices, keep in mind that different learning strategies work for different people. Not all strategies will work for everyone, and not all of the following will work for you.

### Association of Words with Interesting Facts

If you learn an especially unusual, interesting, or curious fact about a word, you'll be more inclined to remember it. Chapter 3 puts this strategy into practice with words that name people and places.

Assume, for example, that you want to learn and remember the word *grebe,* the name of a bird adapted to water. Since lots of birds swim on or feed in the water, we need to find something that makes the *grebe* stand out from all of the other water-dwelling birds. In this case, you might focus on the curious fact that fish-eating grebes also eat large numbers of their own feathers.

The idea behind this learning strategy is that an unusual fact will enhance your memory. It will cause you to pay more attention to the word being learned and to think longer about it. This in turn will plant it more firmly in your mind so that you can more easily recall it later.

### Repetition and Reinforcement

One of the simplest learning strategies is repetition. This book, in fact, uses a three-step learning procedure to encourage repetition and better retention and recall of the words being learned.

If you want to remember the word *grebe*, for example, you might try using it repeatedly in actual sentences. To start, think of three simple sentences that say something about the grebe: "The *grebe* is adapted to water." "The *grebe* swims and dives." "Certain types of *grebes* eat fish."

You don't have to spend a lot of time researching the subject. But unlike some words, the word *grebe* refers to a living thing, something that has a shape, size, and color. Therefore, you can visualize it. The *Clark's grebe,* for example, has a blackish back and a whitish underside. But whether or not you know the precise color, shape, or size of the bird, you can still picture a ducklike bird floating on the water.

The more you repeat or use a word, the better your chances of remembering it. This repetition—with sentences, images, or anything else—will implant, or reinforce, the word in your mind.

### Writing and Spelling the Word

Teachers regularly encourage students to put their words and ideas in writing. The reason they recommend this is that the act of writing something on paper—or, if you're a computer buff, keying it onto a computer screen—will help you remember it.

If you want to remember the word *grebe,* then, you might try taking a pencil and spelling it out on paper or sitting down at your computer and spelling it out with the keyboard. But don't write or spell it merely one time. Write the word several times, following the suggestion of the previous strategy for repetition: *g-r-e-b-e, g-r-e-b-e, g-r-e-b-e.*

Writing and spelling a word on paper or keying it into a computer—preferably several times over—has been known to increase greatly the chances of remembering it. The procedure will help to reinforce the word and its meaning in your mind.

### Pronouncing the Word and Listening to It

Some people find that pronouncing a word silently or aloud, especially the latter, helps them to remember it. They don't think it's enough simply to write the word, even if they write it repeatedly. They also need to *hear* the way the word sounds: *GREEB.*

Repetition is important in matters of pronunciation too. You therefore should say the word you want to remember over and over: *GREEB, GREEB, GREEB.* Consciously *listen* to the sound of it as you say it. This act of pronouncing it repeatedly—and listening to it—will significantly improve your chances of remembering it.

### Mnemonics

The learning strategy of *mnemonics* (neh MAH niks) is a type of association device. The first strategy recommended associating a word with an unusual or interesting fact. With mnemonics, you associate the word with another easy-to-spell word or an easy-to-remember phrase.

This strategy won't work for all words. But it will work well with many of them. The following list has examples of mnemonics that have been widely used in teaching. The first word is the one being learned. The phrase or sentence that follows it is related to the word's definition or its spelling.

The phrase or sentence is meant to be a catchy saying that will stick in your mind. Later, recalling the easy-to-remember catchy phrase will lead you to the less-easy-to-remember word associated with it. The key with using mnemonics is to link certain letters in the phrase—printed here in bold type—with the same letters in the word being learned.

> **complement:** A **comple**ment **comple**tes.
> **foreword:** **Word**s be**fore** make a **foreword.**
> **knowledge:** Know**ledge** gives you the **edge.**
> **rehearse:** **Hear** the choir re**hear**se.
> **relevant:** A picnic is relev**ant** to **ants**.
> **stationary:** A station**a**ry object st**a**nds still.
> **stationery:** Station**e**ry for letters is pap**er.**
> **superintendent:** Pay your **rent** to the superintend**ent.**
> **ware:** Put the **ware**s in the **ware**house.

If you think it's fun to create clever or silly sayings, this strategy is for you. Schoolbooks, office handbooks, and many other types of books describe the device of mnemonics. Entire books have even been written about the subject (check with your local library). It has been popular for decades as an effective tool to help people remember a word's spelling, pronunciation, and definition.

*Strategies for Expanding Your Vocabulary*

The aim of this book is to help you build a bigger and better vocabulary. After you've finished the exercises, you can help yourself in continuing the process on a daily basis. The previous strategies suggested ways to learn and remember words. The following list suggests ways to make vocabulary building an everyday affair.

Leave your mind open to new words, wherever you are, whatever you're doing. Train yourself to *want* to learn more words. When you open yourself to the process of learning new words, your eyes and ears will be continually searching for and learning them. The process will become automatic.

Listen to teachers, television commentators, and others who express themselves intelligently and effectively. Pay attention not only to the type of words they use but to the way they pronounce and use the words. Notice how they apply them—in persuasion, descriptions, explanations, entertainment, or something else.

Develop the habit of reading a variety of material, including newspapers, magazines, and books on different subjects. The more you read, the more you are likely to absorb new words. Usually, readers don't even realize how much is soaking in, but the gain is often substantial.

Learn to figure out the meaning of a word by analyzing the context in which it's used. Sentences, paragraphs, and larger discussions usually contain obvious clues to meaning. Some of the exercises in this book give you a chance to practice determining the meanings of words by studying the sentences using them.

Investigate words that you suspect you have misused, misspelled, or mispronounced. Correct your mistake and learn from it. Then follow the earlier learning strategies, proceeding as though the incorrectly used word is a new word you're learning for the first time.

Set realistic goals. Devise a specific plan for learning one or more new words every day. Keep a notebook or other place where you can record the words and their meanings. Always have a pad and pencil nearby as you read or watch television so that you can jot down unfamiliar words. But don't let too many pile up before you look them up in a dictionary.

Make the dictionary your lifelong friend. Get in the habit of looking up words you definitely don't know and also words you have doubts about. Use the wealth of information in your dictionary to learn other things about a word, such as its origin and its use as different parts of speech.

## Guide to Pronunciation

Have you ever been embarrassed by mispronouncing a word? Ross Joske was. Shortly after his marriage to Anne, he decided that they should take his new in-laws out to dinner. Although Ross and Anne rarely drank wine, he wanted to order a bottle for the meal. Noticing a moderately priced chardonnay on the wine list, he pointed to it and said, "We'd like a bottle of the *'shar DOE ny.'*"

For a moment an awkward silence surrounded the table, and Ross knew something was wrong. But he had to wait until later to find out what. When they got home, Anne told him that *chardonnay* is pronounced "Shar dn AY," not "shar DOE ny," as he had said. "Oh, no," he groaned. "Your parents must think I'm a jerk." "Don't be silly," she said. "But what if you had been out with an important client or your boss?"

Good point. The prospect of a serious blunder worries

many of us. To avoid such mistakes, it's important to learn the pronunciation of a word as well as its meaning. Unfortunately, pronunciations aren't as clear-cut as the meanings of words. But we'll try to make sense out of the subject in the following pages. If the task of learning pronunciation symbols and syllabication is confusing, however, don't let it overshadow your efforts to learn the meanings of new words.

In the beginning, if you have trouble handling the symbols that we'll be using, simply pronounce each word as best you can. Later, when you're more comfortable with the procedure, ease your way into a more precise pronunciation of each word.

By the time you've finished a chapter or two, the basic symbols should start to look very familiar. After seeing them used over and over in different words, they'll soon seem a lot less mysterious and frightening. In fact, you'll soon be correctly pronouncing words with ease and, probably, without even pausing to realize that you're doing it.

## Pronunciation Syllables

A major problem in deciding on the pronunciation of words is that dictionaries don't always agree about such matters. Life would be easier if they used the same pronunciation symbols and the same division of words into syllables (individual units). But they don't. Sometimes the pronunciation and syllabication differences are slight; in other cases they're striking.

To add to the confusion, dictionaries list alternative pronunciations when more than one is correct. They also note differences according to regional varieties of pronunciation, particularly the northern, southern, and midland variations. In this book, however, we'll list only one widely accepted pronunciation for each word.

We'll leave it to you to consult a dictionary if you want to explore the fine points of pronunciation in greater depth.

You may have noticed that dictionaries show two types of syllabication. One type shows places in a word where it may be divided at the end of a line; another type shows the division of the word's pronunciation into syllables.

1. In most dictionaries, if you look up the word *syllable,* you'll see the bold-face entry head **syl·la·ble.** It shows where you can properly divide the word at the end of a line.
2. After the entry head, you'll see the pronunciation of the word *syllable,* which is also divided into units, as in "SI lə bəl," with an emphasis on the first syllable. (We'll explain what the upside-down *e* means in the discussion "Letters With Symbols.")

In this book we'll give *pronunciation* syllables, which sometimes differ from the units that are meant to show where to divide a word at the end of a line.

The differences in pronunciation from one dictionary to another are most obvious when you compare the pronunciation syllables. One dictionary, for example, may break the pronunciation of the word *inactive* after the *i,* as in "i NAK tiv." Another may break it after the *n,* as in "in AK tiv." One may pronounce the word *accept* as "ak SEPT." Another may prefer "ik SEPT."

### Pronunciation Systems

We compared the pronunciation systems used in various dictionaries. Our sources included several

*Webster's* dictionaries, such as *Webster's Encyclopedic Unabridged Dictionary of the English Language* and *Merriam Webster's Collegiate Dictionary*. We also studied *The American Heritage Dictionary of the English Language, The New Shorter Oxford English Dictionary,* and other general dictionaries.

Since certain words and their pronunciations can be found only in specialized dictionaries, we looked at such sources too: new-word dictionaries; dictionaries of information technology, the environment, medicine, and finance; and various foreign-language dictionaries.

After examining the differences and similarities among the various sources, we concluded that their pronunciation systems were too detailed and complex for our purposes. We therefore developed a slightly modified system more suitable for this book. It's primarily a combined and simplified version of several of the more detailed systems used in the major dictionaries.

To take the mystery out of pronunciation, however, even our relatively simple system needs some explanation. So let's go through it step by step, looking at the pronunciation of letters without symbols and then with symbols.

*Letters Without Symbols.* We all know the pronunciation of ordinary words, such as *bet* and *tip*. But if you want to double-check your understanding of ordinary pronunciation, review the following list. It's a collection of alphabet letters *without* symbols and the familiar sounds associated with them.

The words in this list tell you how certain letters are usually pronounced. For example, if you look in a dictionary and see the letter *a,* without any pronunciation symbol attached to it, you should pronounce it as the *a* in *map.*

| a | map | ng | sing |
|---|-----|-----|------|
| b | bake | oi | oil |
| ch | chin | ou | out |
| d | dim | p | pen |
| e | bet | r | red |
| f | file | s | saw |
| g | go | sh | ship |
| h | hat | t | tip |
| hw | whale | th | this |
| i | tip | v | van |
| j | job | w | win |
| k | kit | y | yes |
| l | lid | z | zone |
| m | mud | zh | vision |
| n | no | | |

*Letters With Symbols.* Often the regular pronunciation of unmarked letters isn't sufficient for certain words. In those cases, dictionaries use special symbols to indicate a change in the pronunciation. We've adopted four such symbols to use in this book.

1. One unusual pronunciation symbol is the upside-down *e* called the *schwa*—ə.
2. Another symbol is the straight line over a letter, used with ā, ē, ī, and ō.
3. A third symbol is the single dot over a letter, used with ȯ and u̇.
4. The fourth symbol is the double dot over a letter, used with ä and ü.

Let's find out how to pronounce these symbols. The following table has examples of words that use one or more of the four symbols. It also indicates common pronunciations for the schwa and for the other symbols that are used in conjunction with the vowels *a, e, i, o,* and *u.*

Column 1 lists the four basic pronunciation symbols. Column 2 lists various letters in words that the symbols represent. Column 3 gives an example of a word that has those letters. Column 4 gives the actual pronunciation of the word, using the pronunciation symbols. If this sounds confusing, don't be concerned. It will seem much clearer when you look at the actual columns in the table.

In the exercises throughout this book, the syllables that should receive the greatest amount of stress are printed in all capital letters (behalf/bi HAF). Any that should receive a secondary amount of stress are printed with an apostrophe following the syllable (picnicking/PIK nik′ ing).

| (1) | (2) | (3) | (4) |
|-----|-----|-----|-----|
| ə | a | about | ə BAÜT |
|   | e | shaken | SHĀ kən |
|   | i | April | Ā prəl |
|   | o | collect | kə LEKT |
|   | u | suppose | sə PŌZ |
| ər | er, ur | further | FƏR thər |
| ā | a | day | DĀ |
| ē | e | eat | ĒT |
|   | y | easy | Ē zē |
| ī | eye | eye | Ī |
|   | i | side | SĪD |
|   | y | by | BĪ |
| ō | eau | beau | BŌ |
|   | o | phone | FŌN |
|   | oe | hoe | HŌ |
|   | ow | row | RŌ |

| (1) | (2) | (3) | (4) |
|---|---|---|---|
| ȯ | a | **all** | ȮL |
|  | augh | **caugh**t | KȮT |
|  | aw | **saw** | SȮ |
| u̇ | oo | **woo**d | WU̇D |
|  | u | **pull** | PU̇L |
| au̇ | ou | **out** | AU̇T |
|  | ow | **now** | NAU̇ |
| ä | a | **father** | FÄ ther |
|  | o | **got** | GÄT |
| ü | ou | **youth** | YÜTH |
|  | u | **rule** | RÜL |

Here are a few more examples of the type of pronunciations you'll find in this book. If you want to practice working with the pronunciation symbols a little more before getting into the exercises of the book, read the following examples aloud.

| planet | PLA nət |
| cover | KƏ vər |
| paycheck | PĀ chek' |
| evening | ĒV ning |
| island | Ī lənd |
| clothesline | KLŌZ līn' |
| washbasin | WȮSH bā' sən |
| goodness | GU̇D nəs |
| downtown | dau̇n' TAU̇N |
| flip-flop | FLIP fläp' |
| afternoon | af' tər NÜN |

## Whatever Works for You

If learning, remembering, and pronouncing new words is a challenge for you, try one or more of the common strategies described in this chapter. But don't hesitate to create an entirely new technique or device that you like better. After all, it doesn't matter which strategy or method you use. What matters is whether or not it works for you.

# 2. Take a Preliminary Evaluation Test

*When you're heading toward a goal, don't pause to watch your feet hit the ground. Look over the next hill and around the next bend to see what kind of ground lies ahead.*

So said an English teacher to his new freshman class. It may sound like his warning to be prepared for some rough terrain. But he really wasn't trying to terrify the fainthearted. He simply believed that in matters of learning, people are more likely to stick it out when they know what's coming up. So he was actually giving them a valuable tip.

Let's find out if he's right: Let's look over the next hill and around the next bend. For us that means glancing ahead to see what kind of words and topics we're going to cover in this book.

Since you acquired a vocabulary book, you've apparently decided that you need to enlarge and improve your vocabulary. That's good. Then we won't have to spend time talking you into doing it. Instead, we'll concentrate on getting you off to a good start.

One way to preview what's over the next hill or around the next bend is to test your present understanding of terms we'll be learning in the coming exercises. By taking a few quizzes using a variety of words from throughout the book, you'll find out two things:

First, you'll get an idea of how many words you already know. Second, you'll discover what kind of ground lies ahead.

Remember, though, that you'll have to wait until you get to the appropriate exercises in future chapters to find definitions and pronunciations. But if you simply can't wait until then to learn more about any word, you can locate the word now by looking in the index, where each word is listed along with the page number where it first appears.

Our aim in this chapter, however, is just to shake hands with the words. Later, when we get to the regular exercises in Chapters 3 through 16, we'll take time to get better acquainted with them.

Before you get out your pencil and start writing, we want to tell you something about the tests and your scores:

The following quizzes are *preliminary* tests, introducing words from the main exercises in the following chapters. You'll be taking these tests cold, without having read any definitions or comments about the words. Therefore, no one expects you to score 100 percent on each test.

If you correctly answer 50 percent or more of the questions, congratulations on already having a good understanding of some of the words. If you score below 50 percent, congratulations on being smart enough to buy a vocabulary-building book.

You can evaluate your level of understanding by checking the answer section following each test. At the end of the answers, you'll see a place to record the number of your correct and incorrect answers.

Each test has ten items, so it will be easy to calculate the number or percentage of correct answers. For example, if four out of ten items are answered correctly, you've scored 40 percent correct. If seven out of ten are correct, you've scored 70 percent. If ten out of ten are correct, you've scored 100 percent. Get the idea? Use this guide to evaluate your scores.

| | | |
|---|---|---|
| 0–2 | correct | Inferior |
| 3–4 | correct | Below average |
| 5–6 | correct | Average |
| 7–8 | correct | Above average |
| 9–10 | correct | Superior |

Since you've already decided you want to enlarge and improve your vocabulary, your score may not change your mind about anything—except possibly to make you more determined than ever to learn new words. Either way, we urge you not to let your scores in these preliminary tests occupy all of your attention. The other important purpose of this first chapter is to give you a preview of the words and topics that are waiting over the next hill and around the next bend.

## PRELIMINARY TEST 1

This first preliminary test begins with a group of words and ten test items. Your assignment is to pick from the group the most appropriate word for each test item and write it on the blank line.

Here are the words for you to draw on. Take a moment to look carefully at them before you start writing. When you're ready, get out your pencil, take a deep breath, and begin.

| | |
|---|---|
| alleviate | Badlands |
| apparition | censor |
| asceticism | censure |
| assimilate | contentious |

creationism     ingratiate
decennial     perennial
ephemeral     Philipino
exacerbate     piedmont
Filipino     proscribe

1. The actions of others sometimes make bad things worse. They may make a problem more difficult to solve or make a bitter situation even more bitter. If something will make things worse, it will _____ the situation.

2. People use different tactics to gain something they want. They're not always subtle about it either. In fact, they may take deliberate, obvious steps to gain the favor or good graces of someone, such as going overboard in trying to please a new boss at work. Someone who does this is trying to _____ himself or herself with the other person.

3. People throughout the ages have claimed to have seen a ghostly or unusual figure that appeared unexpectedly. Such a ghost, spirit, or unusual being is commonly referred to as an

_____.

4. Some people practice strict self-denial to bring discipline to their lives. They may live in a sparsely furnished room; wear simple, inexpensive clothes; and eat only very plain, basic foods. This type of person is practicing

_____.

5. Some people just can't get along with others. They seem to like disagreement more than agreement and tend to be quarrelsome or argumentative. This type of person is often described as _____.

6. In southwestern South Dakota you'll find a heavily eroded, dry region of scanty vegetation, an area made popular in the past as the setting for many western movies. This desolate region is best known as the _____.

7. Various words are used in regard to different time periods. For example, a *biannual* event occurs twice a year. A word that means "happening year after year," as with flowers that come up each new year, is _____.

8. From time to time, students, employees, and others have been the subject of strong disapproval, harsh criticism, or even an official rebuke, such as when a legislature criticizes one of its members. To blame or criticize someone in this way is to _____ the person.

9. The previous item described strong disapproval or criticism of someone. Sometimes an action against someone or something is even stronger and more drastic. For example, steps may be taken to banish or outlaw the person or thing. If an organization decides to outlaw or prohibit an unacceptable behavior, such as cursing at others during a meeting, it has decided to _____ the behavior.

10. The Philippines is a republic in eastern Asia consisting of the Philippine Islands in the western Pacific Ocean, southeast of China. A resident of the Philippines is called a _____.

ANSWERS: (1) exacerbate (2) ingratiate (3) apparition (4) asceticism (5) contentious (6) Badlands (7) perennial (8) censure (9) proscribe (10) Filipino
*Correct Answers:* _____ *Incorrect Answers:* _____

## PRELIMINARY TEST 2

How did you do? Perhaps a different type of quiz would suit you better. Throughout the book you'll find a variety of tests, from fill in the blank to column matching to true-false to multiple choice. This time we'll give you a chance to try your luck with a multiple-choice test.

Notice that one word is italicized in the first line of each item in the test. Following this opening line are three choices of definitions. Your task is to circle the one that you think is the best of the three—a, b, or c. Here are the ten words for which you'll be picking appropriate definitions. Study them for a moment before you begin the test.

| | |
|---|---|
| *ad hominem* | downmarket |
| biorhythm | intersession |
| boilerplate | melee |
| canvass | solarium |
| covenant | tort |

1. The word *canvass* means to
    (a) cover something with a rough fabric
    (b) examine carefully or seek opinions
    (c) count the number of residents in an area
2. An *intersession* is
    (a) a time period between sessions
    (b) an intervention between parties in a dispute
    (c) the act of making a plea on another's behalf
3. The French word *melee* refers to a
    (a) confused, often hand-to-hand struggle
    (b) mixture of elements that don't go well together
    (c) household of two or more people

4. The Latin word *ad hominem* means
   - (a) actual or existing in fact
   - (b) pertaining to human beings
   - (c) appealing to emotion instead of logic
5. A *downmarket* is a market
   - (a) for parts and accessories
   - (b) in which sales are declining
   - (c) of lower-income consumers
6. A *boilerplate* refers to
   - (a) a covering for a steam engine
   - (b) a standardized clause or other text
   - (c) X-rated or pornographic material
7. A *biorhythm* is a/an
   - (a) inborn biological (life) cycle
   - (b) musical chord
   - (c) person's natural musical ability
8. A *solarium* is a
   - (a) model of the solar system (sun and other bodies)
   - (b) place for studying the solar system
   - (c) place exposed to solar (sun) rays
9. A *covenant* is a
   - (a) biblical promise or prediction
   - (b) cult or religious group
   - (c) written promise or agreement in a legal paper
10. A *tort* is a
   - (a) prostitute
   - (b) private or civil (noncriminal) wrong
   - (c) type of cake

ANSWERS: (1) b (2) a (3) a (4) c (5) c (6) b (7) a (8) c (9) c (10) b

*Correct Answers:* _____ *Incorrect Answers:* _____

## PRELIMINARY TEST 3

Let's try a matching test. This time you need to match each numbered word in the first column with the most appropriate lettered definition or description in the second column. But notice that column 1 has ten words, whereas column 2 has twelve definitions. Two definitions, therefore, will not be used.

After you select an appropriate definition, look for the letter in front of the column 2 definition—a, b, c, and so on—and write that letter on the short line following the associated word in column 1.

Here are the ten words that need to be matched with the correct definitions in the test. Again, take time to examine these words before you begin.

adaptogen        fiduciary
biodegradable      netiquette
chelation therapy    placebo
demographics       residual value
ecosystem        telephony

1. telephony ____

    a. a person or organization that holds and manages something of value for another person

2. fiduciary ____

    b. a community of living things and their environment functioning as a unit

3. biodegradable ____

    c. the process of removing harmful metals and minerals from the body

4. netiquette ____

    d. something that helps restore health by stimulating the body's own renewal process

5. chelation therapy ____

e. a population of living things that has adapted to a particular set of environmental conditions

6. ecosystem ____

f. the translation of voice and other signals into a form that can travel by wire or radio

7. placebo ____

g. a harmless substance given to a patient instead of an actual drug

8. residual value ____

h. something that adapts to the effects of antibiotics, eventually making them useless

9. adaptogen ____

i. the statistical characteristics of human populations

10. demographics ____

j. capable of being broken down into natural substances by bacteria or other agents

k. short for *Internet etiquette*

l. the existing worth at the end of a period or process

ANSWERS: (1) f (2) a (3) j (4) k (5) c (6) b (7) g (8) l (9) d (10) i

*Correct Answers:* _____ *Incorrect Answers:* _____

## PRELIMINARY TEST 4

This is the last preliminary test. Here, we want you to find words that have meanings similar to those of other words. First, study the group of words preceding the test. Then look at the ten words in column 1 of the test. For each word in column 1, pick a word with a similar meaning from the group of words preceding the test. Write your choice in column 2 across from the word in column 1 that is similar.

Each of the words preceding the test—the words that you'll be choosing from—appears in one of the exercises in this book. The words in column 1 of the test may or may not appear in the book.

To get you started, notice that the word in item 1 of the test is *unfavorable*. Your task is to find a word in the following group that has a similar meaning and write it in column 2.

| | |
|---|---|
| actuate | incisive |
| adverse | incongruous |
| antediluvian | ingenue |
| conciliate | innocuous |
| egregious | legate |
| exacerbate | mettlesome |
| habitué | replete |
| immutable | riparian |
| impugn | taciturn |

1. unfavorable     _____
2. silent     _____
3. antiquated     _____
4. spirited     _____
5. emissary     _____
6. direct     _____
7. serious     _____
8. filled     _____
9. attack     _____
10. pacify     _____

ANSWERS: (1) adverse (2) tactiturn (3) antediluvian (4) mettlesome (5) legate (6) incisive (7) egregious (8) replete (9) impugn (10) conciliate

*Correct Answers:*_____ *Incorrect Answers:*_____

## REVIEW

Before you move on to Chapter 3, take time to review your work. Especially notice the types of words that were previewed here. As you discovered, you'll be learning an amazing variety of words—words that will fortify your vocabulary from every imaginable angle. To get a broad view of what's waiting for you, turn to the table of contents at the beginning of the book or browse the index at the end.

Now that we've looked over the next hill and around the next bend, at least the fear of the unknown should be gone. But we hope more than that happened during this brief trip. We hope you also were a little excited with this glimpse of the powerful new vocabulary you'll possess by the time you finish the book.

So let's buckle up, shift into drive, and climb that next hill to Chapter 3.

# 3. Learn the Words That Name People and Places

> *In the mysterious land of ancient Egypt, the priests are believed to have plucked every hair from their bodies, eyelashes included.*

Eyelashes too? What about other parts of the body that shall remain nameless? Expecting people to go 100 percent hairless—before the age of razors—doesn't seem like a good way to attract new members to any profession. It's hard to imagine masses of young men eagerly waiting in line to start plucking so that they could become priests. One thing is certain, however: Stories like this give new meaning to the words *faith* and *devotion*.

Such stories also remind us that the task of adding more names of people and places to our vocabularies doesn't have to be dull. It's an easy way to pick up interesting tidbits about life and living throughout the ages—facts that will make us seem much more knowledgeable and interesting to others.

Before getting down to the business of learning words that name people and places, however, we need to make a quick point about grammar: The words that name people and places in this chapter are called nouns. Even if you've been out of school a long time, you may recall that *nouns* are words that name persons and places (the subject of this chapter) and physical or nonphysical things (covered in the next chapter).

## People

Let's begin with people: How many people do you know personally? How many do you know of or about as a result of listening to television or reading books, magazines, and newspapers? Too many to count?

You know your friends, relatives, and coworkers. You probably also recognize the names of famous senators and representatives (*Newt Gingrich*), business leaders (*Steve Forbes*), sports figures (*Magic Johnson*), world leaders (*Boris Yeltsin*), and any others regularly in the news. But what about those who aren't regularly or ever mentioned on the nightly news or in a daily newspaper? Does your vocabulary include many of those names?

## EXERCISE 1

Names from the past are always much harder to recognize and remember than are those of people who are currently making headlines. Here are ten such names (nouns) from both the near and the distant past. Some or all of the names may sound familiar. But can you actually describe all of them or relate them to the correct time in history?

Attila the Hun (A′ til ə the HƏN)
Julius Caesar (SĒ zər)
Thomas Edison (ED′ ə sən)

Harry Houdini (Hü DĒ nē)
Huey Long (HYÜ ē)
Nostradamus (Näs' trə DÄ məs)
Pablo Picasso (Pi KÄ sō')
Paul Revere (Ri VIR)
Antonius Stradivarius (Strad' ə VAR ē əs)
Samuel Wilson (Uncle Sam) (WIL sən)

## STEP 1

Did you recognize all of them? How much do you know about each one?

One of the best ways to remember names that aren't household words is to think of them in relation to curious, unusual, or important facts about their lives. An improved memory isn't all you'll gain by doing this. Knowing fascinating bits of information often makes people the life of a party. Read the notable or unusual facts about our ten subjects in the following sentences, and see if this memory device works for you.

1. *Attila the Hun* (about 406–53), king of the primitive and brutal Asiatic Huns, led many merciless invasions that brought terrible devastation to countries between the Black Sea and the Mediterranean Sea. Many people are surprised to learn that such a ruthless and fierce warrior was less than three and a half feet tall.

2. *Julius Caesar* (100–44 B.C.) was a famous Roman statesman and writer. Although the name *Caesar* is still recognized worldwide, few are aware that he had a familiar problem that still afflicts people in the 1990s. He suffered from epilepsy, a disorder affecting body move-

ment and the senses, sometimes accompanied by seizures.

3. *Thomas Alva Edison* (1837–1931), developer of the Edison phonograph and the electric light bulb, lost his hearing at the age of twelve. But this didn't stop him from earning the reputation of being the world's greatest inventor, with more than a thousand creations to his credit.

4. *Harry Houdini* (1874–1926) was a world-famous escape artist. He once stayed under water, sealed in a coffin, for a full hour and a half without evidence of physical harm.

5. *Senator Huey Long* (1893–1935) of Louisiana made one of the longest congressional speeches in history—fifteen and a half hours. His comments filled a hundred pages in the *Congressional Record,* running up $5,000 in printing costs for the government.

6. *Nostradamus* (1503–1566) was an astrologer who studied the effects that stars and planets have on life on earth. He correctly foretold many events that have occurred in modern times and also predicted the arrival of aliens from outer space in 1999.

7. *Pablo Picasso* (1881–1973) was a Spanish painter who changed the course of art throughout the world when he introduced a new style of painting called *cubism.* With this new style, a natural form, such as the human body, is changed into abstract, often separate, parts.

9. *Paul Revere* (1735–1818) was an American patriot who, according to legend, alerted the Minutemen that "the British are coming." But not many know that this patriot was once court-martialed for cowardice. Although he was

cleared of the charges, the scandal followed him for the rest of his life.

9. *Antonius Stradivarius* (1644–1737) is known around the globe for having created the greatest handmade violins in the world. No other violin has ever attained the perfection of a "Stradivarius" in spite of the repeated attempts of others to copy the magnificent beauty and tone of his instruments.

10. *Samuel Wilson* (1800s) was primarily known in his time as a butcher and meat packer. During the War of 1812, the stamp he used to mark barrels of meat for the U.S. Army—*US*—became the inspiration for the symbol of the United States— the character *Uncle Sam*.

## STEP 2

To find out if reading interesting facts about the ten people have helped you to remember them, try matching each one—*Attila the Hun, Julius Caesar, Thomas Edison, Harry Houdini, Huey Long, Nostradamus, Pablo Picasso, Paul Revere, Antonius Stradivarius, Samuel Wilson (Uncle Sam)*—with the correct description in the following list. By writing out each name on the line across from the appropriate description, you'll be more inclined to remember the correct spelling. For most exercises in this book, correct answers are given at the end of each test.

1. _____ Spanish painter
2. _____ man who inspired U.S. symbol
3. _____ American patriot
4. _____ violin maker
5. _____ world's greatest inventor

6. _____  escape artist
7. _____  U.S. senator
8. _____  Roman statesman
9. _____  ruthless king
10. _____  astrologer and prophet

ANSWERS: (1) Picasso (2) Samuel Wilson (3) Paul Revere (4) Stradivarius (5) Thomas Edison (6) Houdini (7) Huey Long (8) Julius Caesar (9) Attila the Hun (10) Nostradamus

## STEP 3

The more you use a word, the better your chances are of remembering it. So let's practice using the ten names again, this time by filling in the correct name— *Attila the Hun, Julius Caesar, Thomas Edison, Harry Houdini, Huey Long, Nostradamus, Pablo Picasso, Paul Revere, Antonius Stradivarius, Samuel Wilson (Uncle Sam)*—in each sentence.

1. Born before Christ, this famous Roman statesman and writer was troubled by a problem—epilepsy—that many people still deal with in the 1990s: _____.
2. Except for practicing magicians, few people can imagine how this famous escape artist could survive sealed in a coffin under water for an hour and a half: _____.
3. Long-windedness was part of this former senator's claim to fame: _____.
4. One of the most important art styles of modern times—cubism—was introduced by this Spanish painter: _____.
5. "Uncle Sam" may be a symbolic figure rather than a real person, but the symbol was inspired

by a meat stamp—*US*—used by this real person:
_____

6. Because of this viciousness toward victims and the destruction he brought to countries he invaded, no one wants to be compared to this ruler:
_____

7. We can be expecting aliens from outer space any day now according to this sixteenth-century astrologer and prophet: _____.

8. Not many know that this famous patriot, who has been credited with alerting the Minutemen that "the British are coming," was court-martialed for cowardice: _____.

9. Although he had been unable to hear since childhood, this talented man was responsible for more than a thousand inventions: _____.

10. The greatest violins ever produced were made by the hands of this creative genius:
_____.

ANSWERS: (1) Caesar (2) Houdini (3) Huey Long (4) Picasso (5) Samuel Wilson (6) Attila the Hun (7) Nostradamus (8) Paul Revere (9) Thomas Edison (10) Stradivarius

## EXERCISE 2

If you're good at remembering names, Exercise 1 was probably easy. But not all nouns referring to people are personal names, such as former president *John F. Kennedy*. Some identify the person in another way, such as by title (the *president of the United States*) or nationality (an *American*). This exercise begins with ten words—all nouns—that identify people by nationality or place of residency.

You'll discover that sometimes the same form may be used both as a noun and as an adjective. You already know the definition of a noun. An *adjective* is a word that describes or limits another word, such as a noun, as a *blue* sky (more about that in Chapter 6). For example:

The form *Saudi* is used as both a noun (a *Saudi*) and an adjective (*Saudi* customs). In other cases, though, the form is different: *Filipino* is a noun (a *Filipino*), and *Philippine* is an adjective (*Philippine* customs). When you're uncertain, check a current dictionary.

Bostonian (Bò STŌ nē ən)
Chicagoan (Shə KÄ go wən)
Cypriot (SIP rē ət)
Filipino (Fil′ ə PĒ nō′)
Indianan (In′ dē AN ən)
Los Angelean (Lòs′ An′ jə LĒ ən)
Milwaukeean (Mil′ WÒK ē ən)
Oregonian (Ōr′ ə GŌ nē ən)
Saudi (SAÛ dē)
Thai (TĪ)

## STEP 1

The ten names and their spellings clearly indicate a person's nationality or the state or city where a person lives. A "Bostonian" is obviously from "Boston," not Chicago. Right? It may seem, then, that tests are not needed in this exercise.

However, if you take time to match the people—*Bostonian, Chicagoan, Cypriot, Filipino, Indianan, Los Angelean, Milwaukeean, Oregonian, Saudi, Thai*—with the places in the next list, it will help you to focus your attention on two things: (1) the differences in spelling between nouns referring to persons and nouns referring to places and (2) how a word describing a person is formed from one representing a place.

A surprising number of people misspell a word such as *Chicagoan* even though they know very well that a "Chicagoan" is from "Chicago." If you want to check your spelling, write the name of the noun indicating a person next to the name of the associated noun indicating a place in the following list.

| | | |
|---|---|---|
| 1. | _____ | Philippines |
| 2. | _____ | Saudi Arabia |
| 3. | _____ | Oregon |
| 4. | _____ | Thailand |
| 5. | _____ | Los Angeles |
| 6. | _____ | Milwaukee |
| 7. | _____ | Chicago |
| 8. | _____ | Boston |
| 9. | _____ | Cyprus |
| 10. | _____ | Indiana |

ANSWERS: (1) Filipino (2) Saudi (3) Oregonian (4) Thai (5) Los Angelean (6) Milwaukeean (7) Chicagoan (8) Bostonian (9) Cypriot (10) Indianan

## STEP 2

Let's mix up the ten words—*Bostonian, Chicagoan, Cypriot, Filipino, Indianan, Los Angelean, Milwaukeean, Oregonian, Saudi, Thai*—into a different order and match them one more time. As you did in Step 1, fill in the names of people in column 1 that will correctly match the places listed in column 2. But try to fill in column 1 without looking back at the answers to Step 1.

| | |
|---|---|
| 1. _____ | Los Angeles |
| 2. _____ | Milwaukee |
| 3. _____ | Oregon |
| 4. _____ | Cyprus |
| 5. _____ | Saudi Arabia |
| 6. _____ | Chicago |
| 7. _____ | Philippines |
| 8. _____ | Indiana |
| 9. _____ | Boston |
| 10. _____ | Thailand |

ANSWERS: (1) Los Angelean (2) Milwaukeean (3) Oregonian (4) Cypriot (5) Saudi (6) Chicagoan (7) Filipino (8) Indianan (9) Bostonian (10) Thai

## STEP 3

For a final check of your memory, circle either true or false for each of the following matches. Try to take this true-false test without glancing back at Step 2 or checking the answers at the end of this list.

| | |
|---|---|
| 1. Cyprus = Cypriot | *True False* |
| 2. Indiana = Indianan | *True False* |
| 3. Milwaukee = Milwaukian | *True False* |
| 4. Oregon = Oregonian | *True False* |
| 5. Los Angeles = Los Angelian | *True False* |
| 6. Thailand = Thailandian | *True False* |
| 7. Boston = Bostonian | *True False* |
| 8. Philippines= Philipino | *True False* |
| 9. Chicago = Chicagoan | *True False* |
| 10. Saudi Arabia = Saudi | *True False* |

ANSWERS: (1) True (2) True (3) False (4) True (5) False (6) False (7) True (8) False (9) True (10) True

## EXERCISE 3

How would you do if you didn't have a list of ten words to guide you? Could you convert names of places to names of people on your own? Let's find out. This time we *won't* begin the exercise with the ten words you'll need. You'll have the names of places to work from, but it will be up to you to convert them to words that name people.

## STEP 1

Are you ready? On each blank line, write what you believe is the correct word for a person who is a resident of the place named in column 2. Be prepared, though, that the spelling of some of the words that name people may be somewhat different from the names of the places on which they're based. If you don't know how to write some of the more difficult ones, check the answers that follow the list. Since we didn't give a beginning list of ten words with pronunciations, you'll find the pronunciations for this group in the answer section.

As you go through the list, remember that it's not a crime to be unaware of the correct word for a native or resident. Even newscasters and reporters sometimes get it wrong. The purpose of this step is not only to help you learn some of these words and how they're formed but also to point out that it may be necessary to consult a dictionary to check unfamiliar cases.

1. _____  Florida
2. _____  Chile
3. _____  Wales

| | |
|---|---|
| 4. _____ | Buffalo (N.Y.) |
| 5. _____ | Paris |
| 6. _____ | Phoenix |
| 7. _____ | Guam |
| 8. _____ | Naples (Italy) |
| 9. _____ | Michigan |
| 10. _____ | San Diego |

ANSWERS: 1. Floridian (Flə RID ē ən)
2. Chilean (CHIL ē ən)
3. Welshman/woman (WELSH mən/wü mən)
4. Buffalonian (Bəf ə LŌ nē ən)
5. Parisian (Pə RI zhən)
6. Phoenician (Fē NI shən)
7. Guamanian (Gwä MÄ nē ən)
8. Neapolitan (Nē′ ə PÄL ə ten)
9. Michigander (MISH ə gan′ dər)
10. San Diegan (San′ Dē Ä gən)

## STEP 2

You may not have guessed correctly with all of the words in the list, so one more time: Fill in the words that name people—*Buffalonian, Chilean, Floridian, Guamanian, Michigander, Neapolitan, Parisian, Phoenician, San Diegan, Welshman/woman*—across from the words that name places. This time, see if you can get 100 percent correct—without looking back at Step 1.

| | |
|---|---|
| 1. _____ | Naples |
| 2. _____ | Phoenix |
| 3. _____ | Buffalo (N.Y.) |
| 4. _____ | San Diego |
| 5. _____ | Florida |
| 6. _____ | Guam |

7. _____  Michigan
8. _____  Paris
9. _____  Chile
10. _____  Wales

ANSWERS: (1) Neapolitan (2) Phoenician (3) Buffalonian (4) San Diegan (5) Floridian (6) Guamanian (7) Michigander (8) Parisian (9) Chilean (10) Welshman/woman

## STEP 3

How did you do in Step 2? Before we leave this group of words, take this easy true-false test as you did in Exercise 2. Circle either true or false depending on whether you believe the match of people with places is correct or incorrect in the following list.

1. Guam = Guamnian                *True   False*
2. Florida = Floridian            *True   False*
3. Phoenix = Phoenicean           *True   False*
4. Chile = Chilean                *True   False*
5. Wales = Walean                 *True   False*
6. Buffalo = Buffaloian           *True   False*
7. San Diego = San Diegoan        *True   False*
8. Paris = Parisian               *True   False*
9. Naples = Neapolitan            *True   False*
10. Michigan = Michiganian        *True   False*

ANSWERS: (1) True (2) True (3) False (4) True (5) False (6) False (7) False (8) True (9) True (10) False

## Places

The English language has tens of thousands of words that name places. If you think that's an exaggeration, page through a national zip code directory or look at the index to a world atlas. The purpose of this section about places, however, is not to persuade you to memorize every city, state, and country in the world; the aim is to help you learn the names of some well-known popular and legendary places. Notice in the next exercise that most of such terms are capitalized, as the *Left Bank* of Paris, an area noted for its artistic atmosphere.

## EXERCISE 4

Do you recognize the following ten words, all nouns that name places? Could you locate them geographically by city, state, region, or country?

Albion (AL  bē  ən)
Badlands (BAD  landz')
Benelux (BEN  ə  ləks')
Delta (DEL  tə)
Foggy Bottom (FÓG  ē  BÄ  təm)
Levant (Lə  VANT)
Loop (LÜP)
Piedmont (PĒD  mänt')
Twin Cities (TWIN  SID  ēs)
the Village (VIL  ij)

## STEP 1

Either in school or since your school days, you've probably heard or read at least some of these names many times. However, professional writers and speakers often use the terms without giving their geographical location. Apparently, they think we already know both the terms and their locations. After completing this exercise, in fact, you *will* know at least some of them.

If you're not sure that you know the meaning and geographical location of each word, first read the following sentences for clues. Fill in the name of the country or other location after each sentence, but wait until Step 2 to find out if your choices are correct.

1. *Albion* is a word sometimes used poetically, instead of the actual name, for this well-known island of English-speaking people in Western Europe: _____.

2. The *Badlands,* the setting for many American westerns, is a desolate area of scanty vegetation in this northern state: _____.

3. *Benelux,* formed in 1947, refers to an economic union of these three European countries: _____, _____, and _____.

4. The fertile region of the *Delta* lies between the Mississippi and Yazoo rivers in this southern state: _____.

5. *Foggy Bottom* is a well-known area near the Potomac River that includes the U.S. Department of State in this important eastern U.S. city: _____.

6. The *Levant* is an old term for the countries from western Greece to Egypt bordering the east side of this great sea: _____.

7. Businesspeople are well aware of the business district called the *Loop* in this large midwestern city: _____.

8. Next to France and Switzerland is an upland region widely known as the *Piedmont* and found in the northwestern section of this southern European country: _____.

9. These two adjoining cities in the northern United States are popularly known as the *Twin Cities:* _____ and _____.

10. The *Village,* short for *Greenwich Village,* traditionally has been a word used to describe the bohemian quarter of this large eastern U.S. city: _____.

ANSWERS: Complete Step 2 and refer to the answers at the end of the next list.

## STEP 2

Here's your chance to find out if the previous sentences helped you locate the ten places geographically. To see if you guessed correctly, match the items in these two columns. Write a, b, c, and so forth on the short line following each term in column 1.

1. Albion ____          a. Mississippi
2. Badlands ____        b. Chicago
3. Benelux ____         c. Washington, D.C.
4. Delta ____           d. Minneapolis and St. Paul
5. Foggy Bottom ____    e. Great Britain; England
6. Levant ____          f. New York City
7. Loop ____            g. South Dakota
8. Piedmont ____        h. Italy
9. Twin Cities ____     i. Mediterranean Sea
10. Village ____        j. Belgium; the Netherlands; Luxembourg

ANSWERS: (1) e (2) g (3) j (4) a (5) c (6) i (7) b (8) h (9) d (10) f

## STEP 3

Do you want to try something different? Here's a true-false test to reinforce your memory.

1. The *Loop* is a bohemian district in Chicago. *True   False*
2. The *Badlands,* located in North Dakota, was the setting for many American western films. *True   False*
3. The U.S. Department of State is located near the Potomac River in Washington, D.C., in an area popularly known as *Foggy Bottom*. *True   False*
4. The two cities of Minneapolis and St. Louis are frequently referred to as the *Twin Cities*. *True   False*
5. Fiction writers often poetically refer to the Isle of Man as *Albion*. *True   False*
6. The economic union of *Benelux* includes Belgium, the Netherlands, and Luxembourg. *True   False*
7. *Levant* is a traditional term for countries along the east side of the Mediterranean Sea. *True   False*
8. The *Village* refers to a well-known business district in New York City. *True   False*
9. An upland region known worldwide as the *Piedmont* is found in northwestern France and Switzerland. *True   False*
10. The fertile region known as the *Delta* lies between the Mississippi and Yazoo rivers. *True   False*

ANSWERS: (1) False (2) False (3) True (4) False (5) False (6) True (7) True (8) False (9) False (10) True

## EXERCISE 5

Like the previous exercises, this one gives you a chance to learn interesting facts about the words. Do you recognize the next group of nouns that name places? Can you place the words geographically?

Bering Strait (BIR ing STRĀT)
Black Forest (BLAK FÒR əst)
Fertile Crescent (FƏR təl KRES ənt)
Great Barrier Reef (GRĀT BAR ē ər RĒF)
Iberian Peninsula (Ī BIR ē ən Pə NIN sə lə)
Occident (ÄK sə dənt)
Orient (ŌR ē ənt)
Persia (PƏR zhə)
South Seas (SAÙTH SĒS)
Windward Islands (WIND wərd Ī lənds)

### STEP 1

Once again, the following sentences contain clues not only to the meaning of each name but also to the geographical location of each place. As you did in Step 1 of the previous exercise, fill in the name of each country or other location, but wait until you've completed Step 2 to check your answers.

1. The *Bering Strait* is a famous water passageway that dissects the Arctic Circle west of Alaska and

separates these two countries: _____
and _____.

2. The *Black Forest,* a forested mountain region, is
located along the upper Rhine in this European
country: _____.

3. The *Fertile Crescent* is a semicircle of fertile land
stretching from the Persian Gulf around the Syrian
desert to the southeastern coast of this great sea:
_____.

4. The *Great Barrier Reef* is the world's largest coral
reef, over a thousand miles long, located along the
state of Queensland off the northeastern coast of
this large island of English-speaking people south
of the equator: _____.

5. The *Iberian Peninsula,* a portion of land nearly
surrounded by water between the Mediterranean Sea and the Atlantic Ocean, is occupied
by these two western European countries:
_____ and _____.

6. The *Occident* is a general term referring to countries with a Western culture, such as the United
States, especially on this continent west of Asia
_____ and in this hemisphere compris-
ing North and South America: _____.

7. The *Orient* is a general term referring to countries
with an Eastern culture, such as Japan, especially
south and southeast of the Himalayas on this large
continent east of Europe: _____.

8. *Persia* is the former name of this Middle Eastern
republic east of Iraq: _____.

9. The *South Seas* refers to the oceans located south
of the equator, including some of the Atlantic and
Indian oceans but especially the southern part of
this major ocean: _____.

10. The *Windward Islands,* consisting of Dominica, St.
Lucia, St. Vincent, and the Grenadines, are lo-

cated in the eastern part of this great sea: _____.

ANSWERS: Complete Step 2 and refer to the answers at the end of the next list.

## Step 2

Were there enough clues for you to fix the locations of the ten places? Match these two columns to double-check your work. Write a, b, c, and so forth on the short line following each term in column 1.

1. Bering Strait ____       a. Australia
2. Black Forest ____        b. Iran
3. Fertile Crescent ____    c. Europe and the Western
4. Great Barrier               Hemisphere
   Reef ____               d. United States and Russia
5. Iberian Peninsula ____   e. Caribbean Sea
6. Occident ____            f. Germany
7. Orient ____              g. Mediterranean Sea
8. Persia ____              h. Pacific Ocean
9. South Seas ____          i. Spain and Portugal
10. Windward Islands ____    j. Asia

ANSWERS: (1) d (2) f (3) g (4) a (5) i (6) c (7) j (8) b (9) h (10) e

## Step 3

Without looking back to Step 2, this time write in the names of the places—*Bering Strait, Black Forest, Fertile Crescent, Great Barrier Reef, Iberian Peninsula, Occident, Orient, Persia, South Seas, Windward Islands*—next to their location.

1. _____ Caribbean Sea
2. _____ Pacific Ocean
3. _____ Australia
4. _____ Germany
5. _____ Asia
6. _____ Europe and the Western Hemisphere
7. _____ Mediterranean Sea
8. _____ Iran
9. _____ United States and Russia
10. _____ Spain and Portugal

ANSWERS: (1) Windward Islands (2) South Seas (3) Great Barrier Reef (4) Black Forest (5) Orient (6) Occident (7) Fertile Crescent (8) Persia (9) Bering Strait (10) Iberian Peninsula

## BONUS WORDS

Following the exercises in each chapter, you'll find a group of bonus words such as the following ten nouns—extra words and definitions for those of you who want to learn more than the words provided in the exercises. Be sure to read each list of bonus words, because some of the words may appear in a review test at the end of a chapter.

1. *Caucasian* (Kò KĀ zhən) a member of the white race (spelled the same whether noun or adjective): a *Caucasian* of European ancestry
2. *Damascus* (Də MAS kəs) capital city of the Middle Eastern republic of Syria; said to be the world's oldest continuously inhabited city

3. *Detroiter* (Dē TRÓID ər) a native or resident of Detroit, Michigan

4. *Down Under* (DAÚN ƏN dər) a reference to Australia or New Zealand

5. *Sigmund Freud (FRÓID), 1856–1939* a specialist in neurology (the human nervous system) and Austrian founder of psychoanalysis (the study and treatment of emotional disorders)

6. *Gandhi* (GÄN dē), *1869–1948* Indian nationalist leader who advocated nonviolent noncooperation to achieve independence for India

7. *Napoléon Bonaparte* (Nə PŌL yən BŌ nə pärt'), *1769–1821* French general, consul, and emperor; defeated by the British at Waterloo in 1815; remembered for the impact of his legal reforms known as the Code Napoléon

8. *Sir Isaac Newton* (Nüt N'), *1642–1727* an English mathematician and physicist who invented differential calculus (a mathematical method of calculation) and developed the theory of universal gravitation, supposedly inspired by a falling apple, a theory that explains why objects near the surface of the earth don't float off into space

9. *Riviera* (Riv' ē ER ə) the Mediterranean coast between France and Italy, famous for its holiday resorts: the French *Riviera*

10. *Albert Schweitzer* (SHWĪT sər), *1875–1965* born in Germany and eventually became a theologian, philosopher, missionary physician, and music scholar; winner of the Nobel Peace Prize in 1952

## REVIEW TEST

At the end of each chapter you'll find a quick review test. You can use this test to monitor your progress and find out how many words you're retaining from previous exercises. The following list has sample sentences with three possible choices for a word that names a person or thing. Circle what you believe is the most appropriate word in each case.

Following the answers at the end of this group of sentences, you'll see a place to record the number of correct and incorrect answers that you gave in the test. As you go through the book, chapter by chapter, the number of *correct* answers you give in these tests should begin to increase. If you find that the opposite trend is occurring—that more of your answers are *incorrect*—return to the beginning and repeat the previous exercises.

1. Having lost his hearing by the age of twelve, this man nevertheless went on to become the world's greatest inventor: *(a) Samuel Wilson (b) Thomas Alva Edison (c) Pablo Picasso.*
2. A resident of Thailand is known as a *(a) Thai (b) Thailander (c) Thailandian.*
3. Sigmund Freud was a specialist in *(a) neurology (b) urology (c) ophthalmology.*
4. The culture of the Occident could best be described as *(a) oriental (b) European (c) Western.*
5. A resident of Florida is known as a *(a) Floridian (b) Florider (c) Floridan.*
6. Albert Schweitzer was awarded this honor in 1952: *(a) Pulitzer Prize (b) Nobel Prize (c) Missionary of the Year.*
7. St. Lucia and St. Vincent are part of an island

group known as the *(a) Wake Islands (b) Windward Islands (c) Virgin Islands.*

8. Many tourists vacation along the Mediterranean between France and Italy at resorts on the *(a) Levant (b) Piedmont (c) Riviera.*

9. The Village is another name for Greenwich Village, onetime bohemian district of *(a) Paris (b) Chicago (c) New York City.*

10. Attila the Hun caused terrible devastation during his invasions near the *(a) Black Sea (b) Persian Gulf (c) Bering Strait.*

ANSWERS: (1) b (2) a (3) a (4) c (5) a (6) b (7) b (8) c (9) c (10) a

*Correct Answers:_____ Incorrect Answers:_____*

# 4. Don't Forget the Other Words That Name

*It took 1,700 years to complete the amazing Great Wall of China, but no one knows for certain why it was built.*

Can you imagine—1,700 years to build a wall? How's that for job security? It's true: The Great Wall of China was started in the third century B.C. and continued into the 1600s. That makes it the longest ongoing construction project in the history of the world. But why was it built? To provide work for the masses? To mark the limits of Chinese territory? No one knows.

We do know, however, that 1,700 years is a long, long time. Either no one was in a hurry in those days, or the wall must be almost endless. It's apparently the latter, because the wall covers about as many miles as the 1,700 years it took to build it. With extensions and branches, in fact, it's closer to 2,500 miles.

We talked about words that name people and places in the previous chapter. Here, we're talking about the Great Wall of China because it's an example of another type of word that names: A *wall* is a "thing," a "structure," and the *Great Wall of China* is the name of a particular thing. It's also a noun, as we learned in Chapter 3. Remember? Nouns name people, places, and physical and nonphysical things. All of these words that name make up a large part of your vocabulary.

Most of us use hundreds of words that name every day—without thinking about them. During a lunch break we might use them to discuss any number of things (the words in italic type are nouns that name):

Who's stealing the morning *newspaper*

The best way to ask the *bank* for a *loan*

What to do about the *fleas* that the *dog* brings in from the *lawn* and deposits in the *bed*

Who's going to pick up the *chips* and *dip* at the *supermarket* after *work*

Whether *stress* will catch up with us before or after *retirement*

Although we may talk about a wide variety of subjects within a very short time, we usually talk about fairly ordinary matters. Words that we use to name familiar things are easy to remember. But when we're talking with others who have a much greater stock of words to draw on, we can't count on every word being familiar. People with a large and rich vocabulary, in fact, often do use words and discuss topics that are unfamiliar. For example:

If your neighbor told you he has *ailurophobia* (ī LÜR ə fō bē ə), would you try to comfort him by asking if he'd like to hold your gentle and loving cat Fluffy? (*Only if you hate your neighbor—an "ailurophobic" person fears cats.*)

If someone said a hippopotamus's sweat is *carmine* (KÄR mən), would you know what that means? (*It refers to color—when a hippo gets excited, its hide oozes a vivid red perspiration.*)

If your son asks you for the name of our own *galaxy* (GAL ək sē)—a large belt of stars and associated matter encircling the heavens—would you know what to tell him? (*Like the familiar candy bar—the Milky Way.*)

As you can see, the English language is loaded with a variety of words that name. To be an interesting conversationalist or writer, you need to have a generous supply of these words in your vocabulary.

## Things You Can See

*Things*—is there any broader category of words? Think about it, or better yet, look around your house or office. Look in your garage or, if you dare, in your closet. Walk through a drugstore or hardware store. Turn on the television—any channel. How many "things" do you see? Dozens? Hundreds? More? It's easy to see why you need a generous supply of these words in your vocabulary to have a good command of the English language.

## EXERCISE 1

Wouldn't it be nice if all words that name things were as simple and easy to remember as the word *thing* itself? But they're not, as you can see from the following ten nouns.

apparition (ap′ ə RI shən)
archetype (ÄR ki tīp′)
artifact (ÄR ti fakt′)
conflagration (kän′ flə GRĀ shən)
contraband (KÄN trə band′)

edifice (ED  ə  fəs)
mosaic (mō  ZĀ  ik)
paraphernalia (par  ə  fər  NĀL  yə)
requiem (REK  wē  əm)
stipend (STĪ  pend′)

## STEP 1

Here are sample sentences with clues to the words'
definitions. As you read the sentences, pronounce the
words, think about them, and notice how they're used.
But even if you see one or more that you're not sure
about, don't reach for your dictionary until you've
completed Step 2.

1. He described the *apparition* as a glowing form
   that hovered near the ceiling.
2. The first superhighway was the *archetype* for a nationwide network of turnpikes and expressways.
3. The museum was filled with wonderful *artifacts*
   from Egypt.
4. The *conflagration* destroyed an entire city block
   before firefighters brought it under control.
5. The border patrol arrested the smugglers and
   seized the *contraband.*
6. The concrete *edifice* reminded me of a huge temple.
7. The students created a *mosaic* on the counter
   surface by arranging small pieces of colored stone
   in the shape of an eagle.
8. The waiting room was so cluttered with *paraphernalia* that one could hardly find a place to sit.
9. The large cathedral was a perfect place to hold
   a *requiem* for the mayor, who died on Monday.
10. If it hadn't been for the help of her *stipend,* she

would have run out of money before the end of her senior year in college.

## STEP 2

Are you ready to double-check the meanings of the ten words you just read? Write each word—*apparition, archetype, artifact, conflagration, contraband, edifice, mosaic, paraphernalia, requiem, stipend*—on the line next to the correct definition.

1. _____ a large, disastrous fire or conflict
2. _____ goods that are smuggled illegally
3. _____ a surface decoration of small, colored pieces of material
4. _____ the original pattern or model
5. _____ a large or massive structure
6. _____ odds and ends
7. _____ a ghostly or unusual figure
8. _____ a periodic payment for services or expenses
9. _____ an object created by a particular culture, often from a certain period
10. _____ a mass or solemn chant for the dead

ANSWERS: (1) conflagration (2) contraband (3) mosaic (4) archetype (5) edifice (6) paraphernalia (7) apparition (8) stipend (9) artifact (10) requiem

## STEP 3

Again, we want to work with the words one more time before leaving them. Use this easy quiz to reinforce your understanding by circling true or false in each sentence.

1. A *mosaic* is a handmade creation from a particular culture. *True False*
2. An *edifice* is a large building or massive structure. *True False*
3. A *conflagration* refers to a large, devastating fire. *True False*
4. A *requiem* is a mass for someone who has died. *True False*
6. *Contraband* refers to goods that are being transported illegally. *True False*
6. An *artifact* usually consists of small colored pieces of material arranged in a pattern. *True False*
7. A *stipend* is a large structure. *True False*
8. The original model for later copies is called the *archetype*. *True False*
9. An *apparition* is a ghostly figure. *True False*
10. *Paraphernalia* refers to mass-produced duplicates. *True False*

ANSWERS: (1) False (2) True (3) True (4) True (5) True (6) False (7) False (8) True (9) True (10) False

## EXERCISE 2

Let's study ten more words, all nouns, that name various things. In this next list the pronunciation of some words, such as *hieroglyphs,* may seem puzzling. If so, you may want to practice saying such words a few times before you move on to Step 1.

appurtenances (ə PƏRT nən səs)
archipelago (är′ kə PEL ə gō′)
biosphere (BĪ ə sfir′)
compendium (kəm PEN dē əm)
emporium (im PŌR ē əm)
hieroglyphs (HĪ rə glifs′)
karaoke (kar′ ē Ō kē)
papyrus (pe PĪ rəs)
protuberance (prō TÜ bər ənts)
syllabus (SIL ə bəs)

## STEP 1

We'll start with brief definitions and examples of the ten nouns that name things.

1. *Appurtenances* are incidental or subordinate rights or possessions attached to property: an estate with *appurtenances* consisting of a garden and a tool shed.
2. An *archipelago* is a large group of islands: the islands of the Philippine *archipelago*.
3. The *biosphere* is that part of the earth and the atmosphere that can support life: the *biosphere* of earth, including the oceans and the immediate atmosphere.
4. A *compendium* is an abstract or a short, complete summary of a larger work or body of knowledge: a *compendium* of tax law in the United States.
5. An *emporium* is a marketplace where goods are bought and sold: an arts and crafts *emporium*.
6. *Hieroglyphs* are characters in a pictorial writing system: the ancient Egyptian *hieroglyphs* written on stone tablets.
7. A *karaoke* is a music device that plays selected

songs while the users sing along and the device records the combined singing and music: *karaoke* music.

8. *Papyrus* is a plant of the Nile valley and a special paper, created from strips of the plant, used for writing and fine art: a *papyrus* scroll.

9. A *protuberance* is a swelling or bulge sticking out from the surrounding surface: the knoblike *protuberance* on a piece of wood.

10. A *syllabus* is an outline or summary of main points in a speech, course of study, or text: the *syllabus* for a lecture.

## STEP 2

Now that you know what the ten words mean, try inserting the correct word—*appurtenances, archipelago, biosphere, compendium, emporium, hieroglyphs, karaoke, papyrus, protuberance, syllabus*—in these sentences.

1. The bump on his chin caused an unsightly _____ for more than a week.

2. Land, water, and air are all part of the _____.

3. The property deed specified land and all _____.

4. I always prepare a _____ of the main points before I give a speech.

5. My daughter and her friends love to sing along with instrumental music, so we bought her a _____ for her birthday.

6. The islands of the Bismarck _____ surround the Bismarck Sea.

7. We opened a booth to sell glassware in the new _____.

8. According to the remaining _____,
   the cave dwellers recorded their activities with
   pictures carved into the walls.
9. A likeness of the Egyptian princess was painted
   on the sheet of _____.
10. The _____ summarizes the treatise
    on the Catholic religion in two pages.

ANSWERS: (1) protuberance (2) biosphere (3) appurtenances (4) syllabus (5) karaoke (6) archipelago (7)
emporium (8) hieroglyphs (9) papyrus (10) compendium

## STEP 3

Here's a matching quiz to reinforce your understanding of the definitions. Match each word in column 1 with the correct definition in column 2, using
the small line after each word to write in the appropriate letter—a, b, c, and so on.

1. appurtenances _____
2. archipelago _____
3. biosphere _____
4. compendium _____
5. emporium _____
6. hieroglyphs _____
7. karaoke _____
8. papyrus _____

a. an abstract or brief summary of a larger work or
   body of knowledge
b. the characters from a
   pictorial writing system
c. a marketplace
d. a plant from the Nile and
   the paper made from it
e. a swelling or bulge
f. the rights and possessions
   attached to property
g. the part of the earth
   and atmosphere supporting life
h. a musical device

9. protuberance ____      i. an outline of main points
                                   in a lecture, course of
                                   study, or text

10. syllabus ____      j. a large group of islands

ANSWERS: (1) f (2) j (3) g (4) a (5) c (6) b (7) h (8) d (9) e (10) i

## Nonphysical Things

Some things are concrete and visible. You can see and touch such things or even hold them—if they're small enough. Although you may get arrested if you try to touch, hold, or pick up a stranger, *people* are real and visible; you can see them walking on the sidewalk and in stores or offices. *Places* are also physically visible; you can visit actual sites such as London or Las Vegas. You can see, touch, and sometimes pick up *objects* (*things*), too, such as a computer or a bar of soap.

In this chapter and the previous one, most of the words we've described so far have referred to concrete, visible people, places, and things. Now it's time to move to the other side and look at words that name things you often *can't* touch physically. But even though you can't reach out and touch some of these things, you can imagine, sense, visualize, and talk about them. Words that name such things often involve concepts, ideas, and processes. For purposes of the next exercise, think of these three categories in the following way.

*Concepts* include definite or developed ideas, thoughts, and theories, frequently abstract or general, such as concepts about the afterlife (heaven or hell) or theories about the origin of human life (whether or not we evolved from apes).

*Ideas* include plans for action, designs, suggestions, and indefinite or undeveloped concepts, such as suggestions for keeping the cat from shredding the couch or thoughts about how to stop vandalism.

*Processes* include natural or planned continuing activities, such as the process (ordeal!) of losing weight or the process of advertising and selling a new mousetrap.

We've all heard or read comments that use these terms to describe something. For example:

"The *concept* that gestures communicate more than words applies to certain types of work, such as directing traffic."

"Your *idea* to serve refreshments during the next meeting sounds great."

"Teenagers can be very rebellious, but it's all part of the *process* of growing up."

Don't worry if you're still not sure whether you know the difference between a concept, an idea, and a process. Sometimes even the experts use these terms to mean the same thing. In the next exercise you need to remember only that we're going to include words that name things we ordinarily can't touch or pick up and often can't see.

## EXERCISE 3

Words that name concepts, ideas, processes, or any other nonphysical entities are often less familiar than words that name physical things. Although the word *idea* should be familiar to most of us, how about *catharsis* or *vicissitude*? Both of these terms, included in the following list, name something nonphysical. They are probably less familiar to you than, say, *New Yorker* or *town house,* both of which name someone or something concrete and physically visible.

Another difference between the two types of words involves spelling and pronunciation. Again, the following ten words, all nouns, may be more difficult to spell and pronounce than many words that name people, places, or physical objects. Yet it's worth the extra effort to master them, because a full and varied vocabulary cannot overlook such words. Without them we would be left out of many of life's most fascinating and important discussions.

With that in mind, try pronouncing each word and repeat it several times. Then mentally spell each one before you begin Step 1 of this exercise.

aberration (ab′ ə RĀ shən)
allusion (ə LÜ zhən)
assimilation (ə sim′ ə LĀ shən)
catharsis (kə THÄR səs)
collusion (kə LÜ zhən)
extrapolation (ik strap′ ə LĀ shən)
genre (ZHÄN rə)
intimation (in′ tə MĀ shən)
narcissism (NÄR sə siz′ əm)
vicissitude (və SIS ə tüd′)

## STEP 1

Let's get right to it. Here—with brief examples—is what the ten words mean.

1. An *aberration* is a deviation from the typical course or a variation from what is normal: an *aberration* such as the unusually odd behavior of a usually normal person.

2. An *allusion* is an indirect reference to someone or something that often doesn't specifically identify the source: an *allusion* to Robert Frost's poem, "Stopping by the Woods on a Snowy Evening," when saying, "I have miles to go before I sleep."

3. *Assimilation* is the process of taking in or absorbing: the *assimilation* of vitamins and minerals in our bodies.

4. A *catharsis* is a freeing or purifying of emotions, which often leads to relief or renewal: the *catharsis* that cancer survivors experience in a support group.

5. *Collusion* is a conspiracy, a secret agreement, or cooperation that often occurs for illegal or deceitful reasons: the *collusion* among businesses to control the supply of a certain product.

6. An *extrapolation* is a prediction, inference, or projection based on something known: a mathematical *extrapolation* of the number of probable car accidents based on the numbers that occurred in previous years.

7. A *genre* is a category or type of artistic, musical, or literary work: the *genre* of science fiction.

8. An *intimation* is a subtle, often tactful, hint, announcement, or suggestion that has enough clues for the receiver to guess what is meant: the *intimation* that she and her spouse might soon start a family.

9. *Narcissism* is excessive self-love or love of one's own body: the *narcissism* evident from numerous

personal photographs, awards, and trophies displayed in his home.

10. *Vicissitude* is a state or quality of being changeable: the *vicissitude* of political life.

## STEP 2

As soon as you're certain that you know what the words mean, test yourself by using them in the next group of sentences. Fill in the blanks with the most appropriate word—*aberration, allusion, assimilation, catharsis, collusion, extrapolation, genre, intimation, narcissism, vicissitude*—in each of the following ten sentences.

1. Neil's house is full of mirrors, and his _____ is so pronounced that he can't pass one without stopping to look at himself.

2. Talking about their problems was a rewarding _____ for members of the support group.

3. In supermarket sales of books, the leading _____ is romance novels.

4. Three straight months without rain in the spring is an _____ in the Midwest.

5. Ben and Marilyn decided on a fixed-rate mortgage because of the _____ of interest rates.

6. Because of his _____ to a recent court case, we wondered if he is planning similar legal action.

7. According to my _____, we can expect 85 percent of the students to finish their freshman year.

8. A familiar characteristic of U.S. society is the _____ of different cultures.

9. Jim wondered if we might each be getting a bonus after hearing the manager's _____ that the company would soon reveal something exciting for its employees.

10. If the downtown hotels are in _____, all rates may remain high this year.

ANSWERS: (1) narcissism (2) catharsis (3) genre (4) aberration (5) vicissitude (6) allusion (7) extrapolation (8) assimilation (9) intimation (10) collusion

## STEP 3

Here's another easy test to reinforce your understanding of the definitions. Circle either true or false after each sentence.

1. A *collusion* is a freeing of emotions leading to a sense of relief. *True False*

2. *Genre* refers to general artistic, musical, or literary work that does not fit in a particular category. *True False*

3. An *extrapolation* is a prediction made on the basis of something already known. *True False*

4. An *aberration* is a deviation from something normal. *True False*

5. *Vicissitude* is a form of self-admiration. *True False*

6. The process of absorbing many different things is called *assimilation*. *True False*

7. An *intimation* is a subtle, often tactful, hint, announcement, or suggestion. *True False*

8. *Catharsis* is a conspiracy for illegal purposes. *True False*
9. The state or quality of being changeable is called *narcissism*. *True False*
10. An *allusion* is an indirect reference to something, often made without mentioning the source. *True False*

ANSWERS: (1) False (2) False (3) True (4) True (5) False (6) True (7) True (8) False (9) False (10) True

## EXERCISE 4

Let's try learning ten more words, all nouns, that name a concept, idea, process, or something else that is generally nonphysical. Again, pronounce each word several times and spell it mentally before you begin

arbitration (är′ bə TRĀ shən)
asceticism (ə SET ə siz′ əm)
avocation (av′ ō KĀ shən)
celibacy (SEL ə bə sē)
clairvoyance (klar VOI ənts)
Darwinism (DÄR wə niz′ əm)
equanimity (ēk′ wə NIM ə tē)
insinuation (in sin′ yə WĀ shən)
largess (lär ZHES)
reincarnation (rē′ in kär NĀ shən)

## STEP 1

Read the following brief definitions and examples of the ten nouns very carefully.

1. *Arbitration* is the process of hearing and deciding a case involving a controversy: the *arbitration* used to settle a labor-management dispute.

2. *Asceticism* is the practice of strict self-denial as a matter of discipline: the *asceticism* evident from a person's sparsely furnished home and his or her refusal to eat anything other than very simple, basic food.

3. An *avocation* is a secondary occupation or activity that a person pursues in addition to his or her regular work: the *avocation* of stamp collecting.

4. *Celibacy* is the practice of refraining from having sex: the *celibacy* practiced in a strict religious group.

5. *Clairvoyance* is the power to be aware of objects or events that the senses (sight, hearing, and so on) don't pick up: one's *clairvoyance* in being able to visualize a disaster one hasn't actually seen.

6. *Darwinism* is a theory of biological evolution developed by Charles Darwin and others: the emphasis on natural selection and survival of the fittest in *Darwinism*.

7. *Equanimity* is the quality of being composed, calm, and even-tempered: showing *equanimity* in spite of extreme pressure at work.

8. An *insinuation* is a suggestion that provokes doubt or suspicion: the *insinuation* that someone is dishonest.

9. *Largess* is generosity or liberality in gift giving, sometimes in a condescending manner: her uncle's almost annoying *largess*.

10. *Reincarnation* is the rebirth of a soul in a different body: the theory of *reincarnation*.

### Step 2

Do you want to try another fill-in-the-blank test? As you did in the previous exercise, pick the most appropriate word—*arbitration, asceticism, avocation, celibacy, clairvoyance, Darwinism, equanimity, insinuation, largess, reincarnation*—for each sentence and write it on the blank line.

1. Since she never arrives at our house without a gift, her _____ obviously isn't confined to holidays.
2. Painting, his _____, has nothing to do with his job as a photocopier service representative.
3. Because of her _____, she was aware of the coming flood although she didn't physically see it with her eyes.
4. After seven weeks of _____, the students' dispute with the university was finally resolved.
5. Considering that Ron is angry at his boss, I'm skeptical of his _____ that the company has mismanaged its pension program.
6. Both of them believe in _____ and claim to have lived many times before.
7. Because of his _____, David continually denies himself many of life's pleasures and comforts.
8. The debate was so heated that her _____ in the midst of it was admirable.
9. According to the theory of _____, very different groups of plants and animals had the same ancestors.
10. The professor was surprised that 20 percent of the

students said they practiced _____ in spite of peer pressure to have sex.

ANSWERS: (1) largess (2) avocation (3) clairvoyance (4) arbitration (5) insinuation (6) reincarnation (7) asceticism (8) equanimity (9) Darwinism (10) celibacy

## STEP 3

To reinforce your understanding, match the words in column 1 with the brief descriptions in column 2. Use the short line after each word to fill in the appropriate letter—a, b, c, and so on.

1. arbitration ____

  a. a secondary occupation or hobby

2. asceticism ____

  b. an ability to sense what one doesn't actually see, hear, and so on

3. avocation ____

  c. the process of hearing and deciding a dispute

4. celibacy ____

  d. calmness and composure

5. clairvoyance ____

  e. self-denial

6. Darwinism ____

  f. a suggestion that arouses suspicion

7. equanimity ____

  g. generosity in gift giving

8. insinuation ____

  h. the rebirth of the soul in another body

9. largess ____

  i. the theory of evolution

10. reincarnation ____

  j. the practice of refraining from having sex

ANSWERS: (1) c (2) e (3) a (4) j (5) b (6) i (7) d (8) f (9) g (10) h

## BONUS WORDS

This list of extra words that name, all nouns, is a bonus for those of you who want to learn more words than the exercises provide. Don't be surprised if some of these words appear in the end-of-chapter review tests along with words from the regular exercises.

1. *altruism* (AL trü iz′ əm) unselfish concern for the welfare of others: the *altruism* of a charitable organization
2. *analogy* (ə NAL ə jē) a comparison to something else based on resemblance to or similarity with the other thing: an *analogy* comparing a slow worker to a turtle
3. *charisma* (kə RIZ mə) personal magnetism, charm, or appeal: an appealing person with a lot of *charisma*
4. *creationism* (krē Ā shə niz′ əm) a theory that the world was created by God as described in Genesis: the theory of *creationism* versus the theory of *evolution*
5. *hiatus* (hī Ā təs) an interruption or break in activity: the *hiatus* taken by television programs each summer
6. *hologram* (HŌ lə gram′) a three-dimensional image created by light from a laser: the lifelike *hologram* in a science fiction film
7. *ideology* (ī dē AL ə jē) a body of ideas that reflect the beliefs and desires of one or more people: republican *ideology* versus democratic *ideology*
8. *nuance* (NÜ änts′) a delicate shade of difference in meaning or color that is difficult to detect

and understand: the *nuances* of color in a painting

9.  *paradox* (PAR ə däks′)  that which seems to be contrary to common sense or opinion but may be true: the *paradox* that prolonged exercise may actually be harmful

10. *Zoroastrianism* (Zōr′ ō AS trē ə niz′ əm) a religious system, founded in Persia by the prophet Zoroaster in the sixth century B.C., based on the worship of a supreme god and focusing on the struggle between good and evil: the similarities between Christianity and *Zoroastrianism*

### REVIEW TEST

Your review test will draw on words from all previous exercises and bonus lists in Chapters 3 and 4. Circle the most appropriate answer—a, b, or c—in each of the following sentences. When you've finished, look for the line below the answer section where you can record your score.

1.  The oceans south of the equator, including parts of the Atlantic and Indian oceans, are popularly known as the *(a) Caribbean Sea (b) Mediterranean Sea (c) South Seas*.

2.  The troubled employee always felt that his sessions with the company counselor led to a *(a) largess (b) catharsis (c) assimiliation*.

3.  Those who believe that God created the world object to the theory of evolution expressed in *(a) narcissism (b) Zoroastrianism (c) Darwinism*.

4.  The astrologer *(a) Nostradamus (b) Stradivarius*

    *(c) Samuel Wilson,* who died in 1566, predicted that aliens from outer space would visit earth in 1999.

5. A/an *(a) archetype (b) edifice (c) syllabus* is a model or pattern for additional copies that follow.

6. Whenever gas prices go up, drivers immediately wonder whether the oil companies or station owners are in *(a) arbitration (b) hiatus (c) collusion.*

7. Seventeen new shops had opened in the *(a) compendium (b) emporium (c) archipelago* by the end of the year.

8. This year a *(a) Filipino (b) Philippine (c) Philippinean* is among the delegates.

9. The largest coral reef in the world, more than a thousand miles long, is the *(a) Great Coral Reef (b) Piedmont Reef (c) Great Barrier Reef.*

10. Someone who shows calmness and composure in the midst of crisis is displaying *(a) asceticism (b) equanimity (c) celibacy.*

  ANSWERS: (1) c (2) b (3) c (4) a (5) a (6) c (7) b (8) a (9) c (10) b
*Correct Answers:*_____ *Incorrect Answers:*_____

# 5. Use Action Words to Energize Your Messages

*Headline:*
AIDE PUTS BUG IN PRESIDENT'S EAR

That's an interesting image—someone stuffing an insect in the president's ear. Fortunately, we all know that the headline means something far less bizarre. The aide was obviously passing on an important suggestion or warning the president about something. Apparently, busy editors don't have time to worry about the strange images that double-meaning headlines create.

Ads are another source of two-sided images. The bug incident reminds us of this one in a Rome (Italy) laundry:

LADIES, LEAVE YOUR CLOTHES HERE AND SPEND THE AFTERNOON HAVING A GOOD TIME!

A "detour" sign posted along a busy Japanese road is equally interesting:

STOP! DRIVE SIDEWAYS!

Whether you decide to poke fun at such bloopers or treat them seriously, they all suggest action. The aide *put* a "bug" in the president's ear. The laundry urged women to *leave* (drop off) their laundry so that they could *spend* the afternoon doing something else. The road sign told drivers to *stop* and *drive* (turn) left or right along the detour route. Suggesting a sense of mental or physical energy or movement is what action words do—they signal activity.

Think about the word *action* itself. It may be the best example of an action word that we can find. When movie director Steven Spielberg shouts "Action!" for example, he's signaling the actors and crew to begin acting and filming. In this sense, the word *action* suggests doing, activity, movement, animation, energy.

Because action words tend to charge our thoughts and feelings in some way, it's not surprising that they can do wonders for conversations and letters. In fact, the more action words you have in your vocabulary, the better.

## Active versus Passive Verbs

If you suspect that people with a rich and powerful vocabulary have done more than simply memorize terms, you're right. For example, successful speakers and writers know when to make their comments passive and when to make them active. They indicate their choice with a grammatical device called "voice." Although you don't have to be a grammar expert to enlarge your vocabulary, knowing the difference between an active and passive voice will help you build a much more effective vocabulary. Here are two easy-to-learn guidelines that will make this chapter more useful.

*Guideline 1—Active Voice:* Using an *active voice* means that the "doer"—the subject of a sentence—is doing the acting or providing the action. This action is indicated by an active *verb*—a word that expresses the action: "He [doer subject] *writes* [active verb] editorials." The subject "he" is the doer, the one who does (writes) the editorials.

*Guideline 2—Passive Voice:* Using a *passive voice* means that the subject of the sentence is passively being acted on instead of actively doing something. "Editorials [inactive subject] *are written* [passive verb] by him." The inactive "editorials" aren't actively *doing* anything; they're just passively sitting there, being acted on (written) by "him."

If all this sounds confusing, just wait. It will become clearer as you move through this chapter. For now, try to remember the basic rule that if you add lively, active verbs to your vocabulary and comment in a lively, active voice, you'll have a much better chance of electrifying your messages. It's common sense that this will help you catch and hold the attention of others.

## EXERCISE 1

Let's see how this active-passive business works. First, learn the following ten verbs. Then we'll use them to put the previous two guidelines into practice.

abridge (ə BRIJ)
amortize (AM ər tīz')
coerce (kō ƏRS)
demote (di MŌT)
integrate (IN tə grāt')
malign (mə LĪN)
precipitate (pri SIP ə tāt)

recant (ri KANT)
synchronize (SIN krə nīz′)
trammel (TRAM əl)


## STEP 1

Before you're tempted to look up the words in a dictionary, take time to pronounce them and notice how they're used in the following sentences. Concentrate on clues to the definitions that the sentences provide. We'll wait until Step 3 to deal with the active and passive voice.

1. The report, which was much too long, *has been abridged* by Tom.
2. By means of monthly payments, they *amortized* the loan in five years.
3. He *coerced* her into opposing the plan by threatening to reveal something unfavorable in her past.
4. I'm afraid the assistant manager *will be demoted* by the president to a lesser position.
5. We *integrated* our word processing and desktop publishing departments into a single production department.
6. She is upset because her reputation *is maligned* by the article.
7. The problem *was precipitated* by the overly strict new policy.
8. After learning that he might also be blamed, he *recanted* his story.
9. We again *synchronized* the film's sound and action to correct some parts where the two didn't match.
10. Since progress *has been trammeled* by the opposition, we may have to start over.

## STEP 2

If the previous sentences gave you some clues to the meanings of the ten verbs, try matching each one—*abridge, amortize, coerce, demote, integrate, malign, precipitate, recant, synchronize, trammel*—with the correct definition in the following list. Write each verb on the line across from the definition it matches. You'll find that writing out each word will help you learn the correct spelling.

1. _____    to cause or throw
2. _____    to make simultaneous with
3. _____    to settle a debt through payments
4. _____    to reduce or shorten
5. _____    to retract or disavow
6. _____    to force or compel
7. _____    to unite or make whole
8. _____    to reduce in grade or status
9. _____    to speak evil of
10. _____    to hinder activity or movement

ANSWERS: (1) precipitate (2) synchronize (3) amortize (4) abridge (5) recant (6) coerce (7) integrate (8) demote (9) malign (10) trammel

## STEP 3

It's time to use the ten verbs you just learned to test whether you can spot the difference between an active and passive voice and an active and passive verb. Remember Guidelines 1 and 2? When a sentence is in the active voice, the subject does the "acting" or "doing": "The students *enjoy* tennis." When a sentence is in the passive voice, the subject does *not* do the acting but instead is acted on: "Tennis *is enjoyed* by the students."

Keeping in mind the distinction explained in Guidelines 1 and 2, reread the same sentences that you first saw in Step 1, repeated here in the following list. This time, circle either (a) active or (b) passive.

1. The report, which was much too long, *has been abridged* by Tom. *(a) active (b) passive*
2. By means of monthly payments, they *amortized* the loan in five years. *(a) active (b) passive*
3. He *coerced* her into opposing the plan by threatening to reveal something unfavorable in her past. *(a) active (b) passive*
4. I'm afraid the assistant manager *will be demoted* by the president to a lesser position. *(a) active (b) passive*
5. We *integrated* our word processing and desktop publishing departments into a single production department. *(a) active (b) passive*
6. She is upset because her reputation *is maligned* by the article. *(a) active (b) passive*
7. The problem *was precipitated* by the overly strict new policy. *(a) active (b) passive*
8. After learning that he might also be blamed, he *recanted* his story. *(a) active (b) passive*
9. We again *synchronized* the film's sound and action to correct some parts where the two didn't match. *(a) active (b) passive*
10. Since progress *has been trammeled* by the opposition, we may have to start over. *(a) active (b) passive*

ANSWERS: (1) b (2) a (3) a (4) b (5) a (6) b (7) b (8) a (9) a (10) b

## EXERCISE 2

Here's a similar exercise, with ten new verbs to learn. Practice pronouncing the words before you begin Step 1.

accede (ak SĒD)
ameliorate (ə MĒL yə rāt')
attenuate (ə TEN yə wāt')
construe (KÄN strü')
eschew (e SHÜ)
exacerbate (ig ZAS ər bāt')
impute (im PYÜT)
juxtapose (JƏK stə pōz')
mitigate (MIT ə gāt')
plagiarize (PLĀJ ə rīz')

### STEP 1

Just as you did in the previous exercise, first read the following sentences. Then try to figure out the definitions of the verbs from the context in which they're used. But wait until Step 3 to decide whether the verbs are active or passive.

1. Against his better judgment, he *acceded* to the client's demands.
2. The serious condition of the animals *has been ameliorated* through the kind efforts of volunteers.
3. The importance of his speech *was attenuated* by the lifeless, boring manner of his delivery.
4. They *construed* her decision to resign as cowardly.
5. Controversy *was eschewed* by my boss before he gained confidence through the company's executive training program.

6. The rent increase only *exacerbates* my financial problems and makes it more difficult to deal with them.

7. Their success *is imputed* by him to their negotiating skills.

8. Rather than separate the two diagrams, she *juxtaposed* them in the appendix.

9. The potentially damaging effects of the computer virus *were mitigated* by your fast corrective action.

10. He shamelessly *plagiarized* his predecessor's writing, repeatedly claiming it as his own work.

## Step 2

Are you ready to match verbs—*accede, ameliorate, attenuate, construe, eschew, exacerbate, impute, juxtapose, mitigate, plagiarize*—with definitions? Write each verb on the line across from the definition that best applies to it.

1. _____ to interpret
2. _____ to moderate the effect of
3. _____ to steal another's ideas or words
4. _____ to agree to
5. _____ to make worse
6. _____ to make weaker or less severe
7. _____ to attribute to
8. _____ to shun
9. _____ to make better
10. _____ to place side by side

ANSWERS: (1) construe (2) mitigate (3) plagiarize (4) accede (5) exacerbate (6) attenuate (7) impute (8) eschew (9) ameliorate (10) juxtapose

## STEP 3

Using the ten verbs you just learned, reread the same sentences first given in Step 1, repeated in the following list. This time, try to distinguish the active from the passive voice and the active from the passive verbs. Circle your choice of "active" or "passive" in each sentence.

1. Against his better judgment, he *acceded* to the client's demands. *(a) active (b) passive*
2. The serious condition of the animals *has been ameliorated* through the kind efforts of volunteers. *(a) active (b) passive*
3. The importance of his speech *was attenuated* by the lifeless, boring manner of his delivery. *(a) active (b) passive*
4. They *construed* her decision to resign as cowardly. *(a) active (b) passive*
5. Controversy *was eschewed* by my boss before he gained confidence through the company's executive training program. *(a) active (b) passive*
6. The rent increase only *exacerbates* my financial problems and makes it more difficult to deal with them. *(a) active (b) passive*
7. Their success *is imputed* by him to their negotiating skills. *(a) active (b) passive*
8. Rather than separate the two diagrams, she *juxtaposed* them in the appendix. *(a) active (b) passive*
9. The potentially damaging effects of the computer virus *were mitigated* by your fast corrective action. *(a) active (b) passive*
10. He shamelessly *plagiarized* his predecessor's writing, repeatedly claiming it as his own work. *(a) active (b) passive*

ANSWERS: (1) a (2) b (3) b (4) a (5) b (6) a (7) b (8) a (9) b (10) a

## Present, Past, and Future Action

People don't express *everything* only in terms of present action—something occurring right now—or do they? Newscasters have an especially annoying habit of saying *"We're back* in thirty minutes" instead of *"We'll be back* in thirty minutes." No wonder some parents of school-age children are tempted to throw their television sets out the window.

When you think how ridiculous it sounds to misstate the time of action—the time when something occurs—it's clear why merely adding words to your vocabulary isn't enough. You have to use verbs in the proper time frame or risk sounding as ignorant as the newscasters who *"are back* in thirty minutes."

To indicate the correct time when some action takes place, verbs have to be expressed in different forms called *tenses*. For example:

> If you want a new car now (in the *present*), you obviously should use the present tense: "I *want* a new car." But if you were looking for a new car last year (in the *past*), you should use the past tense: "I *wanted* a new car last year." If you don't want a new car now, didn't want one last year, but expect to want one next year (in the *future*), you should use the future tense: "I *will* want a new car next year."

It's that simple. Although there are other tenses besides the past, present, and future, these three are enough to demonstrate why the *time* when action oc-

curs is very important if you want to use the verbs in
your vocabulary correctly.

## EXERCISE 3

Here are ten more verbs to learn. But instead of
having you decide if a verb is active or passive in this
exercise, we want you to test your skill at recognizing
the difference between past, present, and future forms
of the verbs. Remember the difference? "I *want*" indicates the present. "I *wanted*" indicates the past. "I
*will want*" indicates the future.

absolve (əb ZÄLV)
acquiesce (ak' wē ES)
capitulate (kə PICH ə lāt')
conjecture (kən JEK chər)
deprecate (DEP ri kāt')
gesticulate (je STIK yə lāt)
impugn (im PYÜN)
lampoon (lam PÜN)
reprove (ri PRÜV)
vindicate (VIN də kāt')

## STEP 1

How many of the ten verbs did you know? Before
looking up the definitions of any you don't know, read
the following sentences in which they're used, pronouncing each of the ten words, and try to decide
their meanings from the context. Don't be concerned
in this step about the time (past, present, or future)
indicated by the verbs—more about that in Step 3.)

1. Jennifer *absolved* Helen of any responsibility for her error in using the wrong mailing list.
2. I *will acquiesce* in this case but do have objections in the other cases.
3. I think he *capitulated* too soon without considering his own chances of winning.
4. Jim *conjectures* that prices will rise, but we need facts, not speculation.
5. Isn't it contradictory that he applauds free thinking but *deprecates* nontraditional procedures?
6. Noreen *gesticulated* frantically when she saw the car skidding toward the crowd.
7. The candidates *impugn* all ads, even those with merit.
8. The television comedy *will lampoon* the president.
9. She *reproved* her old friend for that thoughtless statement.
10. His favorable testimony virtually *vindicates* the defendant.

## STEP 2

Could you figure out the meanings from the sentences in Step 1? Based on your understanding of the words from those sentences, write the appropriate verb—*absolve, acquiesce, capitulate, conjecture, deprecate, gesticulate, impugn, lampoon, reprove, vindicate*—on the line next to the correct definition in the following list.

1. _____     to surrender or give in
2. _____     to express disapproval of
3. _____     to attack the integrity of

4. _____    to forgive or relieve of an obligation
5. _____    to make gestures
6. _____    to satirize or mock
7. _____    to accept quietly without objection
8. _____    to clear of suspicion, especially with proof
9. _____    to criticize mildly
10. _____    to guess or speculate

ANSWERS: (1) capitulate (2) deprecate (3) impugn (4) absolve (5) gesticulate (6) lampoon (7) acquiesce (8) vindicate (9) reprove (10) conjecture

## STEP 3

If you're certain that you know the meaning of each word, let's find out *when* the action takes place. First, reread the sentences from Step 1, stated again in the following list. Then, to reinforce your understanding of when the action takes place, circle the correct tense of each verb: past, present, or future.

1. Jennifer *absolved* Helen of any responsibility for her error in using the wrong mailing list. *(a) past (b) present (c) future*

2. I *will acquiesce* in this case but do have objections in the other cases. *(a) past (b) present (c) future*

3. I think he *capitulated* too soon without considering his own chances of winning. *(a) past (b) present (c) future*

4. Jim *conjectures* that prices will rise, but we need facts, not speculation. *(a) past (b) present (c) future*

5. Isn't it contradictory that he applauds free thinking but *deprecates* nontraditional procedures? *(a) past (b) present (c) future*

6. Noreen *gesticulated* frantically when she saw the car skidding toward the crowd. *(a) past (b) present (c) future*

7. The candidates *impugn* all ads, even those with merit. *(a) past (b) present (c) future*

8. The television comedy *will lampoon* the president. *(a) past (b) present (c) future*

9. She *reproved* her old friend for that thoughtless statement. *(a) past (b) present (c) future*

10. His favorable testimony virtually *vindicates* the defendant. *(a) past (b) present (c) future*

ANSWERS: (1) a (2) c (3) a (4) b (5) b (6) a (7) b (8) c (9) a (10) b

## EXERCISE 4

Before we move on to the next topic, try one more exercise where you pick the tense of the verb: past, present, or future. Here are another ten words to add to your vocabulary and to test how easily you can judge whether a verb refers to past, present, or future action. Remember to pronounce each word and notice its spelling.

alleviate (ə LĒV ē āt′)
expunge (ik SPƏNJ)
foment (FŌ ment′)
ingratiate (in GRĀ shē āt′)
machinate (MAK ə nāt′)
palliate (PAL ē āt′)
preempt (prē EMPT)

protract (prō TRAKT)
usurp (yù SƏRP)
vitiate (VISH ē āt')

## STEP 1

Are you ready? Once again, try to decide what each word means, without using a dictionary, by reading the following sentences.

1. The newer brands of painkiller *alleviate* headaches much faster.
2. We *will expunge* all racial remarks from the record.
3. The charges against the popular singer *fomented* unrest throughout the city.
4. Volunteering to work overtime usually *ingratiates* employees with their employers.
5. He *machinates* more ways to get ahead than anyone else I know.
6. The bank loan *will palliate* his financial constraints.
7. News reports about the disaster *preempted* regular programming.
8. He only *protracts* the proceedings with his endless questions.
9. The rebel forces *will usurp* power the first chance they get.
10. The criminal charges and his conviction *vitiated* their former agreement.

## STEP 2

If the sentences helped you figure out the meanings of the verbs, test your accuracy by writing each word—*alleviate, expunge, foment, ingratiate, machi-*

*nate, palliate, preempt, protract, usurp, vitiate*—on the line across from the definition you believe is correct.

| | |
|---|---|
| 1. _____ | to stir up or arouse |
| 2. _____ | to scheme or plot |
| 3. _____ | to take over or replace |
| 4. _____ | to prolong |
| 5. _____ | to relieve or lessen |
| 6. _____ | to seize wrongfully |
| 7. _____ | to impair or debase |
| 8. _____ | to strike out, delete, or destroy |
| 9. _____ | to relieve or lessen the intensity of |
| 10. _____ | to gain favor through deliberate effort |

ANSWERS: (1) foment (2) machinate (3) preempt (4) protract (5) alleviate (6) usurp (7) vitiate (8) expunge (9) palliate (10) ingratiate

## STEP 3

This is the last step before we leave this topic. Read again the ten sentences from Step 1, listed below. This time, decide when the action in each takes place based on the form of verb that is used. Circle the correct tense—past, present, or future.

1. The newer brands of painkiller *alleviate* headaches much faster. *(a) past (b) present (c) future*
2. We *will expunge* all racial remarks from the record. *(a) past (b) present (c) future*

3. The charges against the popular singer *fomented* unrest throughout the city. *(a) past (b) present (c) future*
4. Volunteering to work overtime usually *ingratiates* employees with their employers. *(a) past (b) present (c) future*
5. He *machinates* more ways to get ahead than anyone else I know. *(a) past (b) present (c) future*
6. The bank loan *will palliate* his financial constraints. *(a) past (b) present (c) future*
7. News reports about the disaster *preempted* regular programming. *(a) past (b) present (c) future*
8. He only *protracts* the proceedings with his endless questions. *(a) past (b) present (c) future*
9. The rebel forces *will usurp* power the first chance they get. *(a) past (b) present (c) future*
10. The criminal charges and his conviction *vitiated* their former agreement. *(a) past (b) present (c) future*

ANSWERS: (1) b (2) c (3) a (4) b (5) b (6) c (7) a (8) b (9) c (10) a

## Productive Words

If you receive two letters today, and both ask for a response, which will you answer first? If nothing in either letter arouses your interest, you may simply answer the one you opened first or the one on the top of the pile. But assume that one letter said, "It is URGENT that I receive your reply by 5 p.m., Thursday, October 5," and the other letter said, "May we hear from you by October 5?" For many people the word *urgent* would stick in their minds, and they would reply to the letter with that word first.

Advertising and sales specialists use such attention-grabbing words intentionally. They know that these words are more likely than others to make us do what they want—thus the term *productive* words.

Words that encourage us to feel, act, or think in a certain way come in all types and sizes, from a two-syllable word such as *prof-it* to a four-syllable word such as *man-u-fac-ture*. Many of these productive words are active verbs, such as *guarantee;* others are nouns, such as *appreciation;* and still others are adjectives, such as *industrious*. (Nouns are defined in Chapter 3 and adjectives in Chapters 3 and 6.)

Productive verbs, nouns, adjectives—they're all excellent choices to add to your vocabulary. A large stock of these productive words will help you in countless situations, both socially and professionally. In fact, you'll find yourself drawing on them every time you want to influence someone or need to encourage someone to respond the way *you* want the person to respond.

## EXERCISE 5

One more time: When a word causes someone to respond the way *you* hoped the person would respond, it has "produced" the desired result. It has been productive. You may want to encourage someone to think or act in a certain way, or you may want the opposite—to discourage someone from thinking or acting in a certain way. The following ten productive words (a mix of verbs, adjectives, and a noun) are frequently used to influence someone positively or to encourage a favorable or friendly response.

accommodate, *vb.* (ə KÄM ə dāt′)
advocate, *vb.* (AD və kāt′)

amenable, *adj.* (ə MĒN ə bəl)
approbation, *n.* (ap′ rə BĀ shən)
conciliate, *vb.* (kən SIL ə āt′)
facilitate, *vb.* (fə SIL ə tāt′)
meritorious, *adj.* (mer′ ə TŌR ē əs)
proficient, *adj.* (prə FISH ənte)
revitalize, *vb.* (rē′ VĪT əl īz′)
scrupulous, *adj.* (SKRÜ pyə ləs)

## STEP 1

Do you know what those ten productive words mean? Did you remember to pronounce and spell each one? Notice how they're used in these sentences before you reach for a dictionary or read ahead in this exercise.

1. We always *accommodate* our guests as much as we can.
2. He strongly *advocates* a balanced budget.
3. Your boss is also *amenable* to my suggestion, so we can proceed with the plan.
4. The crowd showed its *approbation* of the council's position with frequent and heavy applause.
5. A reasonable compromise usually *conciliates* even the strongest opponents.
6. The new postal equipment greatly *facilitates* in-house mail delivery.
7. His speech to the delegates was *meritorious* and, not surprisingly, led to the adoption of many of his proposals.
8. You're our most *proficient* operator and fully deserve the employee-of-the-month award.
9. This plan *revitalizes* a failing segment of the industry.

10. I can assure you that he is always attentive and *scrupulous* in his work.

## STEP 2

Practice spelling the words and at the same time test your understanding of the meanings by writing the appropriate word—*accommodate, advocate, amenable, approbation, conciliate, facilitate, meritorious, proficient, revitalize, scrupulous*—on the line across from its definition.

1. _____ approval or praise
2. _____ to win over or pacify
3. _____ being worthy of honor and esteem
4. _____ to support or recommend
5. _____ to make easier
6. _____ to renew or give new life to
7. _____ to provide what is needed
8. _____ being adept or skilled
9. _____ being upright and painstakingly careful.
10. _____ being agreeable or willing to accept

ANSWERS: (1) approbation (2) conciliate (3) meritorious (4) advocate (5) facilitate (6) revitalize (7) accommodate (8) proficient (9) scrupulous (10) amenable

## STEP 3

Do you feel confident enough to use the same words in *different* sentences? Here are ten new sentences—ready for you to fill in the missing words. Select the most appropriate word—*accommodate, advocate, ame-*

*nable, approbation, conciliate, facilitate, meritorious, proficient, revitalize, scrupulous*—for each sentence. But to make it more challenging, assume that at least one word from the list of ten may be appropriate for more than one sentence and that at least one may not be used at all.

1. Although the policy was discontinued last year, we will _____ it in the spring.
2. When it comes to keeping accurate and detailed records, Bill is _____.
3. In spite of all his training, he never became _____ in written communication and still hates to write letters.
4. Whenever there is a conflict, he thoughtfully _____ our schedule.
5. Adding another work shift will _____ production during the busy season.
6. Your suggestion is clearly _____ and deserves further consideration.
7. The interesting and informative newsletter quickly gained the _____ of the readers.
8. I'm good at poker, but I've never been _____ at chess.
9. I know you like having two work shifts, but would you be _____ to another approach?
10. If you think it will _____ the flow of work to reassign Joe to our department, by all means do so.

ANSWERS: (1) revitalize (2) scrupulous (3) proficient (4) accommodates (5) facilitate (6) meritorious (7) approbation (8) proficient (9) amenable (10) facilitate

## EXERCISE 6

Let's look at another group of words—a mixture of adjectives, nouns, and one verb. These ten are productive words that you can use to prompt a listener or reader to develop a particular image of, feeling about, or response to something you do or say.

assiduous, *adj.* (ə SIJ yə wəs)
auspicious, *adj.* (ȯ SPISH əs)
efficacious, *adj.* (ef′ ə KĀ shəs)
gregarious, *adj.* (gri GAR ē əs)
importune, *vb.* (im′ pər TÜN)
munificent, *adj.* (myü NIF ə sənt)
panacea, *n.* (pa′ nə SĒ ə)
preeminent, *adj.* (prē EM ə nənt)
quintessential, *adj.* (kwin′ tə SENT shəl)
rectitude, *n.* (REK tə tüd′)

## STEP 1

Without using a dictionary or looking ahead, read the following sentences, pronouncing each of the ten words, and try to determine their definitions from the context in which they're used.

1. He's an *assiduous* writer, producing a new novel every year.
2. The new business had an *auspicious* beginning in spite of the competition.
3. The company's ads all proclaim that its herbal pills are *efficacious* for weight reduction.
4. She has always been a *gregarious* individual who is usually the life of the party.
5. I hope you don't mind if I *importune* you once again to join the committee.

6. For all of her life Mrs. Stone was a *munificent* contributor to animal-welfare causes.

7. The professor acts as though his suggestion is a *panacea* for all the country's problems.

8. He's a *preeminent* attorney in a widely recognized law firm.

9. Marlene is the *quintessential* hostess who makes everyone feel welcome.

10. His *rectitude* in a sometimes corrupt world is impressive.

## STEP 2

If the sentences helped you to guess the meanings of the ten words, you're ready to match these words—*assiduous, auspicious, efficacious, gregarious, importune, munificent, panacea, preeminent, quintessential, rectitude*—with their definitions. Practice spelling the words by writing each one on the line next to the appropriate definition.

1. _____ being liberal or generous

2. _____ being outstanding or of high rank

3. _____ being hardworking and busy

4. _____ being the most perfect or representative of

5. _____ moral integrity

6. _____ being effective

7. _____ being sociable

8. _____ being favorable or promising

9. _____ to urge persistently

10. _____ a cure-all or remedy

ANSWERS: (1) munificent (2) preeminent (3) assiduous (4) quintessential (5) rectitude (6) efficacious (7) gregarious (8) auspicious (9) importune (10) panacea

## STEP 3

Here's another fill-in-the-blank exercise to reinforce your understanding of the ten productive words you just learned. Pick the most appropriate word—*assiduous, auspicious, efficacious, gregarious, importune, munificent, panacea, preeminent, quintessential, rectitude*—for each sentence. Again, you may find that a word is suitable for more than one sentence or that one of the ten words isn't used at all in this step.

1.  We need to test whether the process is _____ before announcing it publicly.
2.  The Coldwells are _____ contributors.
3.  The layoffs may have been necessary, but they're hardly a _____ for all of the company's problems.
4.  Calls are running two to one in favor of the tax increase, which is an _____ sign for the mayor.
5.  The sculpture is the _____ form of modern Mexican art.
6.  The farmer tended the crops with _____ attention.
7.  No one as yet has found a _____ for rising teen pregnancy.
8.  I realize you said no, but could I _____ you one more time to reconsider?

9. The keynote speaker is a _____ scientist.

10. His devotion to family and his _____ are qualities that have earned our trust.

ANSWERS: (1) efficacious (2) munificent (3) panacea (4) auspicious (5) quintessential (6) assiduous (7) panacea (8) importune (9) preeminent (10) rectitude

## BONUS WORDS

Here are the bonus words for this chapter—ten action words, all verbs. Bonus words are primarily offered for those of you who want to learn more than the words defined in the exercises. However, everyone is urged to study them, since some of them may be used in the review test at the end of each chapter.

1. *accentuate* (ik SENT shə wāt′) to emphasize or highlight: *accentuate* the benefits of a new policy

2. *actuate* (AK chə wāt′) to move; to put into motion: *actuate* the generator

3. *cajole* (kə JŌL) to coax; to persuade with flattery: *cajole* with repeated appeals

4. *evince* (i VINTS) to show; to reveal: *evince* disapproval with a frown

5. *expedite* (EK spə dīt′) to speed up; to handle promptly: *expedite* a mailing

6. *impeach* (im PĒCH) to accuse; to charge; to remove from office for misconduct: *impeach* a state's governor

7. *intercede* (in′ tər SĒD) to mediate; to inter-

vene to help reconcile differences: *intercede* in a dispute

8. *officiate* (ə FISH ē āt′) to administer; to carry out official duties: *officiate* at a public ceremony

9. *supersede* (sü′ pər SĒD) to replace; to supplant; to make something else obsolete: *supersede* an old product with a new one.

10. *warrant* (WȮR ənt) to guarantee; to secure: *warrant* a product to be free of defects

## REVIEW TEST

The review test in this chapter consists of sample sentences with three possible choices for words drawn from this chapter and Chapters 3 and 4. Circle the word that you believe is most appropriate in each case. When you've finished, don't forget to compare your choices with the answers that follow the test and to record the number of correct and incorrect answers that you gave.

1. I think we should stick to the issues and not *(a) coerce (b) demote (c) malign* someone's character.

2. More taxes will *(a) exacerbate (b) ameliorate (c) eschew* the problem of stagnant wages.

3. David's angry remarks unfairly *(a) gesticulated (b) impugned (c) capitulated* Jeffrey's statement.

4. The *(a) Phoenicean (b) Phoenixer (c) Phoenician* left Phoenix for Detroit on Thursday.

5. His *(a) scrupulous (b) meritorious (c) amenable* presentation won high praise at the meeting.

6. He is the most *(a) munificent (b) gregarious (c)*

*assiduous* employee in the department, the only one who regularly arrives early and works late.

7. Life can exist in many parts of the *(a) genre (b) biosphere (c) mosaic.*

8. The witness later changed her mind and *(a) capitulated (b) palliated (c) recanted* her previous testimony.

9. His *(a) analogy (b) requiem (c) extrapolation* compared the slower old computers to the early steam engines.

10. Introducing too many alternatives may *(a) mitigate (b) attenuate (c) plagiarize* the proposal.

ANSWERS: (1) c (2) a (3) b (4) c (5) b (6) c (7) b (8) c (9) a (10) b

*Correct Answers:*_____ *Incorrect Answers:*_____

# 6. Enrich Your Vocabulary with Words That Describe

*When a black cat crosses your path in Japan, it's considered a sign of good luck.*

It's about time! Why does it have to be a sign of *bad* luck in the United States when a *black* cat crosses your path? Some of us are sick and tired of always worrying about this.

However, you've probably known all along that *black* cats bring *good* luck. Nevertheless, in matters of superstition, *domestic black* cats fare better in Japan than they do in the United States. *Superstitious* people may also fare better in Japan. Think how pleasant it must be for them to view *black* cats crossing their paths as *good* luck.

In spite of Japan's *appealing* attitude and those of you who love *black* cats, it's not likely that *superstitious* Americans will lose their fear of *black* cats crossing their paths. We may be able to learn from the Japanese how to build *better* cars, but changing a superstition from *bad* luck to *good* luck is clearly beyond our capability.

Did you notice the italicized words in the previous paragraphs? The chapter title tells you what purpose they serve. They describe other words, such as nouns.

That means they're *adjectives,* a type of word that was briefly introduced in Chapter 3.

In the previous good luck–bad luck example, the word *cat* by itself doesn't tell you much about the animal, except that it's not a dog or a mouse or something else. But if you add the words *domestic* and *black,* you can visualize the creature—its color and its general size and shape. Adjectives help us to do that: They help us to learn more about something or someone. Most of the time, anything that tells us more is useful, or even essential, so it's understandable why adjectives are such valuable words to add to our vocabularies.

## Descriptive Words

Adjectives say something about the words to which they're applied, such as nouns (*house*) or pronouns (*he*). We already learned about nouns (words that name) in Chapters 3 and 4. Pronouns, such as *she, you, they, we,* and *it,* are words that are used in place of a noun and are just as easy to recognize. For example:

"She [Kim] is intelligent." *She* is a pronoun—it's used in placed of the noun *Kim*. The word *intelligent* describes "she" (Kim), so it's an adjective. This will be easier to understand after you've practiced using some adjectives in the following exercises.

## EXERCISE 1

Both simple and complex words can be used as adjectives. First, look at some simple, familiar adjectives: *large* table, *tall* man, *happy* child, *frightening* storm, *excellent* teacher. The italicized words that describe the nouns "table," "man," and so on are adjectives. That's easy enough, right? The ten adjectives in the next list can also be used in the same way—to describe someone or something.

Since the following adjectives are more difficult to spell and pronounce than simple ones such as *large* or *happy,* it will help you to remember them if you pronounce and spell each adjective before beginning Step 1.

arbitrary (ÄR bə trer′ ē)
capricious (kə PRI shəs)
contentious (kən TENT shəs)
egregious (i GRĒ jəs)
immutable (im MYÜ tə bəl)
intransigent (in TRAN sə jənt)
parsimonious (pär′ sə MŌ nē əs)
punitive (PYÜ nə tiv)
taciturn (TAS ə tərn′)
ubiquitous (yü BIK wə təs)

## STEP 1

Those ten adjectives are used in the following sentences, which may give you a hint about their meanings. After you've read the sentences, go to Step 2 to find out if you really know the definitions.

1. The manager's decision to close the office on Monday was not based on state or national law or on required company policy but rather was strictly *arbitrary*.
2. His explosive reply was unexpected and *capricious*.
3. The two *contentious* neighbors have never been able to get along in all the years I've known them.

4. I'm not surprised that he was fired after committing such an *egregious* error.

5. The school principal's decision is *immutable* in that it is based on state law that is unlikely to change.

6. The *intransigent* council member refused to budge in his position and didn't seem to care whether or not the others liked his views on the city's bond issue.

7. I think Mr. Waxtell, our *parsimonious* neighbor, still has the first penny he ever earned.

8. The court's punishment of the accused included $100,000 in *punitive* damages awarded to the victim.

9. The *taciturn* employee was always alone, perhaps because he never made an effort to join in our conversations.

10. The *ubiquitous* caller-ID device is becoming a standard feature in homes across the country.

## STEP 2

Are you ready to check the definitions? By now you know the procedure: Write each word—*arbitrary, capricious, contentious, egregious, immutable, intransigent, parsimonious, punitive, taciturn, ubiquitous*—on the blank line across from the appropriate definition.

1. _____ very serious
2. _____ refusing to compromise or change
3. _____ impulsive; unpredictable
4. _____ aiming to punish a wrong-doer
5. _____ not likely to change
6. _____ untalkative

7. _____    random; not fixed by law
8. _____    stingy
9. _____    widespread; being every-
                       where
10. _____    argumentative;
                       quarrelsome

ANSWERS: (1) egregious (2) intransigent (3) capricious (4) punitive (5) immutable (6) taciturn (7) arbitrary (8) parsimonious (9) ubiquitous (10) contentious

## STEP 3

Although you may have heard the ten words on television talk shows or have seen them on the editorial pages of newspapers, some may nevertheless be difficult to remember. To be certain the definitions are firmly planted in your mind, let's go through them one more time. This time we'll use a true-false test. Read each sentence and circle your choice of either *true* or *false*.

1. An *immutable* decision is one that is unlikely to change. *True False*
2. An *egregious* error is obvious but not especially serious. *True False*
3. A *parsimonious* person is lavishly generous. *True False*
4. Something *ubiquitous* seems to be everywhere at once. *True False*
5. A decision is considered *arbitrary* when it is based on law or precedent. *True False*
6. *Capricious* behavior is impulsive and unpredictable. *True False*
7. A *taciturn* individual is a very quiet, untalkative person. *True False*

8. *Punitive* damages punish an offender and compensate a victim financially. *True False*
9. An *intransigent* person is prone to change his or her mind. *True False*
10. A *contentious* person is easy to get along with. *True False*

ANSWERS: (1) True (2) False (3) False (4) True (5) False (6) True (7) True (8) True (9) False (10) False

## EXERCISE 2

Here are ten new adjectives to learn. These words, like the previous ten, are not all easy to spell and pronounce. You may, therefore, want to repeat them several times and spell each one mentally before you begin working with the words.

arcane (är KĀN)
cerebral (sə RĒ brəl)
eclectic (e KLEK tik)
evanescent (ev′ ə NES ənt)
innocuous (i NÄK yə wəs)
nefarious (ni FAR ē əs)
propitious (prə PISH əs)
surreptitious (sər′ əp TISH əs)
tenacious (tə NĀ shəs)
unctuous (ƏNGK chə wəs)

## STEP 1

We'll start with brief definitions and examples. Read the following ten sentences and focus on the meaning of each adjective.

1.  *Arcane* means secret or mysterious; known only to a select few: the *arcane* initiation rites of the secret society.

2.  *Cerebral,* referring to the "cerebrum" (brain), means intellectual or brainy: a *cerebral* discussion.

3.  *Eclectic* means drawn from many sources: an *eclectic* art gallery.

4.  *Evanescent* means fleeting, momentary, or very brief: an *evanescent* recollection that was forgotten as fast as it appeared.

5.  *Innocuous* means harmless; unlikely to offend: *innocuous* remarks.

6.  *Nefarious* means evil or obviously wicked: a *nefarious* scheme to gain control of a company.

7.  *Propitious* means tending to favor: a *propitious* time to trade cars.

8.  *Surreptitious* means secret or sneaky: the shoplifter's *surreptitious* behavior.

9.  *Tenacious* means persistent, strong, or stubborn: *tenacious* efforts to score 100 on all tests in this book.

10. *Unctuous* means oily, slick, or insincere: an *unctuous* service representative.


## STEP 2

When you're certain that you understand the meaning of each adjective, fill in the appropriate word—*arcane, cerebral, eclectic, evanescent, innocuous, nefarious, propitious, surreptitious, tenacious, unctuous*—in the following sentences.

1.  The _____ young wrestler was being battered by his older opponent, but he refused to quit.

2. William played the part of the _____ villain in the senior class play.

3. With a sluggish economy, it was not a _____ time to start a new business.

4. The _____ symbols on the scroll were understandable only by members of the secret society.

5. Because of his pushy, hard-sell tactics, everyone disliked the _____ salesperson.

6. Most of the audience was lost and confused by the _____ discussion among the panel of high-level scientists.

7. His _____ movements made us suspect that he was up to no good.

8. The building was painted an _____ beige color that seemed to escape everyone's notice.

9. His nervousness as he began his new job was _____, vanishing as quickly as it appeared.

10. His home study was _____, with furniture and decorations from almost all major design periods.

ANSWERS: (1) tenacious (2) nefarious (3) propitious (4) arcane (5) unctuous (6) cerebral (7) surreptitious (8) innocuous (9) evanescent (10) eclectic

## STEP 3

Are you comfortable with the ten adjectives you just learned? They're all words you may hear at work or over the television, but not all may be words that you yourself regularly speak or write. If you want to reinforce your understanding, here's another true-false test. Read each sentence and circle your choice of either *true* or *false*.

1. A *surreptitious* person is open and forthright. *True False*
2. When *propitious* conditions exist, one has reason to be confident. *True False*
3. Everyone recognizes and understands an *arcane* procedure. *True False*
4. A *tenacious* person gives up easily. *True False*
5. An *evanescent* moment is a fleeting moment. *True False*
6. An *innocuous* comment is not likely to offend anyone. *True False*
7. A *cerebral* discussion may be difficult for the uninformed to understand. *True False*
8. Someone who likes an *eclectic* look in decorating would pick a particular period and decorate with objects only from that period. *True False*
9. *Nefarious* acts are grossly evil. *True False*
10. An *unctuous* politician is not likely to be admired or trusted. *True False*

ANSWERS: (1) False (2) True (3) False (4) False (5) True (6) True (7) True (8) False (9) True (10) True

## Limiting Adjectives

All adjectives tell us more about the words to which they refer. Some of them specifically limit those words as well. For example:

When you say "*two* cars," you don't mean perhaps *three* cars; you mean specifically *two* cars. When you say that a tablecloth is *round,* you don't mean that perhaps it is *square;* you mean specifically that it is *round.*

A limiting adjective, therefore, does as its name suggests: It places a limit on a noun or pronoun. This section will help you think about the importance of using these words carefully and precisely when you want to be very definite and clear about a certain limit, for example: number (*five* people), shape (*round* dish), size (*six*-foot board), amount (*ten*-dollar charge), or quantity (*two*-gallon container). Limiting adjectives are also used to point out a specific frequency or repetition (*weekly* appointments).

## EXERCISE 3

No doubt everyone knows what the simple limiting adjectives, such as the number *one,* mean. It's not likely, though, that everyone knows what the less common ones mean. Look at the following ten words that limit. How many can you define?

concentric (kən SEN trik)
concurrent (kən KƏR ənt)
cubical (KYÜ bi kəl)
quaternary (KWÄ tər ner′ ē)
rectangular (rek TANG gyə lər)
recurrent (ri KƏR ənt)
simultaneous (sī′ məl TĀ nē əs)
spherical (SFIR i kəl)
tertiary (TƏR shē er′ ē)
triangular (trī ANG gyə lər)

## STEP 1

To prepare for the test in Step 2, read the following brief definitions and examples of the ten limiting adjectives. Remember to pronounce any unfamiliar word.

1. *Concentric* means having a common center or axis: a series of *concentric* circles.
2. *Concurrent* means operating or occurring within the same period or at the same time or running side by side: two *concurrent* classes both scheduled in the morning hours. (*Concurrent* is sometimes loosely used interchangeably with *simultaneous*.)
3. *Cubical* means being shaped like a cube with six equal square sides: the *cubical* puzzle.
4. *Quaternary* means consisting of four parts or elements: a *quaternary* program having four sessions.
5. *Rectangular* means having four sides, with adjacent (touching) sides forming right angles, and especially having two adjacent sides of unequal length: the *rectangular* iron box.
6. *Recurrent* means happening repeatedly or being made or done over and over: a *recurrent* request.
7. *Simultaneous* means happening, existing, or being done at the same time or moment: the *simultaneous* use of the telephone lines by numerous people. (*Simultaneous* is sometimes loosely used interchangeably with *concurrent*.)
8. *Spherical* means being shaped like a ball or globe: the *spherical* shape of a planet or moon.
9. *Tertiary* means being third in rank, order, degree, place, and so on: the *tertiary* stage in the development of a species.

10. *Triangular* means having three sides or elements: the *triangular* shape of the side of a pyramid.

## STEP 2

That wasn't so bad, was it? To double-check whether you're correctly remembering the meanings, match the words in column 1 with the definitions in column 2. Write the appropriate letter—a, b, c, and so on—on the short line next to each word in column 1.

1. concentric ____

2. concurrent ____

3. cubical ____

4. quaternary ____

5. rectangular ____

6. recurrent ____

7. simultaneous ____

8. spherical ____

9. tertiary ____

10. triangular ____

a. composed of four parts

b. being shaped like a globe

c. having three sides

d. happening or being done at the same time

e. having six equal square sides

f. being third in rank, order, and so on

g. having the same center or axis

h. having four sides with adjacent sides forming right angles

i. happening again and again

j. occurring within the same period or running side by side

ANSWERS: (1) g (2) j (3) e (4) a (5) h (6) i (7) d (8) b (9) f (10) c

## STEP 3

If you still have doubts about any of the ten words, take the following multiple-choice test. Read each sentence and circle your choice of the most appropriate word.

1. Something composed of four parts would be described as *(a) tertiary (b) quaternary (c) concentric.*
2. When objects have a common axis, they are *(a) concentric (b) cubical (c) spherical.*
3. *Simultaneous* activities are being done *(a) at the same time (b) repeatedly (c) parallel to another activity.*
4. A *tertiary* rank is *(a) above all others (b) equal to another (c) third in line.*
5. An object with six square sides is *(a) spherical (b) cubical (c) quaternary.*
6. A *recurrent* problem occurs *(a) over and over (b) at regular intervals (c) at irregular intervals.*
7. A three-sided object is *(a) tertiary (b) triangular (c) concentric.*
8. The shape of the planet Mars is *(a) spherical (b) concentric (c) quaternary.*
9. Two programs running side by side are *(a) recurrent (b) concurrent (c) concentric.*
10. An object that has four sides with adjacent sides forming right angles is *(a) cubical (b) triangular (c) rectangular.*

ANSWERS: (1) b (2) a (3) a (4) c (5) b (6) a (7) b (8) a (9) b (10) c

## EXERCISE 4

Let's look at another type of limiting adjective, one that refers to a time period or to repetition. This type of adjective can be confusing. For example, do you know the difference between *biannual* and *biennial*? Some people use them to mean the same thing, but they have different meanings, as you'll see in Step 1. The following list contains some of the common yet confusing adjectives that relate to time periods and repetition.

biannual (bī' AN yə wəl)
bicentennial (bī' sen' TEN ē əl)
biennial (bī' EN ē əl)
centennial (sen TEN ē əl)
decennial (di SEN ē əl)
diurnal (dī ƏR nəl)
millennial (mə LEN ē əl)
perennial (pə REN ē əl)
sesquicentennial (ses' kwi sen TEN ē əl)
triennial (trī' EN ē əl)

## STEP 1

Although the adjective forms are defined here (*bicentennial* celebration), some of these words are spelled the same when used as nouns referring to specific anniversaries, celebrations, or the time periods themselves (the *bicentennial*). In other cases the spelling of the noun form is different.

"We will reach the *millennium* [noun] in the year 2000. At that time many *millennial* [adjective] events will take place."

The examples in the following list that have both a noun and adjective form include a note in parentheses telling you whether the noun form is spelled the same as the adjective form.

1. *Biannual* means occurring twice a year: the *biannual* stockholders' meeting.

2. *Bicentennial* means relating to a period of two hundred years: a *bicentennial* celebration (the noun form is spelled the same).

3. *Biennial* means relating to a period of two years: a *biennial* term for members of the board of directors (the noun form is *biennium*).

4. *Centennial* means relating to a period of one hundred years: a *centennial* souvenir poster (the noun form is spelled the same).

5. *Decennial* means relating to a period of ten years: a *decennial* anniversary (the noun form is spelled the same).

6. *Diurnal* means happening every day or in the daytime: the *diurnal* hunting habits of animals.

7. *Millennial* means relating to a period of one thousand years: the *millennial* program scheduled for the year 2000 (the noun form is *millennium*).

8. *Perennial* means happening year after year: *perennial* flowers (the noun form is spelled the same).

9. *Sesquicentennial* means relating to a period of one hundred and fifty years: the *sesquicentennial* celebration that will occur in the year 2150 (the noun form is spelled the same).

10. *Triennial* means relating to a period of three years: a *triennial* rotation period for field employees (the noun form is *triennium*).

## STEP 2

In this step, the first column lists the ten limiting adjectives relating to certain time periods or repetition. The second column briefly notes the times associated with those adjectives. To test how well you remember the definitions given in Step 1, match items in the following two columns the same as you did in the previous exercise, writing your choice of a, b, c, and so forth on the short line in column 1.

| | |
|---|---|
| 1. biannual ____ | a. one hundred years |
| 2. bicentennial ____ | b. daily |
| 3. biennial ____ | c. one thousand years |
| 4. centennial ____ | d. yearly |
| 5. decennial ____ | e. twice a year |
| 6. diurnal ____ | f. one hundred fifty years |
| 7. millennial ____ | g. two hundred years |
| 8. perennial ____ | h. three years |
| 9. sesquicentennial ____ | i. two years |
| 10. triennial ____ | j. ten years |

ANSWERS: (1) e (2) g (3) i (4) a (5) j (6) b (7) c (8) d (9) f (10) h

## STEP 3

To be certain you've remembered all time periods associated with the ten adjectives, take this easy true-false test. Circle either true or false depending on whether you believe the adjectives referring to a particular period and the associated years are correct or incorrect in the following list.

| | | |
|---|---|---|
| 1. millennial—one thousand years | *True* | *False* |
| 2. bicentennial—twice a year | *True* | *False* |

| | | | |
|---|---|---|---|
| 3. diurnal—daily | | *True* | *False* |
| 4. triennial—thirty years | | *True* | *False* |
| 5. biannual—two years | | *True* | *False* |
| 6. sesquicentennial—one hundred fifty years | | *True* | *False* |
| 7. decennial—ten years | | *True* | *False* |
| 8. biennial—two years | | *True* | *False* |
| 9. perennial—one year | | *True* | *False* |
| 10. centennial—one thousand years | | *True* | *False* |

ANSWERS: (1) True (2) False (3) True (4) False (5) False (6) True (7) True (8) True (9) False (10) False

## Words That Are the Most That They Can Be

Does the title of this section remind you of the army's slogan: Be All That You Can Be? Perhaps, but the section title is referring to something different. It means that words can't express more or less than what they already state.

Take the adjective *everlasting,* as in "everlasting faith." If your faith is everlasting, it will continue throughout your life and all eternity. Could your faith possibly last any longer than that? The answer is no: It's the most that it can be—unless you can think of somewhere that it can continue *beyond* "all eternity."

If a friend also has everlasting faith, could yours be any *more* or *less* everlasting than that of your friend, or vice versa? Again, the answer is no: If the word *everlasting* can't be more or less than it already is, it also can't be compared.

Confused? Another example may make clear what the section title means. Consider the adjective *final,* as in "final chapter," meaning the last chapter. If you're reading a book and you reach the final chapter, can this last chapter be any *more* or *less* final? Not if it's really the *last* chapter. That's the most that it can be: It can't be any more final than it already is.

If your friend is also reading a book and reaches the final chapter, is your friend's final chapter *more* or *less* final than yours? Not in this world. Each is a final chapter—the last one in each person's book.

Although some people add *more, most, less,* or *least* before this type of adjective, it usually serves no purpose to do so. For example, why say: "He has the *most* everlasting faith I've ever seen"? Or why say: "I've reached the *most* final chapter in the book"? It makes more sense simply to say: "I've never seen such everlasting faith," and "I've reached the final chapter in the book."

Get the idea? The adjectives in the next two exercises are, in the same respect as *everlasting* and *final,* the most that they can be.

## EXERCISE 5

We'll start with adjectives that are probably more familiar than some of the descriptive adjectives you learned in the first few exercises. But even if you know some or all of the following words, it's important to *re*learn them as words that are the most that they can be. Only then can you be certain that you won't misuse them in a sentence.

absolute (AB sə lüt′)
devoid (di VȮID)
inadmissible (in′ əd MIS ə bəl)
incessant (in′ SES ənt)
indestructible (in′ di STRƏK tə bəl)

omnipotent (äm NIP ə tənt)
replete (ri PLĒT)
ultimate (ƏL ə mət)
unique (yü NĒK)
untouchable (ən' TƏCH ə bəl)

## STEP 1

The following sentences may help you figure out the meaning of any of the ten adjectives that you don't know. After you've read these sentences, check your understanding of the words in Step 2.

1. He has *absolute* authority in matters involving hiring and firing and doesn't even need the president's approval.
2. It was a harsh speech *devoid* of compassion for anyone having financial problems.
3. Since the evidence was *inadmissible,* the jury never had a chance to hear about it.
4. Her *incessant* chatter gives me a headache.
5. Although the steel frame is *indestructible,* the plastic covering may eventually crack.
6. The way he acts, you would think he and God are the only *omnipotent* beings in the universe.
7. The warehouse was *replete* with unsold merchandise, leaving no place to store the new goods.
8. He paid her the *ultimate* compliment when he said her work was perfect in every way.
9. Singer Ella Fitzgerald had a *unique* voice and singing style.
10. His argument was so strong and persuasive that it seemed *untouchable* by the critics.

## STEP 2

To test whether you know the definitions, write each adjective—*absolute, devoid, inadmissible, incessant, indestructible, omnipotent, replete, ultimate, unique, untouchable*—on the line across from the most appropriate meaning.

As you fill in the adjectives, remind yourself that each word is already the most that it can be. If you use it in a sentence, then you won't add *more, most, less,* or *least.* For example, if you talk about an indestructible hammer, you won't say that it's the *most* indestructible hammer you could find. A hammer is either indestructible or it isn't.

1. _____ continuing without interruption

2. _____ being greatest or last

3. _____ all-powerful; having unlimited authority

4. _____ impossible to destroy

5. _____ complete, total, or unlimited

6. _____ being the only one of its kind

7. _____ empty or completely lacking

8. _____ out of reach; beyond criticism or attack

9. _____ not accepted or admitted

10. _____ filled to capacity

ANSWERS: (1) incessant (2) ultimate (3) omnipotent (4) indestructible (5) absolute (6) unique (7) devoid (8) untouchable (9) inadmissible (10) replete

## STEP 3

A final check to reinforce your understanding of the ten words: Read each statement in the following list and circle your choice of either true or false.

1. A painting that is the only one of its kind is *unique. True False*
2. A computer disk that is *replete* with data has no information stored on it. *True False*
3. An *omnipotent* god is all-powerful. *True False*
4. An object that cannot be ruined by any known act or effort is *indestructible. True False*
5. *Absolute* authority is limited only by constitutional restrictions. *True False*
6. *Inadmissible* evidence in a court trial can be introduced by a judge but not by any attorney. *True False*
7. An *untouchable* argument is beyond criticism. *True False*
8. Someone who is *devoid* of sympathy has it but doesn't know how to show it. *True False*
9. The *ultimate* test in a series of exercises is the one given before all others. *True False*
10. Activity that continues without interruption is *incessant. True False*

ANSWERS: (1) True (2) False (3) True (4) True (5) False (6) False (7) True (8) False (9) False (10) True

## EXERCISE 6

Now that you know what it means for an adjective to be the most that it can be, you'll probably zip through the next ten words.

enduring (in DÚR ing)
eternal (i TƏR nəl)
extinct (ik STINGKT)
illimitable (il' LIM ə tə bəl)
inestimable (in ES tə mə bəl)
infinitesimal (in fi' nə TES ə məl)
irreversible (ir i VƏR sə bəl)
perpetual (pər PECH ə wəl)
terminal (TƏR mə nəl)
unanimous (yú NAN ə məs)

## STEP 1

Here are ten sentences that may give you clues to
the meanings of the adjectives. But wait until Step 2
to find out if you understand each word.

1. The *enduring* struggle to survive is part of the
   human condition and never changes.
2. He compared timeless *eternal* truths to those that
   have been developed at specific times throughout history.
3. The bones of the *extinct* animal revealed that it
   had lived during the time of dinosaurs.
4. Career opportunities in the United States are *illimitable* today and will probably continue to be
   limitless for years to come.
5. The flood caused *inestimable* damage to more
   than fifty thousand acres, so no realistic estimates
   are available.
6. The odds of contracting a disease that has not
   existed for more than a hundred years is so *infinitesimal* that no one worries about it.
7. The disease is *irreversible,* although the doctors
   will try to slow its progress.
8. The sculpture's *perpetual* motion reminds me of

a modern timepiece that continues to move precisely without interruption.

9. Of the building's one dozen columns, the twelfth, or *terminal*, column is there primarily for decoration.

10. Because of the *unanimous* agreement among the members, no debate was necessary.

## STEP 2

Any problems? Once again, you can double-check whether you correctly remember the meanings with the following fill-in definitions. Write each adjective—*enduring, eternal, extinct, illimitable, inestimable, infinitesimal, irreversible, perpetual, terminal, unanimous*—on the line across from the most appropriate definition.

1. _____  no longer active or in existence

2. _____  too tiny to measure

3. _____  impossible to estimate

4. _____  lasting; continuing

5. _____  being in complete accord or harmony

6. _____  continuing without interruption

7. _____  without beginning or end

8. _____  representing or situated at the end

9. _____  impossible to reverse

10. _____  limitless; impossible to limit

ANSWERS: (1) extinct (2) infinitesimal (3) inestimable (4) enduring (5) unanimous (6) perpetual (7) eternal (8) terminal (9) irreversible (10) illimitable

## STEP 3

Let's end this last exercise of the chapter with a multiple-choice test. Circle your choice of the most appropriate word in each of the following sentences.

1. Something lasting or continuing is *(a) enduring (b) irreversible (c) illimitable.*
2. That which has no beginning or end is *(a) terminal (b) extinct (c) eternal.*
3. Anything too small to measure must be *(a) infinitesimal (b) terminal (c) illimitable.*
4. When an animal no longer exists anywhere on earth, it is classified as *(a) irreversible (b) extinct (c) terminal.*
5. If something cannot be limited, it is *(a) terminal (b) illimitable (c) perpetual.*
6. When everyone agrees with a decision, the decision is *(a) unanimous (b) irreversible (c) inestimable.*
7. Something that cannot be computed or measured is *(a) irreversible (b) enduring (c) inestimable.*
8. The part of a task that occupies the final stages would be *(a) irreversible (b) illimitable (c) terminal.*
9. When something moves continually, without interruption, the motion is said to be *(a) perpetual (b) irreversible (c) illimitable.*
10. A disease that cannot be cured is *(a) extinct (b) irreversible (c) perpetual.*

ANSWERS: (1) a (2) c (3) a (4) b (5) b (6) a (7) c (8) c (9) a (10) b

## BONUS WORDS

Here are your bonus words for this chapter—ten extra adjectives to add to your vocabulary before moving on to a new topic in Chapter 7.

1. *consummate* (KÄN sə mət)   complete or perfect in every way: *consummate* happiness
2. *deleterious* (de′ lə TIR ē əs)   having an injurious or harmful effect: an undesirable, *deleterious* policy
3. *ephemeral* (i FEM ər əl)   lasting only a very short time: *ephemeral* youth
4. *impetuous* (im PECH ü əs)   impulsive and impatient: an *impetuous* shopper
5. *incongruous* (in KÄNG grü əs)   incompatible; lacking in harmony: two *incongruous* personalities
6. *obsequious* (əb SĒK wē əs)   fawning; acting subservient: an annoyingly *obsequious* employee
7. *pernicious* (pər NISH əs)   deadly; very destructive: *pernicious* anemia
8. *proprietary* (prə PRĪ ə ter′ ē)   of or relating to owning and managing a business; owned exclusively: a *proprietary* interest in a business venture
9. *provincial* (prə VINT shəl)   having a narrow outlook; appearing unfashionable and unsophisticated: a *provincial* resident in a remote rural area
10. *specious* (SPĒ shəs)   deceptively attractive; having a ring of truth while actually being false: a *specious* argument that isn't as good as it sounds.

## REVIEW TEST

As you take this test, keep in mind that the words chosen for all review tests may come from any previous chapter, exercise, or list of bonus words. Use the following multiple-choice questions to find out if you're remembering the words you've learned so far. The word to be defined will be stated first, followed by three possible brief definitions. After you've picked the most appropriate definition for each word, circle a, b, or c.

Don't forget to record the number of your correct and incorrect answers and to compare the results with those in previous chapters. Is your work improving? Are you getting more correct answers each time? If the answer is no, don't hesitate to repeat previous exercises—as often as necessary.

1. To *amortize* a loan is to
    (a) reduce or shorten it
    (b) settle it through payments
    (c) forgive or free one from the obligation
2. *Huey Long* (1893–1935)
    (a) is known as the world's greatest escape artist
    (b) was the inspiration for the U.S. symbol "Uncle Sam"
    (c) gave the longest speech in congressional history
3. A series of *concentric* squares means that each
    (a) has two adjacent sides of unequal length
    (b) has a common center
    (c) consists of four parts
4. An *immutable* decision is
    (a) unlikely to change

      (b) obvious but not serious

      (c) based on many sources

5. To *juxtapose* the pictures is to

      (a) interpret them

      (b) renew or give life to them

      (c) place them side by side

6. To *actuate* the conveyor belt is to

      (a) speed it up

      (b) move it or put it into motion

      (c) slow it down

7. His employer's *approbation* indicated

      (a) approval or praise

      (b) disapproval

      (c) forgiveness

8. An *allusion* is a/an

      (a) indirect reference to something

      (b) thing that is not typical

      (c) suggestion that provokes doubt

9. An *incongruous* couple is

      (a) secret or sneaky

      (b) not likely to change

      (c) incompatible

10. To *conciliate* opponents is to

      (a) coax or persuade them

      (b) win them over or pacify

      (c) provide what is demanded by them

ANSWERS: (1) b (2) c (3) b (4) a (5) c (6) b (7) a (8) a (9) c (10) b

*Correct Answers:*_____ *Incorrect Answers:*_____

# 7. Watch for Easily Confused Words

*Everyone wanted to know why Sally was so thrilled about her husband's recent condemnation at work.*

We also want to know why Sally was so happy that her husband was condemned at work. Most people in her position would have been mortified. So is Sally a little strange, or does she simply hate her husband—or none of the above?

Here's what really happened: At a neighborhood party, Sally could hardly wait to tell her friends about her husband's "good" fortune. As salesperson of the month, Art had been honored at a recent company event. But after Sally explained what happened to him, her friends put their arms around her and told her not to worry—plenty of others had been in the same position, and in time, everything would get better.

Puzzled that people were trying to comfort her instead of congratulate her, Sally took a friend aside and quietly asked what was going on. "Well, you did say that Art got a *condemnation*," the friend whispered. "Everyone is just trying to be understanding and sympathetic."

When Sally still didn't catch on, the friend suddenly

realized what the problem was. She gently explained that *condemnation* means blame for doing something wrong. Sally had confused the word *condemnation* with *commendation,* which means praise. So naturally her friends thought that Art had been harshly criticized rather than praised.

Are you shaking your head, thinking that no one could make such a mistake? You'd be surprised. Certain words are so frequently confused, in fact, that numerous dictionaries have been devoted especially to this subject. Perhaps, then, we should call this chapter "How to Avoid Sounding Stupid." Embarrassment is often what comes when you confuse two words, choosing one that means something very different from what you intend to say.

Because the problem of confusing two or more words is so widespread, it's best to deal with it as soon as possible in your vocabulary-building program. After all, adding new words to your vocabulary won't help if one day you confuse the new words with other words that seem similar.

This chapter and the next one, therefore, take aim at the problem of commonly confused words. This chapter looks at a variety of misused words, and Chapter 8 focuses on two specific types of confusing words—lookalikes and soundalikes.

## Words with the Same Beginning

To help you remember the words in this chapter, they're divided into two groups. In this first group of commonly confused words—including nouns, verbs, and adjectives—the first part of each word in a pair is the same, but the endings are different, as ap*praise* and ap*prise,* defined in Exercise 1.

In the second group, discussed in Exercises 3 and 4, the first part of each word in a pair is different, but the endings are the same, as *bilateral* and *unilateral*, defined in Exercise 3. This will be much easier to follow when you actually see the pairs. So let's move on to Exercise 1 and the first group of words.

## EXERCISE 1

Like all exercises, this one begins with ten words. However, the words are listed in five pairs instead of as ten unrelated words. Otherwise, the same general pattern that was used in previous exercises is followed here.

With these first ten words you'll want to pay special attention to pronunciation and spelling. Since the word beginnings are the same within a pair, the two words may also seem the same at first glance—that's why they're so easily confused. So how will you remember the difference? The key is to focus on the *endings*, which are different.

app*raise*, *vb.* (ə PRĀZ)
app*rise*, *vb* (ə PRĪZ)

cred*ible*, *adj.* (KRED ə bəl)
cred*itable*, *adj.* (KRED i tə bəl)

ingen*ious*, *adj.* (in JĒN yəs)
ingen*uous*, *adj.* (in JEN yə wəs)

judi*cial*, *adj.* (jù DISH əl)
judi*cious*, *adj.* (jù DISH əs)

offi*cial*, *adj.* (ə FISH əl)
offi*cious*, *adj.* (ə FISH əs)

## STEP 1

We'll start with brief definitions and examples so that you can immediately understand the difference between two words in a pair. Be prepared that sometimes the difference is significant; in other cases, it is slight.

1. The verb *appraise* means to evaluate or estimate, especially in an official capacity; *appraise* property for tax assessment. The verb *apprise* means to inform or give notice: *apprise* staff members of a decision.

2. The adjective *credible* means believable and reliable: a *credible* account of an accident. The adjective *creditable* means worthy of belief or praise: a *creditable* proposal that met with everyone's approval.

3. The adjective *ingenious* means clever and imaginative: an *ingenious* idea for increasing sales. The adjective *ingenuous* means naive or unsophisticated: an *ingenuous* young man away from home for the first time.

4. The adjective *judicial* means relating to courts of law or the judicial system and the administration of justice: depending on *judicial* proceedings to settle a matter. The adjective *judicious* means having or making sound judgment: a *judicious* strategy that is sure to work.

5. The adjective *official* means relating to an office or authority: *official* business. The adjective *officious* means being overly, and sometimes annoyingly, eager to help: an *officious* assistant who tries too hard.

## STEP 2

Now you know why these words can't be substituted one for another, but it won't be surprising if you hear them misused from time to time. Use the next group of sentences to see if you can avoid the same mistake.

In each sentence, fill in what you believe is the most appropriate word—*appraise, apprise, credible, creditable, ingenious, ingenuous, judicial, judicious, official, officious.* So that the test isn't too easy, the words won't be kept together in pairs within a single sentence but will be separated in different sentences.

1. With her imaginative and inventive mind, she should be able to devise an _____ marketing plan.
2. Sam is known to be very reliable, so I'm sure his account of the accident would be completely _____.
3. The Office of the Chief Inspector is sending an _____ investigator to evaluate conditions on the plant floor.
4. Now that _____ proceedings have begun, my boss will be in court every morning.
5. We think the committee's idea is _____ and deserves the respect and praise of the entire board.
6. It's budgeting time, so we should _____ management of the unexpected decrease in sales this month.
7. We can always depend on Joe to make a _____ decision backed by careful analysis and full safeguards.
8. I finally left the store without buying anything because the _____ clerk kept interrupting me with her advice.

9. Since we're eager to set a selling price, do you know how soon someone can _____ the property?

10. The senator is _____ when he says that homelessness is a myth.

ANSWERS: (1) ingenious (2) credible (3) official (4) judicial (5) creditable (6) apprise (7) judicious (8) officious (9) appraise (10) ingenuous

## STEP 3

How did you do? Are you satisfied that you know the difference between the words in each of the five pairs? If you're not 100 percent certain, don't feel bad. As we indicated earlier, the problem of choosing the wrong word is widespread.

This third step has a true-false test to give you a chance to reinforce your understanding. Reach each sentence and circle either *true* or *false*.

1. An *official* capacity means that it relates to an office or authority. *True False*
2. A *credible* proposal is believable and reliable. *True False*
3. An *ingenuous* person is clever and imaginative. *True False*
4. To *appraise* means to inform or give notice. *True False*
5. A *judicial* decision is a decision made by a court of law. *True False*
6. An *officious* person means someone in a position of authority. *True False*
7. A *creditable* act is one that is worthy of praise. *True False*

8. An *ingenious* idea appears clever and inventive. *True False*

9. To *apprise* means to estimate or evaluate. *True False*

10. A *judicious* judgment is a sound decision. *True False*

ANSWERS: (1) True (2) True (3) False (4) False (5) True (6) False (7) True (8) True (9) False (10) True

## EXERCISE 2

Are you getting the hang of this? The aim is to learn how to focus on the part of two similar words that is different. The difference in spelling is a signal that there may be a difference in meaning too.

Here are more pairs of words that are frequently confused. Like the previous pairs, the words in the following five pairs have the same beginning but different endings. Before starting Step 1, therefore, it will help to study the different word endings and also the different pronunciations.

censor, *vb.* (SEN sər)
censure, *vb.* (SEN shər)

deposi*tary*, *n.* (di PÄZ ə ter' ē)
deposi*tory*, *n.* (di PÄZ ə tōr' ē)

exten*ded*, *adj.* (ik STEND ed)
exten*sive*, *adj.* (ik STEN sive)

luxuri*ant*, *adj.* (ləg' ZHU̇R ē ənt)
luxuri*ous*, *adj.* (ləg' ZHU̇R ē əs)

var*ied, adj.* (VER    ēd)
var*ious, adj.* (VER    ē    əs)

## STEP 1

Again, we'll start with brief definitions and examples so that you will know immediately how the words in each pair differ in meaning.

1. The verb *censor* means to examine and remove anything that is objectionable: *censor* the questionable dialogue in the script. The verb *censure* means to criticize harshly or to rebuke officially: *censure* someone for unacceptable behavior during a meeting.

2. The noun *depositary* primarily means someone who cares for or safeguards something (sometimes also used to mean a "depository"): the person who serves as the *depositary*. The noun *depository* primarily means a place where something is cared for or safeguarded (sometimes also used to mean a "depositary"): the place designated as the *depository*. For clarity, use *depositary* in reference to a person and *depository* in reference to a place.

3. The adjective *extended* means stretched, pulled out, or continued a long time: an *extended* tour of duty. The noun *extensive* means large, vast, or broad: *extensive* training in medicine.

4. The adjective *luxuriant* means having rich, profuse, or abundant growth: the *luxuriant* gardens. The adjective *luxurious* means marked by luxury, particularly if costly or rich: the *luxurious* yacht.

5. The adjective *varied* means diverse, with miscellaneous or numerous kinds or forms and distinct characteristics: a *varied* selection of antique bottles. The adjective *various* means different and

separate, being more than one: *various* people who attended the concert.

## STEP 2

As you do this step, keep in mind that in some word pairs the differences in meaning are significant, whereas in others they're slight. Again, in each sentence, fill in the most appropriate word—*censor, censure, depositary, depository, extended, extensive, luxuriant, luxurious, varied, various.* But don't expect the two words in a pair to be used in the same sentence or in one sentence following the other.

1. He delivered the inactive records to the _____, an elderly man who explained the new transfer and storage procedure for public records.
2. Have you ever seen such thick, _____ plant growth?
3. The college has _____ divisions for the different disciplines—law, engineering, and so on.
4. When the car antenna is _____, it is possible to pick up thirty radio stations.
5. After years as a writer, her new assignment as editor means that she will _____ other people's material instead of having her own work subjected to possible deletions.
6. He delivered the old records to the _____, a place with endless rows of files and boxes.
7. Their new condo, overlooking the Pacific in an upper-class neighborhood, is _____.
8. After the unanimous vote it was clear that the organization would _____ the unruly member.

9. Her personnel file indicates an _____ background in accounting, with fifteen years' service as a certified public accountant in another firm.

10. The wallpaper samples are _____, with miscellaneous patterns and colors.

ANSWERS: (1) depository (2) luxuriant (3) various (4) extended (5) censor (6) depository (7) luxurious (8) censure (9) extensive (10) varied

## STEP 3

Here's another true-false test to reinforce your understanding of the differences in meaning. Read each new sentence and circle either *true* or *false*.

1. A *depositary* usually refers to the building or other place where records are stored. *True False*
2. If someone plans an *extended* visit, it will be one that is continued a long time. *True False*
3. To *censor* means to rebuke someone. *True False*
4. Rich, abundant plant life could be described as *luxurious*. *True False*
5. If a company has several departments, you could say that it has *various* departments. *True False*
6. A *depository* usually refers to the person who stores and safeguards material. *True False*
7. Someone with *extensive* training has a lot of training. *True False*
8. To *censure* means to examine and remove anything offensive. *True False*
9. Someone who likes a *luxurious* atmosphere would enjoy pleasure, comfort, and elegance. *True False*

10.   A workshop with several miscellaneous sessions, each having a different kind of presentation, has a *varied* program. *True False*

ANSWERS: (1) False (2) True (3) False (4) False (5) True (6) False (7) True (8) False (9) True (10) True

## Words with Different Beginnings

We've been looking at commonly confused words that have the same beginning but different endings. Some frequently misused words are the opposite: They have different beginnings but the same ending, as *prescribe* and *proscribe*, defined in the next exercise.

## EXERCISE 3

As in the first two exercises, the ten words in this exercise are listed in pairs. In this case the best way to remember the difference between two words in a pair is to focus on the *beginnings,* which are different. Practice pronouncing and spelling the words to help you remember the differences.

bi*lateral, adj.* (bī′ LAT  ər  əl)
uni*lateral, adj.* (yü′ ni  LAT  ər  əl)

con*notation, n.* (kȧn′  ə  TĀ  shən)
de*notation, n.* (dē′  nō  TĀ  shən)

dis*ability, n.* (dis′  ə  BIL  ə  tē)
in*ability, n.* (in′  ə  BIL  ə  tē)

pre*scribe*, *vb.* (pri SKRĪB)
pro*scribe*, *vb.* (prō SKRĪB)

sub*conscious*, *adj.* (səb′ KÄNT shəs)
un*conscious*, *adj.* (ən′ KÄNT shəs)

## STEP 1

Let's start by finding out the difference between the two words in each pair. Read each brief definition and example before taking the quiz in Step 2.

1.  The adjective *bilateral* means two-sided, affecting both sides equally: the *bilateral* agreement between the company and the union. The adjective *unilateral* means one-sided, affecting only one side: the school superintendent's *unilateral* decision to close the debate club.
2.  The noun *connotation* means a suggested meaning beyond or in addition to a dictionary definition: the *connotation* of being snobbish associated with the word *aloof.* The noun *denotation* means the primary dictionary definition: for the word *aloof,* a *denotation* of being physically and emotionally distant.
3.  The noun *disability* means physical impairment; a condition of inadequate strength or ability: a physical *disability* caused by a car accident. The noun *inability* means lack of power, resources, or capacity, usually mental: the *inability* to concentrate during lectures.
4.  The verb *prescribe* means to set forth as a guide or to order: *prescribe* peace and quiet. The verb *proscribe* means to condemn or outlaw: *proscribe* the destructive behavior.
5.  The adjective *subconscious* means consisting of

mental activities of which one is not wholly conscious or aware: *subconscious* desire to become famous. The adjective *unconscious* means having a loss of consciousness or awareness: being *unconscious* during surgery.

## Step 2

This time let's try a matching test. As soon as you feel comfortable with the word pairs, write each word—*bilateral, unilateral, connotation, denotation, disability, inability, prescribe, proscribe, subconscious, unconscious*—on the line next to the appropriate brief definition.

1. _____ to set forth or order
2. _____ an additional suggested meaning
3. _____ physical impairment
4. _____ being two-sided
5. _____ not being wholly aware
6. _____ the dictionary definition
7. _____ being one-sided
8. _____ having a loss of consciousness
9. _____ to condemn or outlaw
10. _____ inadequate mental capacity

ANSWERS: (1) prescribe (2) connotation (3) disability (4) bilateral (5) subconscious (6) denotation (7) unilateral (8) unconscious (9) proscribe (10) inability

## Step 3

Use the fill-in test in this step to reinforce your understanding. For each sentence, pick the most appropriate word—*bilateral, unilateral, connotation, denotation, disability, inability, prescribe, proscribe, subconscious, unconscious*—from the group of ten that you just learned.

1. His physical _____ did not stop him from operating the large press.
2. The school should _____ all pornographic literature.
3. The term *South Seas* has a _____ of sparkling blue waters, friendly natives, unhurried days, and romantic nights.
4. He believes that some stories of past lives are _____ memories brought out under hypnosis.
5. He may have a good idea, but I don't think his _____ decision should be imposed on others.
6. According to my dictionary, the word *data* has the _____ of "factual information."
7. The director may _____ other measures to control the problem.
8. The hit-and-run victim was _____ for several hours.
9. The two sides issued a _____ statement on Tuesday.
10. He failed to get the job because of his _____ to understand spreadsheet accounting.

ANSWERS: (1) disability (2) proscribe (3) connotation (4) subconscious (5) unilateral (6) denotation (7) prescribe (8) unconscious (9) bilateral (10) inability

## EXERCISE 4

By now you should be much more aware of words that are sometimes confused and what to look for to tell the difference. Here's another group of ten words, listed in pairs, all with the same ending but different beginnings. Practice spelling and saying each word aloud before you begin Step 1.

de*cisive, adj.* (di SĪ siv)
in*cisive, adj.* (in SĪ siv)

de*duction, n.* (di DƏK shən)
in*duction, n.* (in DƏK shən)

dis*interested, adj.* (dis′ IN trə stəd)
un*interested, adj.* (ən′ IN trə stəd)

dis*organized, adj.* (dis ȮR gə nīzd′)
un*organized, adj.* (ən′ ȮR gə nīzd′)

quali*tative, adj.* (KWÄL ə tā′ tiv)
quanti*tative, adj.* (KWÄN tə tā′ tiv)

## STEP 1

Are you ready to begin? Read the following brief definitions and examples. As you read, remember to focus on the different beginnings to help keep the words separate in your mind.

1. The adjective *decisive* means determined and conclusive: a *decisive* majority vote. The adjective *incisive* means direct and clear-cut: easy-to-follow *incisive* comments.
2. The noun *deduction* means reasoning by moving from the general to the specific: a *deduction* based on the general collection of evidence. The noun

*induction* means reasoning by moving from the specific to the general: an *induction* arising from a particular example.

3. The adjective *disinterested* means objective and free of bias: the *disinterested* position of a debate moderator. The adjective *uninterested* means not interested: an *uninterested* person who's bored with the subject.

4. The adjective *disorganized* means not having a logical, orderly system: a messy, *disorganized* file system. The adjective *unorganized* means not having unity or representation: an *unorganized* group of people, without a leader, standing outside the auditorium.

5. The adjective *qualitative* means involving quality or kind: a *qualitative* examination of the applicants' experience and education. The adjective *quantitative* means involving quantity or amount: a *quantitative* examination of the school's enrollment figures by class.

## STEP 2

Do you have the differences in meaning fixed firmly in your mind? Test yourself by writing each word— *decisive, incisive, deduction, induction, disinterested, uninterested, disorganized, unorganized, qualitative, quantitative*—across from the brief definition that best describes it.

1. _____ being direct and clear-cut
2. _____ not being interested
3. _____ being without an orderly system
4. _____ involving quantity or amount

5. _____ being determined and conclusive

6. _____ reasoning from general to specific

7. _____ being objective and free of bias

8. _____ not having unity or representation

9. _____ involving quality or kind

10. _____ reasoning from specific to general

ANSWERS: (1) incisive (2) uninterested (3) disorganized (4) quantitative (5) decisive (6) deduction (7) disinterested (8) unorganized (9) qualitative (10) induction

## STEP 3

Before we leave this exercise, here's a final fill-in test for you to reinforce your understanding of the differences in meaning. From the group of ten words—*decisive, incisive, deduction, induction, disinterested, uninterested, disorganized, unorganized, qualitative, quantitative*—that you just learned, pick the most appropriate word for each sentence.

1. His science project included a _____ analysis of the containers' size and volume.

2. Everyone agreed that the judges for the art show were _____ and fair.

3. We appreciate his _____ instructions, which are always clear and straightforward.

4. All fax machines accept both text and graphics; by the process of _____, therefore,

he concluded that the X1400 should also accept text and graphics.

5. I've never seen such chaos as we found in his messy, _____ office.

6. The report included a _____ analysis of copier resolution and quality.

7. He examined four top brands of fax machines, each of which accepts both text and graphics; by the process of _____, therefore, he concluded that all fax machines should handle both text and graphics.

8. Jim is a very _____ manager who has no trouble evaluating the facts and reaching a firm decision.

9. The protesters were _____ at the time but since then have formed an association to represent their cause.

10. We've tried repeatedly to get her interested in buying season tickets, but she always seems _____.

ANSWERS: (1) quantitative (2) disinterested (3) incisive (4) deduction (5) disorganized (6) qualitative (7) induction (8) decisive (9) unorganized (10) uninterested

## BONUS WORDS

As you continue to build a larger and more effective vocabulary, regularly remind yourself of what this chapter has demonstrated—that some words are easily confused with others that seem to be similar. Two words may have the same beginning but different endings, or they may have the same ending but different beginnings. Since you are likely to find more of the latter, the ten bonus words in this chapter, listed in five pairs, have different beginnings and the same ending.

1. *adverse, adj.* (ad VƏRS) being unfavorable: *adverse* conditions
   *averse, adj.* (ə VƏRS being strongly opposed to: *averse* to public speaking

2. *amend, vb.* (ə MEND) to change or improve: *amend* an outdated rule
   *emend, vb.* (ē MEND) to improve by critical editing: *emend* a carelessly written article

3. *covert, adj.* (KŌ vərt) being secret or hidden: *covert* military operations at night
   *overt, adj.* (ō VƏRT) being open for all to see: *overt* assistance and support to freedom fighters opposing a dictatorship.

4. *explicit, adj.* (ik SPLIS ət) fully and clearly defined or expressed; *explicit* instructions that cover everything
   *implicit, adj.* (im PLIS ət) understood but not directly expressed: an *implicit* understanding that everyone will support a new plan

5. *mystical, adj.* (MIS ti kəl) having a spiritual or mysterious reality not apparent to the senses: a *mystical* quality in the dark, old house
   *mythical, adj.* (MITH i kəl) existing in myth (fictional story): *mythical* Greek legends

## REVIEW TEST

This is your check-up test for Chapters 3 through 6. It's a multiple-choice quiz in which you choose the correct definition for a word stated in the brief opening phrase. Circle your choice of a, b, or c in each item. After you've finished making your choices, check the answer section and record your score below it.

1. An *ingenuous* suggestion is
    (a) honest
    (b) brilliant
    (c) naive
2. An *aberration* indicates something
    (a) typical
    (b) not typical
    (c) illegal
3. To *mitigate* is to
    (a) help resolve a dispute
    (b) moderate the effect of something
    (c) make something better
4. *Scrupulous* attention is
    (a) worthy of praise
    (b) persistent
    (c) especially careful
5. To *evince* shock is to
    (a) show it
    (b) administer it
    (c) compare it to something else
6. An *egregious* mistake is one that is
    (a) impulsive
    (b) serious
    (c) random
7. To *absolve* is to
    (a) forgive
    (b) justify
    (c) surrender
8. A *provincial* resident
    (a) resides in a province

      (b) is known only to a select few
      (c) is unworldly

9. An *incisive* person is
      (a) direct
      (b) mean-spirited
      (c) objective

10. Someone *averse* to socializing is
      (a) inclined toward it
      (b) opposed to it
      (c) dependent on it

ANSWERS: (1) c (2) b (3) b (4) c (5) a (6) b (7) a (8) c (9) a (10) b
*Correct Answers:* _____ *Incorrect Answers:* _____

# 8. Beware of Tricky Soundalikes and Lookalikes

*As the war continued, the natives lived in fear of a ruthless band of gorillas terrorizing their village.*

Who wouldn't be afraid—all those big, hairy apes sneaking into villages and terrorizing innocent people? It would be bad enough having to worry about warring *guerrillas* roaming the countryside.

Yes, you guessed it. This is another mix-up. The comment should have referred to a band of *guerrillas*, not *gorillas*. Although some guerrillas may behave like gorillas, the former refers to humans and the latter to apes.

Did you notice that *gorillas* and *guerrillas* (also spelled *guerillas*) are pronounced the same? That's what causes the problem. It makes us forget that the spelling and the meaning are different. In the previous chapter we learned about different types of words that are sometimes confused. Those words, however, weren't spelled or pronounced the same. In this chapter we're going to look at some words that definitely sound or look the same.

These soundalikes and lookalikes can be your worst enemy. Because they have the same, or nearly the same, spelling (lookalikes) or pronunciation (soundalikes), it takes extra effort to keep them separate. But there's a bright side to this picture. Once you become aware that there are such things as soundalikes and lookalikes, watching for them and recognizing them eventually becomes much easier.

Let's learn a couple words right now—no, not two soundalikes or lookalikes but, rather, the formal names for soundalikes and lookalikes.

The formal name for a soundalike is *homophone*. An easy-to-remember example is *cite/site*. Both are pronounced the same (*SĪT*), but *cite* is a verb meaning "to call attention to" (to *cite* an article) and *site* is a noun meaning "a location" (*site* of the new hotel). A homophone, therefore, is a word that is pronounced like another word but has a different spelling and meaning.

The formal name for a lookalike is *homograph*. An easy-to-remember example is *wind*. When used as a noun and pronounced as *WIND*, the word refers to "the movement of air" (*wind* blowing the leaves around). When used as a verb and pronounced *WĪND*, it refers to "making a circular motion" (*wind* the string around the spool). A homograph, therefore, is a word that is spelled like another word but has a different pronunciation and meaning.

Before we forget the two definitions, let's hurry on to Exercise 1 and see if we can cope with this annoying problem of words that sound or look the same.

## Soundalikes (Homophones)

Have you ever read a dictionary from cover to cover? We assume the answer is no. But if you were to page through a large dictionary, such as the *Oxford English Dictionary,* you would find far more soundalikes than lookalikes. This chapter follows that general pattern, with three times as many soundalikes as lookalikes.

## EXERCISE 1

If you're ready, here are the first ten soundalikes, or homophones. They're listed in five pairs so that you can easily see both the similarities and the differences. Notice that the two words in each pair look and sound similar but actually have different spellings.

acclamation, *n.* (ak' lə MĀ shən)
acclimation, *n.* (ak' lə MĀ shən)

adherence, *n.* (ad HIR ənts)
adherents, *n.* (ad HIR ənts)

canapé, *n.* (KAN ə pē)
canopy, *n.* (KAN ə pē)

canvas, *n.* (KAN vəs)
canvass, *vb.* (KAN vəs)

complementary, *adj.* (käm' plə MEN tə rē)
complimentary, *adj.* (käm' plə MEN tə rē)

## STEP 1

We'll start with brief definitions and examples of the ten soundalikes. You'll want to give special attention to the difference in spelling, however slight, since that's the best way to tell the words in these pairs apart.

1. The noun *acclamation* means loud or enthusiastic approval: *acclamation* of the supportive audience. The noun *acclimation* refers to the process of becoming accustomed to a new situation or environment: *acclimation* to a higher altitude.

2. The noun *adherence* refers to the process of being devoted to someone or something or to the condition of sticking fast, such as by suction or glue: *adherence* to the new rules. The noun *adherents* means those who support and uphold someone or something: *adherents* of the former Indian leader Gandhi.

3. The noun *canapé* refers to an appetizer consisting of a cracker or thin piece of bread spread with something tasty: the cheese *canapé*. The noun *canopy* means a covering spread or suspended over something to form a roof: the *canopy* over the outdoor stage.

4. The noun *canvas* refers to heavy, usually rough fabric, such as that used for tents or sails: walking shoes made of *canvas*. The verb *canvass* means to examine carefully or discuss fully; to seek votes or opinions: *canvass* the residents of the neighborhood.

5. The adjective *complementary* means serving to complete or add to a thing to strengthen the whole: a *complementary* frame around the picture. The adjective *complimentary* means expressing praise: his *complimentary* remarks about our work.

## STEP 2

While the definitions are still fresh in your mind, test yourself by matching the words and their meanings in the following two columns. Write the correct word—*acclamation, acclimation, adherence, adherents, canapé, canopy, canvas, canvass, complementary, complimentary*—in column 1 on the line across from the definition that most closely matches it.

1. _____    a covering or roof
2. _____    serving to complete
3. _____    supporters
4. _____    enthusiastic approval
5. _____    the process of becoming accustomed to
6. _____    the act of being devoted to or sticking to
7. _____    serving to express praise
8. _____    an appetizer
9. _____    to examine carefully; to seek opinions
10. _____    a heavy fabric such as that used for tents and sails

ANSWERS: (1) canopy (2) complementary (3) adherents (4) acclamation (5) acclimation (6) adherence (7) complimentary (8) canapé (9) canvass (10) canvas

## STEP 3

Do you have the differences between the words in the five pairs firmly in mind? If you're not sure, fill in the most appropriate word—*acclamation, acclimation, adherence, adherents, canapé, canopy, canvas, canvass, complementary, complimentary*—in the following ten sentences.

1. At the meeting the measure was passed by _____, with a strong majority expressing loud approval.

2. If they hold the wedding outdoors, I hope they'll have a large _____ over the wedding party in case of rain.

3. The addressing and mailing functions are _____.

4. The faculty expects strict _____ to the school's rules and regulations.

5. I'm sure they'll like living in a desert area after the usual period of _____.

6. Mike thinks we should _____ the residents to be certain public opinion is on our side.

7. Was that meat or a soy product on that _____?

8. Jean did such a good job that her boss was very _____ in his comments.

9. Considering how dark the sky looks, I'm glad that our tent is made of waterproof _____.

10. The reformers clearly had many _____ who willingly contributed more than enough campaign money.

ANSWERS: (1) acclamation (2) canopy (3) complementary (4) adherence (5) acclimation (6) canvass (7) canapé (8) complimentary (9) canvas (10) adherents

## EXERCISE 2

As you discovered in Exercise 1, the problem with soundalikes is not that the words are exceptionally complex or unfamiliar; confusion arises primarily because some words sound almost the same, and that means they're more likely to be misused. This exercise has ten more soundalikes, again listed in easily confused word pairs. Take special note of the difference in spelling, even when slight, because that's the best clue to the difference in meaning.

contingence, *n.* (kən TIN jəns)
contingents, *n.* (kən TIN jənts)

depravation, *n.* (dep′ rə VĀ shən)
deprivation, *n.* (dep′ rə VĀ shən)

intercession, *n.* (in′ tər SESH ən)
intersession, *n.* (IN tər sesh′ ən)

meddlesome, *adj.* (MED əl səm)
mettlesome, *adj.* (MET əl səm)

veracious, *adj.* (və RĀ shəs)
voracious, *adj.* (vò RĀ shəs)

## STEP 1

First, review these brief definitions and examples for the ten words, presented in pairs. Then try to select the definitions on your own in Step 2.

1. The noun *contingence* means a joining or touching: the *contingence* of the two angles. The noun *contingents* means events or conditions that are likely to occur: the *contingents* that could affect the outcome of negotiations.

2. The noun *depravation* means corruption or perversion: the *depravation* of the gang members. The noun *deprivation* means the act of taking something away or condition of having something taken away: the *deprivation* experienced by those who are homeless.

3. The noun *intercession* means the act of making a plea on another's behalf or coming between two

parties in the hope of helping them settle a dispute: his *intercession* on behalf of the unhappy couple. The noun *intersession* means the time or period between two academic or other sessions: the *intersession* between the morning and afternoon sessions.

4. The adjective *meddlesome* means being inclined to interfere: a *meddlesome* busybody. The adjective *mettlesome* means being spirited or having spirit: the *mettlesome* cheerleaders.

5. The adjective *veracious* means honest or accurate: her trustworthy, *veracious* character. The adjective *voracious* means greedy or having an appetite that can't be satisfied: the football player's *voracious* appetite.

## STEP 2

If you can correctly match words with definitions in these two columns, you'll know that the differences in the word pairs has stuck in your mind—for now. Write the most appropriate word—*contingence, contingents, depravation, deprivation, intercession, intersession, meddlesome, mettlesome, veracious, voracious*—in column 1 across from the matching definition.

| | |
|---|---|
| 1. _____ | the act of making a plea for another |
| 2. _____ | the act of taking something away or condition of having something taken away |
| 3. _____ | being greedy or endlessly hungry |
| 4. _____ | likely occurrences |
| 5. _____ | a joining or touching |

| | |
|---|---|
| 6. _____ | being spirited |
| 7. _____ | the space between sessions |
| 8. _____ | being honest |
| 9. _____ | corruption or perversion |
| 10. _____ | being inclined to interfere |

ANSWERS: (1) intercession (2) deprivation (3) voracious (4) contingents (5) contingence (6) mettlesome (7) intersession (8) veracious (9) depravation (10) meddlesome

## STEP 3

To fix the definitions firmly in your mind, take this easy true-false test. Read each sentence carefully, notice the spelling of the italicized word, and circle either true or false.

1. When a person is accused of *depravation,* he or she has been caught in the act of taking something away. *True False*
2. Conferences may have an *intersession* between program sessions. *True False*
3. The *contingence* of two lines refers to their separation. *True False*
4. If Paul has a *voracious* appetite, he's always hungry. *True False*
5. It's flattering to be thought of as a *meddlesome* person. *True False*
6. Someone who has experienced *deprivation* has lost something. *True False*
7. You can't be *veracious* and honest at the same time. *True False*
8. An *intercession* in a dispute usually represents an effort to help solve the problem. *True False*

9. *Contingents* are highly improbable events that will not likely take place. *True False*

10. A *mettlesome* person tends to be full of vigor and has a strong spirit. *True False*

ANSWERS: (1) False (2) True (3) False (4) True (5) False (6) True (7) False (8) True (9) False (10) True

## Lookalikes (Homographs)

Get ready to change course. We've been working with words that sound similar but have different spellings and different meanings. Now we're going to look at the other troublemaker: lookalikes. Although there aren't as many lookalikes as soundalikes, there are enough to cause problems. Lookalikes, or homographs, are words that are spelled the same but have different pronunciations and different meanings.

## EXERCISE 3

Here are five pairs of lookalikes. As you can immediately see, the spelling of the two words in each pair is identical. Therefore, the best clue to the difference in meaning is the pronunciation. In some cases the part of speech—noun, adjective, or verb—is also an indicator. In the following list, for example, *legate* means something different when used as a noun than when used as a verb. You'll see what we mean as you move through each step of this exercise.

adage, *n.* (AD ij)
adage, *n.* (àd DÁÁZH)

epicrisis, *n.* (ə PIK rə səs)
epicrisis, *n.* (ep′ ə KRĪ səs)

legate, *n.* (LEG ət)
legate, *vb.* (lə GĀT)

recession, *n.* (ri SESH ən)
recession, *n.* (rē′ SESH ən)

resoluble, *adj.* (ri ZÄL yə bəl)
resoluble, *adj.* (rē SÄL yə bəl)

## STEP 1

Without taking any more time to talk about look-alikes, let's see what the words in this group mean. As you read the brief definitions and examples, pronounce the pairs of words one after another, noting the difference.

1. When the noun *adage* is pronounced *AD ij,* it refers to a saying that summarizes a general truth: the *adage* about a penny saved being a penny earned. When the noun is pronounced *à DÁÁZH,* it is an alternative spelling of *adagio* (ə DÄ jō), a direction in music meaning easy and graceful or a slow tempo: the part of the musical score marked *adage.*
2. When the noun *epicrisis* is pronounced *ə PIK rə səs,* it means an analytical summary of a medical case history: the *epicrisis* on John Doe. When the noun is pronounced *ep′ ə KRĪ səs,* it means a secondary crisis: an *epicrisis* that followed soon after the initial crisis.

3. When *legate* is used as a noun and pronounced *LEG ət*, it means an official emissary or representative of the pope: the arrival of the new *legate*. When it is used as a verb in a legal context and pronounced *lə GĀT*, it means to bequeath or will: to *legate* her personal property to her son.

4. When the noun *recession* is pronounced *ri SESH ən*, it means a period of reduced economic activity: the *recession* of the 1980s. When the noun is pronounced *rē' SESH ən*, it means the act of yielding to or transferring something back to the party that previously possessed it: the *recession* of his land to the prior owner.

5. When the adjective *resoluble* is pronounced *ri ZĀL yə bəl*, it means capable of being resolved or settled: a legal problem that is *resoluble*. When the adjective is pronounced *rē SĀL yə bəl*, it means capable of being dissolved again: the thick paste that is *resoluble*.

## STEP 2

More than any other exercise, this one should underline the importance of pronunciation in matters of vocabulary. Let's double-check if you can successfully use pronunciation to tell apart the five pairs of words—*adage, epicrisis, legate, recession, resoluble*. Match the pronunciations given in the first column with the brief definitions in the second column. Write a, b, c, and so forth on the short line following each term's pronunciation.

1. lə GĀT _____
   a. an official emissary

2. ri ZĀL yə bəl
   _____
   b. the act of transferring something back to a former owner

3. ri SESH ən ___    c. the musical direction meaning easy and graceful

4. AD ij ___    d. a period of reduced economic activity

5. LEG ət ___    e. capable of being settled

6. rē′ SESH ən ___    f. a secondary crisis

7. ə PIK rə səs ___    g. to bequeath or will

8. rē SÄL yə bəl ___    h. a saying that summarizes a general truth

9. ä DÁÁZH ___    i. a summary of a medical case history

10. ep′ ə KRĪ səs ___    j. capable of being dissolved again

ANSWERS: (1) g (2) e (3) d (4) h (5) a (6) b (7) i (8) j (9) c (10) f

## STEP 3

It's hard enough to remember new words and meanings without having to pay such strict attention to pronunciation. But that's the burden we have to bear with lookalikes. So here's one more test—a true-false quiz—for you to be certain that you know the meanings based on pronunciation.

1. A *rē SÄL yə bəl* substance can be dissolved more than one time. *True   False*
2. A *LEG ət* might be a representative of the pope. *True False*
3. An *ep′ ə KRĪ səs* is a medical case history summary. *True   False*
4. A *ri SESH ən* is a period of reduced economic activity. *True   False*

5. The term *à DÀÁZH* means the same thing as *adagio*—easy and graceful. *True False*
6. In legal matters, to *lə GĀT* is to will something to another party. *True False*
7. An *ə PIK rə səs* is a secondary crisis. *True False*
8. An *AD ij* is a slow tempo. *True False*
9. When something is *ri ZĀL yə bəl*, it can be resolved. *True False*
10. The act of yielding something back to a former owner is called *rē' SESH ən*. *True False*

ANSWERS: (1) True (2) True (3) False (4) True (5) True (6) True (7) False (8) False (9) True (10) True

# BONUS WORDS

Your ten bonus words for this chapter consist of five pairs of soundalikes (homophones)—nouns, verbs, and an adjective. Like those in the first two exercises, these soundalikes have a very similar pronunciation but look different. Spelling, therefore, is the key to their different meanings.

1. *ordinance, n.* (ÒRD nənts) an official order or public law: a city *ordinance*
   *ordnance, n.* (ÒRD nəns) military supplies and equipment: army *ordnance*
2. *penance, n.* (PEN əns) an act expressing sorrow for wrongdoing: doing *penance* for committing a sin
   *pennants, n.* (PEN ənts) long, tapering flags used on ships for identification and signaling: the navy vessel's *pennants*

3. *pervade, vb.* (pər VĀD) to spread or be found throughout: a scent that *pervades* the atmosphere
   *purveyed, vb.* (pər' VĀD) to have supplied or obtained something: to have *purveyed* food

4. *saccharin, n.* (SAK ə rən) a white, powdered substance that is much sweeter than sugar: the artificial sweetener *saccharin* found in grocery stores
   *saccharine, adj.* (SAK ə rən) having an especially sweet taste or character: a *saccharine* smile

5. *triptik, n.* (TRIP tik') a series of road maps: a *triptik* provided by an auto club to members planning a trip
   *triptych, n.* (TRIP tik') painted or carved artwork in three panels or compartments that are displayed side by side and sometimes are hinged together: a *triptych* of angels

## REVIEW TEST

As usual, the review test draws on words from previous chapters as well as the current chapter, including bonus words. This is a multiple-choice quiz, so you should circle your choice of answers a, b, or c in each sentence and record your score after the answer section.

1. A swelling or bulge sticking out from the surrounding surface is called a/an *(a) hologram (b) protuberance (c) aberration.*

2. Someone who is impulsive and unpredictable is considered *(a) capricious (b) parsimonious (c) taciturn.*

3. When conditions are favorable to start a new

business, they are said to be *(a) proprietary (b) propitious (c) unctuous.*

4. Something that continues without interruption is *(a) incessant (b) ephemeral (c) synchronized.*

5. When you force or compel someone to do something, you have done the following: *(a) coerce (b) trammel (c) reprove.*

6. To guess or speculate is to *(a) vitiate (b) importune (c) conjecture.*

7. To gain favor through deliberate effort is to *(a) vitiate (b) ingratiate (c) capitulate* oneself.

8. A person who tends to interfere in the business of others is *(a) meddlesome (b) mettlesome (c) officious.*

9. Something that is worthy of belief or praise is *(a) munificent (b) complimentary (c) creditable.*

10. To shun something or someone is to do the following; *(a) attenuate (b) impugn (c) eschew.*

ANSWERS: (1) b (2) a (3) b (4) a (5) a (6) c (7) b (8) a (9) c (10) c

*Correct Answers:* _____ *Incorrect Answers:* _____

# 9. Practice Using Some Common Foreign Words

*Millions of people carry the words* e pluribus unum *with them every day of their lives.*

Surprised? Don't be, because you're one of the millions who carry around the words *e pluribus unum,* at least most of the time. We'll prove it if you'll take time to look in your purse or wallet. If you have a dollar bill in there—and most of you will have—take it out and look at the side that has the Great Seal of the United States printed on it. Then look at the banner in that seal. See anything?

You may not have noticed before, but every time you look at the greenish side of a dollar bill, the Latin expression *e pluribus unum* is staring back at you. Pronounced *Ē plür' ə bəs YÜ nəm,* the phrase means "one out of many."

Can you find it? The words are printed on the banner that an eagle is holding in its mouth in the middle of the Great Seal. The type on the banner is very small, however, so those of us who have entered the age of bifocal and multifocal glasses may need a magnifying glass to read it.

The words "one out of many" have a special meaning in U.S. history. If you haven't already guessed what it is, think back to the early, pre–Civil War days—before there were such things as "states" in the United States. The *many* refers to the original thirteen colonies of the United States, and the *one* refers to the union they agreed to form.

This bit of history surrounding the use of the phrase *e pluribus unum* in the United States makes an important point: Other words and expressions besides English have been part of American culture for a long time.

Only a few decades ago, however, the general public used very few of such words or phrases. Usage was limited to the very common terms, such as *alma mater* (al′ mə MÄ tər), referring to the educational institution one attended. We didn't feel as connected to the rest of the world then. But nowadays increasing international trade and instant computer connections have caused us to feel very connected.

In fact, we need to know a number of foreign terms just to understand the daily news. Socially, too, if we don't have a basic stock of common foreign words and expressions in our vocabularies, we risk appearing to be out of touch or behind the times. It gives us cause to worry that somewhere there's a blunder waiting to happen—or should we say a *faux pas* (FŌ pä′) waiting to happen?

## Common French Expressions

Most of the foreign terms that we need to know are of French or Latin origin. French expressions have always been common both socially and professionally in the United States. Social usage of French has often been spurred on by a belief that the use of French expressions makes us sound more worldly and sophisticated.

For example, you've no doubt heard the expression *haute couture* (ōt′ kù TÜR), referring to the houses or designers of exclusive women's fashions. To most people, using the French term sounds much more impressive than using the English words "high-class dressmaker."

Like French, Latin has been used heavily in the United States. Although it is taught less often in universities today, it is still firmly entrenched in U.S. business law, medicine, and other areas. In fact, dictionaries of foreign words and expressions used in the United States consist mostly of French and Latin terms, with a much smaller mix of other languages, such as Spanish, German, and Italian.

Today, our dictionaries include thousands of *Anglicized words*—words from other cultures that are used so often in the United States that we have adapted them to the English language. We'll begin the chapter with French words, follow with Latin words, and end with bonus words consisting of miscellaneous terms from other languages.

Before you begin the first exercise, however, we need to talk about the use of accents and italic type with foreign words. The following are the main points you need to consider.

First, should you use accents (called "diacritical marks," such as *é*) in foreign words and type or print them in an italic face? The rule on this isn't clear, but generally, if a foreign word is not Anglicized, it definitely should have accents and be printed in italics.

Second, how do you know whether a term is Anglicized? Some follow the rule that anything found in a standard English dictionary is Anglicized and need not be accented or printed in italics. Others believe that all but the most widely used foreign terms should be accented and italicized even if they are Anglicized.

Third, all of the words in this chapter can be found in standard English dictionaries, so you can point to that fact if you choose not to use accents or italics with them. But in case you decide to use them, we'll include the accents that are most commonly used.

Finally, the diacritical marks that we've included in this chapter are the acute accent, as in é; the grave accent, as in è; and the circumflex, as in ê. In the exercises that follow, notice how the words with these marks are pronounced.

## EXERCISE 1

If you're a little nervous about learning foreign words, don't be. It's not going to be any harder than learning new English words. For each group of ten foreign words, for example, you'll be given spelling and pronunciation, the same as with each group of English words.

You may enjoy the sense of power you'll feel at knowing words and expressions from other languages. If you already have some knowledge of another language, look on the exercises in this chapter as a way to fill in the gaps with some words you may have missed.

Here are ten French words—all nouns. Practice pronouncing and spelling each word before you begin Step 1. Even though these terms are Anglicized, the pronunciation of some of the words may surprise you.

*aperitif* (ə per′ ə TĒF)
*consummé* (kön′ sə MĀ)
*cortege* (kòr TEZH)
*coup d'état* (kü′ dä TÄ)
*debacle* (dē BÄ kəl)
*élan* (ā LÄN)
*ingenue* (AN jə nü′)
*mélange* (mä LÄNZH)
*melee* (MĀ lā′)
*pièce de résistance* (pēs′ də re zē′ STÄNTS)

## STEP 1

First, the definitions and examples—we'll make them as brief and as easy to learn and remember as possible.

1. An *aperitif* is a small alcoholic beverage served before a meal as an appetizer: enjoying a delightful *aperitif* before the meal.
2. *Consommé* is a clear, well-seasoned soup made from meat or vegetable stock, sometimes served cold as jelly: his favorite *consommé*.
3. A *cortege* is a train of attendants; a funeral procession: the influential senator's *cortege*.
4. A *coup d'état* is the sudden overthrow of a government, frequently by a small group of people who are or were in a position of authority: the unexpected *coup d'état*.
5. A *debacle* is a disaster or violent disruption: the *debacle* that brought everything to a halt.
6. *Élan* is enthusiastic spirit: the obvious *élan* of the happy guests.
7. An *ingenue* is a simple, unworldly girl or woman: the innocence of the *ingenue*.
8. A *mélange* is a mixture of elements that are in

conflict, lack harmony, and are usually unsuitable together: the odd *mélange* in the store window.

9. A *melee* is a confused, often hand-to-hand struggle among several people: the *melee* that broke out after the game.

10. A *pièce de résistance* is an outstanding item or accomplishment: the *pièce de résistance* that won an award.

## STEP 2

Let's see if you remember the meanings of the ten French words. On each line, fill in the term—*aperitif, consommé, cortege, coup d'état, debacle, élan, ingenue, mélange, melee, pièce de résistance*—that best matches the brief definition next to it. Use this step also to practice spelling the ten words.

1. _____ an unsuitable mixture of elements

2. _____ the overthrow of a government by a small group

3. _____ enthusiastic spirit

4. _____ a simple girl or woman

5. _____ something that is outstanding

6. _____ a before-meal alcoholic beverage

7. _____ a confused struggle

8. _____ a clear, well-seasoned soup

9. _____ a train of attendants or a funeral procession

10. _____ a disaster or violent disruption

ANSWERS: (1) *mélange* (2) *coup d'état* (3) *élan*
(4) *ingenue* (5) *pièce de résistance* (6) *aperitif* (7) *melee*
(8) *consommé* (9) *cortege* (10) *debacle*

## STEP 3

If you remember all of the words, you should be
ready to reinforce your understanding by filling in the
correct word—*aperitif, consommé, cortege, coup d'état,
debacle, élan, ingenue, mélange, melee, pièce de résistance*—in each of the following sentences.

1. Before the _____ was over, Tim had
   a bloody nose.
2. The former army generals planned the South
   American country's _____ months
   before the actual overthrow took place.
3. Your report is brilliant—a _____ for
   all to behold!
4. In the school play Janice took the role of an
   _____ who had never been beyond
   the limits of the small village.
5. At the dinner the appetizer consisted of a rum-
   based _____.
6. The company takeover turned into a
   _____; nothing went as planned.
7. The restaurant's delicious _____ was
   made from vegetable rather than beef stock.
8. She acted like the happiest person in the world
   and made no effort to hide her _____
   _____.
9. The ambassador's _____ included
   fourteen aides and attendants.
10. The sculptor's studio was crowded with a
    _____ of twisted metal scraps, rough
    pieces of lumber, and beautifully finished sculptures.

ANSWERS: (1) *melee* (2) *coup d'état* (3) *pièce de résistance* (4) *ingenue* (5) *aperitif* (6) *debacle* (7) *consommé* (8) *élan* (9) *cortege* (10) *mélange*

## EXERCISE 2

Even if you've seldom or never worked with foreign words, you apparently survived the first exercise or you wouldn't be reading this. Exercise 2 may then seem a little less frightening. Here are ten more French words for you to study—again, all nouns.

*appliqué* (ap′ lə KĀ)
*cause célèbre* (kòz′ sə LEB rə)
*déjeuner* (dā zhə NĀ)
*denouement* (dā′ nü′ MÄN)
*habitué* (hə BICH əw ā′)
*ménage* (mā NÄZH)
*mésalliance* (mā′ ZAL′ ē əns)
*portiere* (pōr TYER)
*table d'hôte* (tä bəl DŌT)
*tête-à-tête* (tet′ ə TET)

## STEP 1

Did you practice pronouncing and spelling the ten terms? Say each word again as you read these brief definitions and examples.

1. An *appliqué* is a smaller decoration attached to a larger piece of material: the animal-shaped *appliqué* sewed onto the tablecloth.
2. A *cause célèbre* is an incident that creates widespread interest: the exciting announcement that became a *cause célèbre* throughout the city.

3. *Déjeuner* is breakfast or lunch; a form of service in which breakfast is served on a tray: the hotel plan including *déjeuner*.

4. A *denouement* is the final outcome or resolution in a sequence of events or in a literary work: a surprising *denouement* in the last act of the play.

5. A *habitué* is someone who frequents a certain place, especially a place of entertainment: the *habitué* known by all in the club.

6. A *ménage* is a household: a *ménage* of four people.

7. A *mésalliance* is a marriage to someone who is socially inferior: the earl's much criticized *mésalliance*.

8. A *portiere* is a heavy curtain that is hung across a doorway: the gold *portiere* at the dining room entrance.

9. *Table d'hôte* is a hotel or restaurant meal, with usually limited choices, served to all guests at a particular time and at the same price: a business lunch served *table d'hôte*.

10. A *tête-à-tête* is a private conversation between two persons: the *tête-à-tête* between the owner and one of the secretaries.


## STEP 2

Try this multiple-choice quiz to test whether you're remembering the definitions. Circle your choice of a, b, or c in each sentence.

1. A *habitué* is a
   (a) place that many people frequent
   (b) person who frequents a particular place
   (c) person whose habits are well known to others

2. An *appliqué* is a
   (a) heavy curtain hung across a doorway
   (b) final outcome or resolution
   (c) small decoration fastened to a larger item

3. A *ménage* is a
   (a) place where people live together
   (b) place that people regularly visit
   (c) marriage to someone of lower social status

4. A *table d'hôte* is a
   (a) communal table for fixed-price meal service
   (b) meal table for people who frequent a place
   (c) table for meals in a household

5. A *tête-à-tête* is a
   (a) romantic affair between two people
   (b) regular meeting place of two people
   (c) private conversation between two people

6. *Déjeuner* is a
   (a) person who frequents a place of entertainment
   (b) breakfast or lunch service
   (c) service of meals in the dining room

7. A *portiere* is a
   (a) heavy curtain across a doorway
   (b) household
   (c) portable breakfast tray

8. A *cause célèbre* is a/an
   (a) romantic affair between two people
   (b) marriage to someone who is inferior
   (c) incident causing widespread attention

9. A *denouement* is a
   (a) final outcome or resolution
   (b) marriage agreement
   (c) communal household

10. A *mésalliance* is a
   (a) household with two unmarried people

    (b) marriage to someone of a lower social standing

    (c) household with several married couples

ANSWERS: (1) b (2) c (3) a (4) a (5) c (6) b (7) a (8) c (9) a (10) b

## STEP 3

Before leaving this group of words, reinforce your understanding of the meanings with this matching test. Write the correct word—*appliqué, cause célèbre, déjeuner, denouement, habitué, ménage, mésalliance, portiere, table d'hôte, tête-à-tête*—in column 1 to match the appropriate brief definition in column 2.

1. _____ a household
2. _____ a final outcome
3. _____ someone who frequents a place
4. _____ a hotel or restaurant meal for all at a fixed price
5. _____ a private conversation of two persons
6. _____ an event creating a lot of attention
7. _____ breakfast or lunch
8. _____ a heavy curtain across a doorway
9. _____ a marriage to someone who is socially inferior
10. _____ a small decoration attached to a larger item

ANSWERS: (1) *ménage* (2) *denouement* (3) *habitué* (4) *table d'hôte* (5) *tête-à-tête* (6) *cause célèbre* (7) *déjeuner* (8) *portiere* (9) *mésalliance* (10) *appliqué*

## EXERCISE 3

Is it getting any easier? We'll keep at it until it is. Here are ten more French words to learn—eight nouns and two adjectives. Don't forget to spell each word mentally and to pronounce it several times before beginning Step 1.

*bête noir, n.* (bet′ NWÄR)
*carte blanche, n.* (KÄRT BLÄNSH)
*chef d'oeuvre, n.* (shā DEU vrə)
*connoisseur, n.* (kän′ ə SƏR)
*dossier, n.* (DȮS ē ā)
*laissez-faire, adj.* (les′ ā FAIR)
*nom de plume, n.* (näm′ di PLÜM)
*nouveau riche, n.* (nü′ vō′ RĒSH)
*par excellence, adj.* (PÄR ek′ sə LÄNS)
*raison d'être, n.* (rā′ zōn′ DET rə)

## STEP 1

All set? As usual, we'll begin with brief definitions and examples. Say each word aloud as you read the ten definitions.

1. The noun *bête noir* means someone or something that is strongly disliked and to be avoided: the unpopular novel that was the *bête noir* of romantics everywhere.
2. The noun *carte blanche* means full, unrestricted power or authority to act: *carte blanche* to adjust prices as needed.
3. The noun *chef d'oeuvre* means a masterpiece, especially one that is artistic or literary: the writer's acclaimed *chef d'oeuvre*.

4. The noun *connoisseur* means an expert: a *connoisseur* of fine art.

5. The noun *dossier* means a file with detailed information about someone or something: the diplomat's *dossier*.

6. The adjective *laissez-faire* refers to a kind of doctrine or philosophy that opposes unnecessary governmental regulation or a philosophy that opposes interference in the affairs of others: the government's *laissez-faire* policy toward its territories.

7. The noun *nom de plume* means a pen name (pseudonym): the novelist's *nom de plume*.

8. The noun *nouveau riche* means the newly rich: the *nouveau riche* who flaunted their new wealth.

9. The adjective *par excellence* means being the best of a kind: a speech *par excellence*.

10. The noun *raison d'être* means the reason for being or existing: the company's *raison d'être*.

## STEP 2

Here's another chance to practice your spelling. Write the correct term—*bête noir, carte blanche, chef d'oeuvre, connoisseur, dossier, laissez-faire, nom de plume, nouveau riche, par excellence, raison d'être*—across from the appropriate matching definition.

1. _____  a masterpiece
2. _____  the reason for being or existing
3. _____  being the best of a kind
4. _____  a file of detailed information on someone or something
5. _____  the newly rich

6. _____ full authority to act
7. _____ a pen name
8. _____ an expert
9. _____ something or someone to be avoided
10. _____ referring to a philosophy of noninterference

ANSWERS: (1) *chef d'oeuvre* (2) *raison d'être* (3) *par excellence* (4) *dossier* (5) *nouveau riche* (6) *carte blanche* (7) *nom de plume* (8) *connoisseur* (9) *bête noir* (10) *laissez-faire*

## STEP 3

Do you feel confident enough to use the words in actual sentences? To reinforce your understanding, try inserting the most suitable word—*bête noir, carte blanche, chef d'oeuvre, connoisseur, dossier, laissez-faire, nom de plume, nouveau riche, par excellence, raison d'être*—in these sentences.

1. He took a _____ detailing his work experience with him to the interview.
2. He is well known as a _____ of fine wines.
3. The main sales office has always had a _____ policy toward the field representatives, who enjoy their freedom from headquarters' control.
4. He believes that devoting his life to medical science is his _____ and that he has no other purpose for being on earth.
5. The new secretary was given _____ to select and train her own assistant.

6. Her painting is a _____ and clearly belongs in a fine gallery.

7. Her novel was published under a _____ rather than her own name.

8. The play may have been a _____ in most U.S. cities, but it received rave reviews in Paris.

9. He is a composer _____ and is admired around the world.

10. We should have guessed from the way she flaunted her wealth that she was among the _____.

ANSWERS: (1) *dossier* (2) *connoisseur* (3) *laissez-faire* (4) *raison d'être* (5) *carte blanche* (6) *chef d'oeuvre* (7) *nom de plume* (8) *bête noir* (9) *par excellence* (10) *nouveau riche*

## Common Latin Expressions

People don't carry on a conversation in Latin the way that they might speak French or Spanish. Latin isn't a "living" language in that sense. But the English language is generously supplied with Latin words and phrases, and certain expressions are therefore intermixed with English in speech and writing.

Some words derived from Latin, such as *consensus* (kən SENT səs), meaning general agreement, are so common in English usage that most of us don't even think of them as anything but English words. Others sound and look more like Latin expressions, and those are the ones we're going to learn in the next two exercises.

Although language authorities believe that Latin usage is declining, it shows no sign of disappearing from various U.S. professions anytime soon. It's still firmly entrenched in religion, law, literature and the arts, and many scientific fields, such as medicine and botany.

For example, think of all the plant and animal classifications in Latin, such as *Hedera helix* (HED ə rə HĒ liks), the Latin name for common ivy. If you look for common ivy in a nursery, the identification tag on the plant will likely give the Latin name as well as the popular name.

With such widespread infiltration into English, Latin occupies a well-earned place in our vocabularies. But it's not always treated in the same way that French is treated. Whereas French tends to be appealing for social reasons, the attraction to Latin seems to be on an intellectual level. For example, just as some people believe that using French expressions makes them appear refined and worldly, others believe that using Latin expressions makes them appear well educated and intellectual.

Don't misunderstand: We're not recommending that you use French and Latin words and expressions to show off. Those who *overuse* such language seem snobbish and pretentious. Instead, we urge you to use the words and expressions to help you understand what others who do use these terms are saying. However, don't be afraid to use them yourself if you find just the right occasion when a little foreign flavor is needed.

## EXERCISE 4

Here are your first ten Latin words and expressions—a mix of five nouns and five adjectives. As you practice pronouncing these terms, notice how different they sound from the French words you just learned.

*ad hominem, adj.* (AD HÄM ə nem′)
*bona fide, adj.* (BŌ nə fīd′)
*caveat emptor, n.* (KA vē ät′ EMP tər)
*de facto, adj.* (dē FAK tō′)
*de jure, adj.* (dē′ JÚR ē)
*Homo sapiens, n.* (HŌ′ mō SĀ pē enz′)
*mea culpa, n.* (mā′ ə KÚL pə)
*nolo contendere, n.* (NŌ lō kən TEN də rē)
*pro forma, adj.* (prō′ FÓR mə)
*vox populi, n.* (VÄKS PÄP yü lī′)

## STEP 1

Shall we begin? Don't forget to say each word again while you're reading the following definitions and examples.

1. The adjective *ad hominem* means appealing to personal feelings rather than logic or reason: an *ad hominem* argument that ignored common sense.
2. The adjective *bona fide* means sincere; made in good faith: a *bona fide* suggestion worth considering.
3. The noun *caveat emptor* refers to a business principle stating that a buyer takes a risk when buying goods or services that aren't warranted (guaranteed) by the seller or producer ("Let the buyer beware"): the store's blatant attitude of *caveat emptor*.
4. The adjective *de facto* means actual; existing in "fact," though not legal or formally recognized: a *de facto* business still preparing for incorporation.

5. The adjective *de jure* means by right; legal; existing by right or according to law: a fully formed *de jure* corporation.

6. The noun *Homo sapiens* means human beings: the tendency of *Homo sapiens* to live among others of their kind.

7. The noun *mea culpa* refers to an acknowledgment of personal error or fault ("my fault"): his sincere *mea culpa* to the angry employees.

8. The noun *nolo contendere* refers to a defendant's plea in a criminal case that, without admission of guilt, subjects the person to conviction ("I do not wish to contend [contest]"): a decision to plead *nolo contendere* rather than "not guilty."

9. The adjective *pro forma* means done or made as a formality: a *pro forma* letter of agreement following their decision by telephone.

10. The noun *vox populi* means popular opinion ("voice of the people"): a decision based on the *vox populi*.

## STEP 2

It's matching time again. Find out how well you remember the definitions by connecting each word in column 1 with the appropriate brief definition in column 2. Write your choice of a, b, c, or so forth on the short line following each term in column 1.

| Column 1 | Column 2 |
|---|---|
| 1. *de facto* _____ | a. "I don't wish to contend" |
| 2. *Homo sapiens* _____ | b. popular opinion |
| 3. *nolo contendere* _____ | c. done as a formality |
| 4. *ad hominem* _____ | d. by right; legal |
| 5. *vox populi* _____ | e. "my fault" |
| 6. *bona fide* _____ | f. "let the buyer beware" |

7. *pro forma* ___
8. *de jure* ___
9. *mea culpa* ___
10. *caveat emptor* ___

g. actual; in fact
h. genuine
i. human beings
j. appealing to emotions instead of logic

ANSWERS: (1) g (2) i (3) a (4) j (5) b (6) h (7) c (8) d (9) e (10) f

## STEP 3

Did you miss any answers in the Step 2 quiz? Let's see if you can score 100 in this reinforcement fill-in test. Write your choice—*ad hominem, bona fide, caveat emptor, de facto, de jure, Homo sapiens, mea culpa, nolo contendere, pro forma, vox populi*—in each of the following sentences.

1. If it's what the public wants, who are we to argue with the _____?
2. Scientists have identified several upright beings as forerunners of modern _____.
3. It was already agreed that David would be the group's next president, but the board held a _____ election anyway.
4. The sophomore's study group was asked to analyze a _____ corporation that was legally formed and operating in the state.
5. The defendant entered a plea of _____ so that she could deny the charges later in other proceedings.
6. The buyer should have heeded the well-known warning, _____, before buying a car that had no warranty.
7. His argument was purely _____ and had no logical basis.

8. We felt they had made an attractive and
   _____ offer and were sorry we had
   to turn it down.
9. The organizers of the _____ corporation were open for limited business even
   though they had numerous papers to file before
   achieving full legal status.
10. What can I say except _____? No
    one else is responsible for the problem.

ANSWERS: (1) *vox populi* (2) *Homo sapiens* (3)
*pro forma* (4) *de jure* (5) *nolo contendere* (6) *caveat
emptor* (7) *ad hominem* (8) *bona fide* (9) *de facto* (10)
*mea culpa*

## EXERCISE 5

So how do you like Latin so far? Many people either love it or hate it. But the people who work in
professions that use numerous Latin terms don't seem
to mind it or at least accept it as a part of their working lives. However the rest of us feel, let's press on
and try another ten words and expressions—four
nouns and six adjectives.

*ad hoc, adj.* (AD HÄK)
*amicus curiae, n.* (ə MĒ kəɛ KYÚR ē ī′)
*a priori, adj.* (Ä prē ŌR ē)
*deus ex machina, n.* (DĀ əs eks′ MÄ ki nə)
*ex gratia, adj.* (eks GRĀ shē ə)
*ex officio, adj.* (eks′ ə FISH ē ō′)
*modus operandi, n.* (mō′ dəs äp′ ə RAN dē)
*persona grata, adj.* (pər SŌ nə GRÄ tə)

*persona non grata,* adj. (pər SŌ nə nän′ GRÄ tə)

*sine qua non,* n. (sin′ i kwä′ NÄN)

## Step 1

Did you remember to pronounce each word in the list and mentally spell it? We keep asking this because studies show that it's very important to say each word mentally or aloud to remember it and ensure that you'll pronounce and spell it correctly in the future. So keep on saying the words as often as necessary and repeat them again as you read the following definitions and examples.

1. The adjective *ad hoc* means concerned with or formed for a specific purpose: an *ad hoc* staff at the convention.
2. The noun *amicus curiae* refers to a party not involved in a lawsuit but allowed to advise the court ("friend of the court"): he testified as *amicus curiae.*
3. The adjective *a priori* means based on or proceeding from a known cause: *a priori* reasoning based on his theory but not supported by experiment or experience.
4. The noun *deus ex machina* means an unlikely person or event that provides a solution to a problem or difficulty: the novel's silly *deus ex machina.*
5. The adjective *ex gratia* means as a favor; not being required by law: an unexpected *ex gratia* payment for his outstanding service.
6. The adjective *ex officio* means because of an office or a position: the director's *ex officio* appointment as secretary on the board of directors.

7. The noun *modus operandi* means method of operating: the manager's well-known *modus operandi*.

8. The adjective *persona grata* means an acceptable or welcome person: a good friend who is *persona grata*.

9. The adjective *persona non grata* means an unacceptable or unwelcome person: a noisy neighbor who is *persona non grata*.

10. The noun *sine qua non* means something that is absolutely essential: the main ingredient that is the *sine qua non* of the recipe.

## STEP 2

Let's use a matching test in this step. Connect each word in column 1 with the most appropriate brief definition in column 2. Write your choice of a, b, c, and so forth on the short line following each term in column 1.

1. *persona grata* ____       a. method of operating
2. *deux ex machina* ____     b. something absolutely essential
3. *ad hoc* ____              c. an unacceptable person
4. *modus operandi* ____      d. an acceptable person
5. *sine qua non* ____        e. reasoned from a known cause
6. *amicus curiae* ____       f. an unlikely person or event that solves a problem
7. *persona non grata* ____   g. formed for a specific purpose
8. *a priori* ____            h. as a favor

9. *ex officio* ___         i. by virtue of an office
10. *ex gratia* ___         j. "friend of the court"

ANSWERS: (1) d (2) f (3) g (4) a (5) b (6) j (7) c (8) e (9) i (10) h

## STEP 3

This fill-in test will give you a chance to practice spelling the terms as well as reinforce your understanding of their meanings. Write the most appropriate term—*ad hoc, amicus curiae, a priori, deus ex machina, ex gratia, ex officio, modus operandi, persona grata, persona non grata, sine qua non*—in each of the following sentences.

1. Mutual respect is the _____ of any successful relationship.
2. Her boss rejected her _____ argument because it was based on a faulty assumption.
3. We enjoy his company so much that he is always _____ at our house.
4. The function of an _____, though not a party to a lawsuit, is to call the court's attention to some matter that might otherwise escape its attention.
5. All the employees happily shared the _____ payments from the entertainment fund.
6. The president of the finance committee was _____ chairman of the subcommittee on budgeting.
7. The vandals' _____ was to spray paint on the walls and toss the empty cans in the nearest Dumpsters while running away.

8. The pushy, obnoxious salesperson is
   _____ in our office.
9. The _____ task force was formed
   especially to review the bylaws for possible
   revisions.
10. The stranded campers were almost ready to give
    up hope of ever being rescued when a hunter
    walked into their camp like a _____.

ANSWERS: (1) *sine qua non* (2) *a priori* (3) *persona grata* (4) *amicus curiae* (5) *ex gratia* (6) *ex officio* (7) *modus operandi* (8) *persona non grata* (9) *ad hoc* (10) *deus ex machina*

## BONUS WORDS

For your bonus words in this chapter, we've drawn on eight languages other than Latin and French. English spelling is used for the Japanese and Chinese words. As you pronounce languages such as German and Spanish, notice the differences in sound between them.

1. *a capella (Italian), adj.* (ä′ kə PEL ə) not having instrumental accompaniment: an *a capella* choir consisting of voices only
2. *aficionado (Spanish), n.* (ə fish′ ē ə NÄ dō′) someone who deeply appreciates and enthusiastically pursues an interest or activity: an *aficionado* of African art who avidly collects pieces from different countries in Africa
3. *apartheid (Afrikaans), n.* (ə PÄRT hīt) an official policy of racial segregation and discrimination against non-European groups in the Republic of South Africa: the economic oppression

that many suffered when *apartheid* was officially endorsed by the South African government

4. *chutzpah (Yiddish), n.* (HŪT spə) utter nerve; excessive self-confidence: the *chutzpah* of someone who boasts about having superior intelligence

5. *ersatz (German), adj.* (ER zäts') being a usually inferior substitute or imitation: an *ersatz* cheese spread made of nondairy substances

6. *junta (Spanish), n.* (HŪN tə) a group of military officers that controls a government after seizing power: the ruling *junta* following a revolution

7. *kimono (Japanese), n.* (kə MŌ nə') a long robe with wide sleeves worn with a sash as an outer garment; a loose robe worn mostly by women: a *kimono* worn as a dressing gown or jacket

8. *ombudsperson (Swedish), n.* (ÄM bŭdz' pər sən) someone who investigates citizen complaints, reports findings, and works out settlements: the *ombudsperson* who helps to resolve a dispute between a student and university officials

9. *Tao (Chinese), n.* (TAŪ) the right way; the guiding principle of all reality: the *Tao* philosophy of harmony with nature (capitalized in reference to the beliefs of Taoists; often not capitalized in reference to the beliefs of other groups)

10. *Weltschmerz (German), n.* (VELT shmerts') sadness over the state of the world: the *Weltschmerz* caused by increasing terrorism around the globe

## REVIEW TEST

Let's try a true-false quiz this time. As usual, the words in the test may come not only from this chapter but also from any previous chapter. A place to record the number of correct answers you score follows the answer section. If you don't get 100 percent correct, compare your score with that for previous review tests. If it isn't an improvement, you may benefit from repeating some of the previous exercises.

1. A practice of strict self-denial and severe, disciplined economy is known as *asceticism*. *True False*

2. An *insinuation* is a subtle announcement about a pleasurable event or action that will soon occur. *True False*

3. A supply room that is *replete* with cartons is full with cartons. *True False*

4. A *judicious* decision is one that is made in a court of law. *True False*

5. A person with a huge appetite has a *veracious* appetite. *True False*

6. An official order or public law is called an *ordinance*. *True False*

7. A *ménage* is a mixture of elements that are frequently unsuitable together. *True False*

8. Spain and Portugal occupy the *Iberian Peninsula*. *True False*

9. *Inadmissible* evidence is presented in court for a jury's consideration, but it is not used by a judge in sentencing defendants. *True False*

10. To *impute* something is to steal another's words or ideas. *True False*

ANSWERS: (1) True (2) False (3) True (4) False (5) False (6) True (7) False (8) True (9) False (10) False

*Correct Answers:* _____ *Incorrect Answers:* _____

# 10. Weed Out the Words You Should Avoid

> *The mobile reptile traveled up and down the West Coast but never ventured east across the Rockies.*

What do we have here: a lizard on the move? A misplaced alligator that can't climb mountains? A territorial-minded snake or turtle patrolling the coastline? Some other cold-blooded creature that's riding on a truck going up and down the coast?

It's hard to tell, unless you know the popular language of the 1990s. A *mobile reptile* is a novel, intentionally colorful, and not very flattering word for a traveling sales representative. It's really a *buzzword,* which is an imprecise, flashy substitute for a more specific, ordinary term (see the definition in the upcoming list). The English language includes many such nonstandard popular words and expressions. Some, such as *mobile reptile,* are well outside the realm of proper or standard English. But others, such as *white paper* (an official government report), are now widely considered acceptable English terms.

Every vocabulary, including that of well-educated professionals, has nonstandard as well as standard terms in it. We would find it very hard to carry on a conversation without knowing what some of the more common nonstandard terms mean. In addition to buzzwords, just mentioned, this variety of everyday language includes jargon, clichés, slang, and idioms.

Do you know the difference between the various types of nonstandard English? With some words there is no difference. A word may fit into all or most of the above categories. *Long shot* (something unlikely to succeed), for example, can be found in dictionaries of jargon, clichés, slang, and idioms. Before we say any more, however, let's be certain we agree on what these terms generally mean.

*Buzzwords,* such as *trash stash* (landfill), are voguish, sometimes sarcastic words or phrases or important-sounding but imprecise terms connected with a specialized field or group. Some authorities consider buzzwords to be a form of jargon or slang. People primarily use them to try to be clever and impress others.

*Jargon,* such as *fallout* (consequences), is the language of a special group or profession that often coins new words to explain aspects of its activity. As such, jargon is sometimes a form of professional shorthand. It's generally acceptable when used among members of the same group. But when it's used outside, with people who don't understand it, it's pretentious, confusing, and therefore unacceptable.

*Clichés,* such as *the fair sex* (women), are trite, overused, unimaginative expressions. This type of language should be treated as unacceptable anywhere beyond one's immediate family and friends. Even they are likely to find it stale and boring.

*Slang,* such as *big gun* (important person), is another type of language associated with a certain group or class of people. The users of slang typically coin new words to be different or to shock others. Young people, who want their own exclusive language, develop many slang expressions, some of which are vulgar and crude and are therefore not widely used in ordinary society.

*Idioms,* such as *follow suit* (do what someone else just did), are expressions that are peculiar to a people or a language. Although they are not necessarily offensive, they are usually difficult to translate into another language literally or logically. The words *follow suit,* for example, are meaningless when taken literally.

*Discriminatory language,* such as *brotherly love* (kindheartedness, compassion), is any language—standard or nonstandard—that suggests a bias for or against someone or something or that excludes a particular group. To some, the term *brotherly love* indicates a bias in favor of men to the exclusion of women. Such negative impressions can be avoided by substituting a neutral expression instead of referring exclusively to either men or women.

Most nonstandard English, not just idioms, is difficult to translate literally. Can you imagine people in other countries trying to translate an English expression such as *rip-off* (theft or deception) into their own language? When expressions are not widely familiar, or when they're dull, vulgar, or discriminatory, it's best to weed them out of your vocabulary. You'll be much more successful if you get in the habit of using ordinary, standard English.

## Using Jargon Wisely

It would be a mistake to give you the impression that all jargon is bad. For example, if you're an accountant, you're going to have to use specialized accounting terms to communicate with other members of your profession. The same situation exists in other professions. So we simply urge you to file jargon in a special place in your vocabulary where you go only in the company of others who use the same language.

But keep in mind that since jargon consists of words being coined for specialized occasions or activities, it includes many of the new words we hear over television or read in the newspapers every day. Since we all want and need to know these terms, the second half of this book lets you taste some of the new words and expressions. Chapter 13, for example, introduces some new information-technology terms, Chapter 15 has a number of new environmental terms, and various other chapters also include 1990s language, including professional jargon. But before we get into those areas, let's look at the good, the bad, and the ugly of nonstandard English.

## EXERCISE 1

We're starting with jargon because it's one of the most acceptable of the questionable types of words described in this chapter. Not that it's all desirable, mind you. Using a buzzword such as *mobile reptile*, for example, would not endear you to traveling salespeople. But the jargon listed in this exercise isn't offensive in that sense. The main problem with the following expressions—all nouns—is that some of the words aren't widely used or known. Therefore, we should follow the rule of using them only among others who share the same technical or professional vocabulary.

ageism (Ā jiz′ əm)
boilerplate (BŎI lər plāt′)

cocooning (kə KÜN ing)
cohousing (KŌ haus' ing)
demarketing (dē MÄR kət ing)
disinformation (dis' in' fər MĀ shən)
factoid (FAK toid')
infomercial (IN fō mər' shəl)
morphing (MORF ing)
outplacement (aut' PLĀS mənt)

## STEP 1

How many of the words did you know? All of them have been used in television news programs and have appeared in daily newspapers. See if the meanings are evident in the following sentences.

1. We need to avoid *ageism* or anything else that suggests discrimination against a certain age group.

2. The *boilerplate* stating the cancellation procedure can be repeated in each of our insurance policies.

3. The couple used to go to bars after dark, but now that they have children, *cocooning* has replaced their wild nights on the town.

4. A *cohousing* policy ensures that potential residents of a new community can participate in development decisions that will affect them later.

5. In recent years we have seen marketing that discourages public interest in a harmful product, as in the *demarketing* of cigarettes.

6. The spread of *disinformation* caused public opinion to turn against the 'legislation, even though the distorted facts were easily disproved.

7. Although the *factoid* appeared on the editorial page of the newspaper, and many of us knew it was merely the writer's opinion, a large segment

of the population foolishly assumed that it must be a valid fact simply because it was printed in the paper.

8. The advertisers bought thirty minutes of television time on Saturday mornings to air the *infomercial* (*info*rmation com*mercial*) promoting their new exercise equipment.

9. The computer technique of *morphing* was used in the science fiction program *Star Trek: Deep Space Nine* to make characters called "shape-shifters" appear to change shape easily and fluidly into another object, animal, or person.

10. Because of the company's *outplacement* policy, executives were given help in finding new jobs each time the firm decided to end their employment.

## Step 2

Most of those sentences had very specific clues to the meanings of the ten terms. But to be certain that you know each definition, match the words in column 1 with the brief definitions in column 2. Write your choice of a, b, c, and so forth on the short line after each term in column 1.

1. demarketing \_\_\_\_

2. outplacement \_\_\_\_

3. factoid \_\_\_\_

4. ageism \_\_\_\_

5. cocooning \_\_\_\_

a. discrimination against a certain age group

b. standardized text

c. marketing that tries to discourage public interest

d. a television program that is really an extended ad

e. a brief news item assumed to be true simply because it was printed

6. morphing ____

f. the "dehiring" process of helping employees being fired find another job

7. infomercial ____

g. the practice of spending leisure time at home with one's family

8. disinformation ____

h. computer process that makes something appear to change shape into something else

9. cohousing ____

i. false information willfully spread to influence public opinion

10. boilerplate ____

j. a process whereby potential residents help design their prospective community

ANSWERS: (1) c (2) f (3) e (4) a (5) g (6) h (7) d (8) i (9) j (10) b

## STEP 3

Here's a final test for anyone who still isn't completely comfortable with the terms. Decide whether the term used in each sentence is the best possible choice and then circle either true or false at the end of each statement.

1. *Disinformation* is factually correct information aimed at discouraging public interest in someone or something. *True False*
2. A *factoid* is a standardized news item. *True False*
3. *Outplacement* is the practice of helping an em-

ployee who is being let go find another job. *True False*

4. *Cocooning* is the practice of spending leisure time at home with one's family. *True False*

5. *Ageism* is discrimination against a particular age group, such as teenagers or the elderly. *True False*

6. *Demarketing* is the spread of information to influence public opinion favorably or unfavorably. *True False*

7. A *boilerplate* is a brief news item assumed to be true simply because it appeared in print. *True False*

8. *Cohousing* is a process in which potential residents help plan their prospective community. *True False*

9. *Morphing* is a computer technique that makes objects appear to change into something else before our eyes. *True False*

10. An *infomercial* is an extended informative commercial. *True False*

ANSWERS: (1) False (2) False (3) True (4) True (5) True (6) False (7) False (8) True (9) True (10) True

## EXERCISE 2

Here are ten more words—nine nouns and an adjective—that qualify as jargon. Do any look familiar?

advertorial, *n.* (ad′ vər TŌR ē əl)
aftermarket, *n.* (AF tər mär′ kət)
autofacturing, *n.* (o′ tō FAK chər ing)
backselling, *n.* (BAK sel′ ing)

broad-brush, *adj.* (BRȮD brəsh′)
copreneur, *n.* (kō′ prə NƏR)
downmarket, *n.* (DAÚN mär′ kət)
flatliner, *n.* (FLAT līn ər)
Generation X, *n.* (jen′ ə RĀ shən EKS)
outsourcing, *n.* (AÚT sōr′ sing)

## STEP 1

Let's begin with brief definitions and examples. Read each sentence for meaning and use the information to prepare for the tests in Steps 2 and 3.

1. The noun *advertorial* (*adver*tisement edi*torial*) refers to an advertisement that is written in an editorial format and appears to contain objective commentary while it really consists of the advertiser's own publicity material: the vitamin manufacturer's two-page *advertorial.*

2. The noun *aftermarket* refers to a market for parts and accessories used to repair or enhance something: the *aftermarket* for air conditioners to be installed in used cars.

3. The noun *autofacturing* (*auto*mation manu*facturing*) refers to all the activities in an automated factory, from computerized materials acquisition to robotic loading of finished products: the *autofacturing* of automobiles.

4. The noun *backselling* refers to indirect marketing by reverse promotion, such as from a retailer back to a manufacturer rather than to a consumer, or by promotion to any target other than the actual buyer: manufacturers who use *backselling* by promoting their products directly to consumers, instead of to the retailers who actu-

ally buy from them, in the hope that the consumers will ask the retailers to carry the goods.

5. The adjective *broad-brush,* derived from the idea of a painter's broad brush strokes, means being rough, general, or incomplete: a *broad-brush* account of the new policy.

6. The noun *copreneur* (*co*uple entre*preneur*) refers to a married couple who set up and run their own business as partners: the *copreneurs,* Mr. and Mrs. Davis.

7. The noun *downmarket* refers to a market characterized by lower-income consumers: the *downmarket* for low-income housing.

8. The noun *flatliner* refers to a person, product, or idea that is unsuccessful or sluggish: the company's admission that the new model was a *flatliner.*

9. The noun *Generation X* refers to the generation born after 1965 whose interests and buying habits as a group are often hard to identify: the advertiser's unsuccessful attempts to appeal to *Generation X* buyers.

10. The noun *outsourcing* refers to the business practice of sending work to be done to outside sources, such as to foreign firms, instead of hiring employees to do the work within the company: the loss of jobs because of the practice of *outsourcing.*

## STEP 2

What do you think? Are you familiar with this collection of jargon? Let's find out. For Step 2, write each of the ten words—*advertorial, aftermarket, autofacturing, backselling, broad-brush, copreneur, downmarket, flatliner, Generation X, outsourcing*—in column 1 across from the most appropriate brief definition in column 2.

1. _____    a seller's indirect marketing to someone other than the actual buyer

2. _____    a married couple who operate a business as partners

3. _____    sending work to be done outside the firm

4. _____    a low-income market

5. _____    someone or something unsuccessful or sluggish

6. _____    the generation born after 1965

7. _____    being general or incomplete

8. _____    an editorial-style advertisement

9. _____    automated-manufacturing factory

10. _____    the market for parts and accessories used to repair or enhance products

ANSWERS: (1) backselling (2) copreneurs (3) outsourcing (4) downmarket (5) flatliner (6) Generation X (7) broad-brush (8) advertorial (9) autofacturing (10) aftermarket

## STEP 3

Here's your last chance to reinforce your understanding of the current ten terms—a multiple-choice quiz. Circle the most appropriate choice—a, b, or c—in the following sentences.

1. Robots commonly load trucks in *(a) aftermarkets (b) outsourcing (c) autofacturing.*

2. With a/an *(a) broad-brush (b) advertorial (c) backselling* account, the company avoided revealing too many specifics to its customers.

3. The married couple operated their new service establishment as business *(a) outsourcers (b) copreneurs (c) backsellers.*

4. The failed product was the company's third *(a) broad-brush (b) downmarket (c) flatliner.*

5. Many companies have trouble determining how to market products successfully to buyers in the elusive *(a) Generation X (b) autofacturing (c) advertorials.*

6. Seat covers for new and used cars is a booming *(a) aftermarket (b) downmarket (c) flatliner.*

7. The appealing *(a) advertorial (b) outsourcing (c) broad-brush* led to a huge sales volume last month.

8. The inexpensive tennis shoes were targeted to the Midwest's *(a) Generation X (b) aftermarket (c) downmarket.*

9. With so much *(a) outsourcing (b) backselling (c) autofacturing* nowadays, U.S. workers are losing jobs to low-cost factories in other countries.

10. Through *(a) advertorials (b) backselling (c) outsourcing,* the retailer's sales message was aimed at the manufacturer of the product instead of the consumer.

ANSWERS: (1) c (2) a (3) b (4) c (5) a (6) a (7) a (8) c (9) a (10) b

## Avoiding Questionable Language

So much for jargon. In the next two exercises we'll look at four types of questionable language: discriminatory language, idioms, slang, and clichés. Although careful writers and speakers try to avoid this type of language, except when used for humor or another special purpose, we all want to know what the words and expressions mean. Otherwise, we won't understand what the people who do use such language are saying.

## EXERCISE 3

We learned earlier what type of words constitute discriminatory language, idioms, slang, and clichés. This exercise has at least two examples of each type of language, including seven nouns, two adjectives, and one verb. Each term is identified by type of language—idiom, cliché, and so on. Keep in mind, however, that some authorities may place a word in more than one category.

bachelor's degree (discrim. lang.), *n.* (BACH ə lərs di GRĒ)

backpedal (idiom), *vb.* (BAK ped′ əl)

boondoggle (slang), *n.* (BÜN däg əl)

copasetic (slang), *adj.* (KŌP ə sət′ ik)

elbow grease (idiom), *n.* (EL bō GRĒS)

eloquent silence (cliché), *n.* (EL ə kwənt SĪ ləns)

indelible impression (cliché), *n.* (in DEL ə bəl im PRESH ən)

motherland (discrim. lang.), *n.* (MƏ thər land′)

tailor-made (idiom), *adj.* (tā′ lər MĀD)

time immemorial (cliché), *n.* (TĪM im′ ə MŌR ē əl)

## STEP 1

Before we can decide on a more acceptable substitute for the ten questionable terms, we need to be certain that the definitions are clear. If you don't already know what the ten expressions mean, the following sentences may help.

1. After four busy years at U.S. University, Tim received a *bachelor's degree* in economics on June 14 this year. (Although some consider *bachelor* to be sexist, the expression *bachelor's degree* is the official designation in many colleges and universities and should be used in those cases.)

2. It seems that they always *backpedal* just after making a commitment to something. Why do they keep reversing their opinion?

3. That project is the worst *boondoggle* I've ever seen. What a waste of money.

4. Everything is *copasetic* here—no problems so far.

5. He had to use a lot of *elbow grease* in waxing the car. It was hard work just watching him.

6. Sometimes, *eloquent silence* is the best choice. It can say more than all the words in the world.

7. The movie made an *indelible impression* on her. She still gets tears in her eyes when someone mentions it.

8. After spending seven years in Japan, he longed for the day when he would see his *motherland* again.

9. The Saturday computer courses are *tailor-made* for busy executives who don't have time to attend weekday classes.

10. People have been predicting the end of the world since *time immemorial.*

## STEP 2

We need to accomplish two things in this step: double-check the meanings of the ten expressions and find more appropriate substitutes. The standard English phrases in column 2 not only serve to define the ten expressions but also represent acceptable substitutes for them.

To complete this step, fill in the expressions of discriminatory language, idioms, slang, and clichés—*bachelor's degree, backpedal, boondoggle, copasetic, elbow grease, eloquent silence, indelible impression, motherland, tailor-made, time immemorial*—across from acceptable substitutes.

1. _____ satisfactory; agreeable
2. _____ homeland; native land
3. _____ ancient times; time long past
4. _____ well-suited; perfectly fitted to
5. _____ baccalaureate; undergraduate degree
6. _____ wasteful project; impractical activity
7. _____ silence; silence that conveys more than words
8. _____ retreat; reverse action or opinion
9. _____ lasting impression; unforgettable impression
10. _____ hard work; vigorous physical labor

ANSWERS: (1) copasetic (2) motherland (3) time immemorial (4) tailor-made (5) bachelor's degree (6) boondoggle (7) eloquent silence (8) backpedal (9) indelible impression (10) elbow grease

## STEP 3

In Step 2 we learned some acceptable substitutes for the questionable language. This time, without glancing back to that step, fill in *one* substitute for each of the ten questionable expressions listed in column 2. Since this is a reverse quiz—the opposite of the pattern we've followed thus far—we'll supply the first one as an example. Again, we're looking for *acceptable substitutes* for the ten questionable expressions listed in column 2.

1. <u>baccalaureate</u>       bachelor's degree
2. _____   eloquent silence
3. _____   backpedal
4. _____   indelible impression
5. _____   copasetic
6. _____   time immemorial
7. _____   boondoggle
8. _____   tailor-made
9. _____   motherland
10. _____   elbow grease

ANSWERS: (1) baccalaureate *or* undergraduate degree (2) silence *or* silence that conveys more than words (3) retreat *or* reverse action or opinion (4) lasting impression *or* unforgettable impression (5) satisfactory *or* agreeable (6) ancient times *or* time long past (7) wasteful project *or* impractical activity (8) well-suited *or* perfectly fitted to (9) homeland *or* native land (10) hard work *or* vigorous physical labor

## EXERCISE 4

Did you make it through the last step of Exercise 3? If you did, this exercise will seem even easier. Here are ten more examples of discriminatory language, idioms, slang, and clichés—nine nouns and an adjective. We've again identified each one according to type of language—idiom, slang, and so on. But some authorities may disagree or may consider the term applicable to more than one category.

Also, for this exercise we again need to develop a dual line of thinking. It's important to know what the questionable expressions mean because other people use them. But our goal should be to use acceptable *substitutes* in our own conversations and letters.

Achilles' heel (cliché), *n.* (ə KIL ēz HĒl)
chairmanship (discrim. lang.), *n.* (CHER mən ship')
droid (slang), *n.* (DRÓID)
jaundiced eye (cliché), *n.* (JÓN dəst Ī)
man-made (discrim. lang.), *adj.* (MAN mād)
meteoric rise (cliché), *n.* (mē' tē ÓR ik RĪZ)
poetic justice (idiom), *n.* (pō ET ik JƏS təs)
Shangri-la (idiom), *n.* (Shang' gri LÄ)
siege mentality (cliché), *n.* (SĒJ men TAL ə tē)
wuss (slang), *n.* (WƏS)

## STEP 1

Some of you have no doubt heard these expressions many times before. But if any of them are unfamiliar, the following sentences should suggest the meaning.

1. The undeniable fact that he once violated the tax law will forever be his *Achilles' heel.*
2. He's such a *droid* with his nose always stuck in a book.
3. Today, she resigned the *chairmanship* of the conference committee.
4. He has always looked upon the poor with a *jaun-*

    *diced eye,* perhaps because he grew up in a preju-
dicial upper-middle-class neighborhood.

5. All of the flowers and plants in the store are
   *man-made,* except for one living cactus.

6. The young actor's *meteoric rise* to fame apparently happened too fast, because he soon became
   caught in a tangle of drug use and emotional
   upheavals.

7. She was so ruthless in firing everyone who dis-
   agreed with her that her own dismissal following
   an argument with her boss seems like *poetic
   justice.*

8. This resort may not be *Shangri-la,* but it's the
   most perfect place I've ever found.

9. His *siege mentality* prevents him from acting con-
   fidently and forcefully; it makes him a prisoner
   of his own exaggerated fears.

10. I wish he would get some backbone and stand
    up for himself, but he's such a *wuss.*

## Step 2

To double-check the meanings, match the expressions in column 1 with the appropriate definitions in
column 2. Write your choice of a, b, c, and so forth
on the short line after each column 1 definition.

1. Achilles' heel ＿＿＿   a. prejudiced view
2. chairmanship ＿＿＿   b. sudden and swift rise
3. droid ＿＿＿   c. weak person
4. jaundiced eye ＿＿＿   d. a dull, bookish, or robotlike person
5. man-made ＿＿＿   e. suitable, though acciden-
   tal or unrelated, pun-
   ishment

6. meteoric rise ____     f. defensive attitude; overly fearful attitude

7. poetic justice ____     g. an imaginary perfect place

8. Shangri-la ____     i. a vulnerable (open to attack) point

9. siege mentality ____     h. artificial; synthetic; constructed

10. wuss ____     j. the chair; leadership; presidency

ANSWERS: (1) h (2) j (3) d (4) a (5) i (6) b (7) e (8) g (9) f (10) c

## STEP 3

Again, we want to use this step to reinforce the *acceptable substitutes* for the questionable language. So without glancing back to Step 2, see if you can fill in *one* appropriate substitute for each of the questionable expressions listed in column 2. We'll get you started by filling in the first item.

1. <u>dull person</u>     droid
2. _____     meteoric rise
3. _____     wuss
4. _____     Achilles' heel
5. _____     Shangri-la
6. _____     siege mentality
7. _____     chairmanship
8. _____     man-made
9. _____     poetic justice
10. _____     jaundiced eye

ANSWERS: (1) dull, bookish, *or* robotlike person (2) sudden rise *or* swift rise (3) weak person (4) vulnerable point (5) perfect place (6) defensive attitude *or* overly fearful attitude (7) chair, leadership, *or* presidency (8) artificial, synthetic, *or* constructed (9) suitable punishment (10) prejudiced view

## BONUS WORDS

Your bonus collection in this chapter consists of ten words and expressions drawn from jargon, clichés, idioms, and slang. Each word is classified by type of language. But keep in mind that experts sometimes disagree in the selection of a category or may put a word in more than one category.

1. *boiler room* (jargon), *n.* (BŌI lər RŪM)   a place of high pressure and sometimes illegal telephone selling by salespeople, each of whom sits in a small room or cubicle equipped with telephones: the *boiler room* set up by a group selling counterfeit musical compact disks.
2. *checkered career* (cliché), *n.* (CHEK ərd kə RIR)   a background of successes and failures, often with more failures: the congressional representative with a *checkered career*
3. *false start* (idiom), *n.* (FÒLS STÄRT)   an unsuccessful beginning that has to be repeated: a *false start* in designing a word processing program
4. *gentrification* (jargon), *n.* (jen' trə fə KĀ shən)   the process of rebuilding a lower-income area, causing an influx of middle- and higher-income residents who displace the previous poorer residents: the *gentrification* that turned the run-down neighborhood into an area of expensive town houses
5. *hyphenates* (jargon), *n.* (HĪ fə nāts')   a refer-

ence to people who have more than one heritage
or job function: the photographer-editor *hyphenates* who were African-Americans

6. *infotainment* (jargon), *n.* (in' fō' TĀN mənt)
a type of television program that presents factual information, such as news, as entertainment (*info*rmation enter*tainment*): the chatty,
joking atmosphere created by the *infotainment*'s hosts

7. *mousemilking* (jargon), *n.* (MAÚZ MILK ing)
investing maximum time and effort for something
that produces a minimum return: his admission
of *mousemilking* when he spent $500 worth of
sales effort that produced a $2 sale

8. *subemployment* (jargon), *n.* (səb' im PLÓI
mənt) any form of inadequate employment or
actual unemployment: the *subemployment* of
people who aren't receiving a proper living wage

9. *word engineering* (jargon), *n.* (WƏRD en'
jə NIR ing) the process of deceptively alter-
ing information so that the people reporting say
only what they want to reveal: the *word engineering* practices in the government

10. *yenta* (slang), *n.* (YEN tə) a degrading term
of Yiddish origin for someone who gossips or
meddles: the *yenta* who was known throughout
the neighborhood

## REVIEW TEST

Are you ready to check your progress so far? This
multiple-choice test will cover Chapters 3 through 9
as well as the present chapter. Circle your choice of
a, b, or c in each item.

As usual, a place is given after the answer section

for you to record the number of correct and incorrect answers you give. If you're not scoring well above 50 correct answers or are not doing better than you did on the previous chapter's test, you may want to repeat some of the earlier exercises.

1. *Hieroglyphs* are
    (a) small pieces of colored stone
    (b) possessions attached to property
    (c) pictorial characters
2. To *vitiate* is to
    (a) impair or debase
    (b) stir up or arouse
    (c) make easier
3. Something *infinitesimal* is
    (a) too small to measure
    (b) impossible to limit
    (c) lacking in harmony
4. A *disinterested* person is
    (a) not interested
    (b) objective
    (c) indifferent
5. An *intercession* is an
    (a) interim period between sessions
    (b) incidental session between two other sessions
    (c) intervention in someone's behalf
6. *Ordnance* refers to
    (a) supplies and equipment
    (b) a city law
    (c) military flags
7. The Chinese word *Tao* refers to
    (a) a long robe worn as an outer garment
    (b) a guiding principle
    (c) sadness over the state of the world

8. *Demarketing* is
    (a) an effort to discourage public interest
    (b) false information aimed at discouraging interest
    (c) marketing to a target other than one's customers
9. *Acclamation* means
    (a) the process of adjusting to a new environment
    (b) unenthusiastic agreement to something
    (c) loud or enthusiastic approval
10. A *sesquicentennial* event occurs every
    (a) fifteen years
    (b) one hundred fifty years
    (c) fifty years

ANSWERS: (1) c (2) a (3) a (4) b (5) c (6) a (7) b (8) a (9) c (10) b

*Correct Answers:* _____ *Incorrect Answers:* _____

# 11. Expand Your Vocabulary with Prefixes and Suffixes

*The category of "nonsporting dog" now includes the bulldog and poodle, once bred for a form of outdoor entertainment popularly known as "field sports."*

One has to wonder what *kind* of field sport was suitable for a pudgy, stocky bulldog or a dainty, well-groomed poodle. They obviously were looked upon differently then—and looked different too. But it's still hard to picture a lumbering bulldog quietly flushing pheasants or quail from a thicket or a graceful poodle menacing a cougar or bear in the wilderness—at least not the bulldogs and poodles that most of us have known and loved.

We're delighted, however, that these onetime working dogs are now enjoying lives of leisure as our household pets and companions. Some owners, in fact, now doubt that their little friends would know what to do even if they tripped over a bird or animal in the wild.

Whether they now fit in the sporting or nonsporting category, what do bulldogs and poodles have to do with prefixes and suffixes? In this chapter the opening comment about dogs has other significance: It includes a common prefix and suffix.

Can you find them? If they aren't obvious, some

definitions may help: A *prefix* is one or more letters attached to the *beginning* of a word or the main part of it. A *suffix* is the same type of attachment, but it's positioned at the end rather than the beginning.

Now, can you find the two attachments in the opening statement? One is *non-* in *nonsporting;* the other is *-ment* in *entertainment.* The English language has many such words with letters affixed to the beginning or end, as you'll see in the following discussions of prefixes and suffixes.

## Using Prefixes to Enlarge Your Vocabulary

Attaching prefixes to already existing words, thereby forming new words, is a surprisingly effective way to enlarge your vocabulary. For example: *anti-* + *government* = *antigovernment; micro-* + *computer* = *microcomputer; semi-* + *formal* = *semiformal; pre-* + *school* = *preschool.* Get the idea? It's a little like two or more words for the price of one.

In those examples, did you notice that there is no hyphen between a prefix and the main word to which it's attached (*semiformal,* not *semi-formal*)? A hyphen would be necessary, though, if the prefix were attached to a capitalized word, such as *anti-American* (not *antiAmerican*).

## EXERCISE 1

Before you start this exercise, we want to alert you that this is a chapter on word forming. So extra steps will be involved in each exercise. But don't worry about it. Just take your time, and it will work out fine.

Here are the first ten prefixes. A brief description

follows each one to indicate common meanings. For pronunciation, refer to the pronunciations of newly formed words containing these prefixes in this exercise.

ante-: before or earlier
bio-: life or living
chrono-: time
counter-: contrary or equal
extra-: outside or beyond
geo-: earth
hydro-: hydrogen or water
mono-: one
neo-: new or recent
supra-: above or greater than

## STEP 1

Let's see how we can use those prefixes to create different words. We'll give you ten basic words, and your task will be to attach a prefix to each of the basic words to form a new word.

You may decide that some prefixes will work with more than one word. That situation is common with prefixes and suffixes. For purposes of the test, however, we want you to use each prefix only once.

Most of the basic words will be familiar to you. But if you don't know their meanings, you should be able to find clues in the column 2 new-word definitions of the next test. If you're still uncertain, however, pull out your trusty dictionary and look up any word that remains a mystery.

After you've combined prefixes with basic words, write each new word you create in column 1 of the test across from the appropriate matching definition in column 2. To get you started, we'll go through the steps of forming one of the new words.

First, notice the definition of test item 1, which refers to the *center* of the *earth*.

Next, review the list of basic words preceding the test; one word (*centric*) is clearly related to the word *center*.

Then, review the list of prefixes preceding the test (definitions were given at the beginning of this exercise); one prefix (*geo-*) means "earth."

Finally, put the two together (prefix + basic word), and you have a new word, *geocentric,* that fits the column 2 definition.

Keep in mind that in all of the word-forming tests in this chapter, each column 2 definition contains obvious clues to the appropriate prefix and basic word to use.

To find pronunciations and parts of speech for the newly formed words, check the answer section beneath each test.

Here are the ten prefixes and the ten basic words you'll need to form new words that match the column 2 definitions in the upcoming test.

| | |
|---|---|
| ante- | active, *adj.* |
| bio- | balance, *vb.* |
| chrono- | centric, *adj.* |
| counter- | classical, *adj.* |
| extra- | curricular, *adj.* |
| geo- | date, *vb.* |
| hydro- | drama, *vb.* |
| mono- | dynamic, *adj.* |
| neo- | logical, *adj.* |
| supra- | national, *adj.* |

1. _geocentric_ — regarding the center of the earth

2. _____ — to offset or balance with an equal or contrary force

3. _____ — relating to the force, or dynamics, of liquid or water in motion

4. _____ — concerning a new interest in or revival of traditional, classical style

5. _____ — a drama written for one performer

6. _____ — concerning a substance affecting, or acting on, living tissue

7. _____ — being greater than national borders or spheres of influence

8. _____ — being outside a school's regular curriculum

9. _____ — to be of, or to give, an earlier date

10. _____ — being arranged logically according to time of occurrence

ANSWERS: 1. geocentric, *adj.* (jē′ ō SEN trik)
2. counterbalance, *vb.* (KAÜN tər bal′ əns)
3. hydrodynamic, *adj.* (hī′ drō dī NAM ik)
4. neoclassical, *adj.* (nē′ ō KLAS i kəl)
5. monodrama, *n.* (MÄN ə drä mə)
6. bioactive, *adj.* (bī′ ō AK tiv)
7. supranational, *adj.* (sü′ prə NASH ə nəl)
8. extracurricular, *adj.* (ek′ strə kə RIK yə lər)
9. antedate, *vb.* (AN ti dāt)
10. chronological, *adj.* (krä′ nə LÄJ i kəl)

## STEP 2

How did you do? By now you've discovered that word forming involves extra thought, time, and steps beyond simply learning the definition of an already existing word. But even if you had trouble creating the new words in Step 1, don't give up. Simply realizing how you can use prefixes to create new words with different meanings is important in itself.

Let's use the same ten prefixes one more time. But for this test, try combining the prefixes with a different group of words. Again, use each prefix only once even if you think it would work with more than one word.

Follow the same procedure as in Step 1. If you've forgotten the definitions of the prefixes, return to the start of Exercise 1 and refresh your memory about them. Then read the definitions in column 2 of the next test and create a new word—prefix + existing word—to match each of those definitions. Write the newly formed word in column 1.

Again, we'll work out the first one to get you started.

First, check the definition of test item 1, which refers to a *culture* that is *contrary* to established culture.

Next, review the list of basic words preceding the test; the word *culture* is on that list.

Then, review the list of prefixes preceding the test (definitions were given at the beginning of this exercise); one prefix (*counter-*) means "contrary or equal."

Finally, put the two together (prefix + basic word), and you have a new word, *counterculture*, that fits the column 2 definition.

After you finish forming the other nine words in this way, check the answer section following the test for pronunciations and parts of speech.

Here are the ten prefixes and the ten words you'll need to form new words that match the column 2 definitions.

| | |
|---|---|
| ante- | conservative, *n.* |
| bio- | culture, *n.* |
| chrono- | diluvian, *adj.* |
| counter- | electric, *adj.* |
| extra- | genesis, *n.* |
| geo- | legal, *adj.* |
| hydro- | magnetic, *adj.* |
| mono- | meter, *n.* |
| neo- | rational, *adj.* |
| supra- | rhythm, *n.* |

1. <u>counterculture</u>    a culture with values and lifestyles contrary to established culture

2. _____    relating to the magnetism, or attractive force, of the earth

3. _____    a former liberal, or new conservative, who supports intellectual and political conservatism

4. _____    being extremely old and antiquated; existing before the so-called biblical diluvial deluge (the great flood)

5. _____    a theory stating that the origin, or genesis, of all

things is a single ancestor or cell

6. _____ greater than the rational or what can be decided by reason alone

7. _____ generating electricity by converting the energy of running water

8. _____ an inborn biological (life) cycle or rhythm

9. _____ occurring outside the law, or not being regulated or permitted by law

10. _____ a timepiece; an exceptionally precise device, or meter, that measures time

ANSWERS: 1. counterculture, *n.* (KAÙN tər kəl′ chər)

2. geomagnetic, *adj.* (jē′ ō mag NET ik)
3. neoconservative, *n.* (nē′ ō kən SƏR və tiv)
4. antediluvian, *adj.* (an′ ti də LÜ vē ən)
5. monogenesis, *n.* (män′ ə JEN ə səs)
6. suprarational, *adj.* (sü′ prə RASH ə nəl)
7. hydroelectric, *adj.* (hī′ drō i LEK trik)
8. biorhythm, *n.* (BĪ ō rith′ əm)
9. extralegal, *adj.* (ek′ strə LĒ gəl)
10. chronometer, *n.* (krə NÄM ə tər)

## STEP 3

You did it! In Steps 1 and 2 you doubled the number of words you were given. By combining the ten prefixes with twenty words, such as *balance* and *electric,* you ended up with a total of forty words (twenty basic words + twenty new words). Not bad! That's the magic of knowing how to create new words by attaching prefixes to already existing words.

Let's use the final step of this exercise to reinforce your understanding of the ten prefixes and some of the new words you just formed. The following multiple-choice questions will draw on the two groups of newly formed words. Circle the most appropriate choice—a, b, or c—in each sentence.

1. Something that acts on living tissue is *(a) antediluvian (b) monogenesis (c) bioactive.*

2. The files were arranged by date in a/an *(a) chronometric (b) chronological (c) antedated* pattern.

3. We have recently seen interest increasing in the *(a) neoclassical (b) chronological (c) biorhythmic* art style.

4. She went beyond logic and used a *(a) suprarational (b) geomagnetic (c) hydrodynamic* analysis to explain the strange lights in the night sky.

5. If the theory of *(a) biorhythms (b) bioactivity (c) monogenesis* is correct, my pet rabbit and I both descended from the same single cell or ancestor.

6. The one-person play was the first *(a) monogenesis (b) monodrama (c) bioaction* he ever produced.

7. Because the advertising was not permitted by law, the public objected to the company's *(a) extralegal (b) antediluvian (c) countercultural* publicity campaign.

8. This year's comedy is a good *(a) antedate (b) chronometer (c) counterbalance* to last year's murder mystery.

9. The *(a) geocentric (b) geomagnetic (c) hydrodynamic* storm was caused by a change in the earth's magnetism, associated with solar flares.

10. The *(a) hydroelectric (b) chronometric (c) hydro-*

*dynamic* plant generated power from running water.

ANSWERS: (1) c (2) b (3) a (4) a (5) c (6) b (7) a (8) c (9) b (10) a

## Using Suffixes to Enlarge Your Vocabulary

For this part of the chapter, we need to stop thinking about the front, or beginning, of words and start thinking about the rear, or ending, of words. A suffix, as we learned earlier, is one or more letters attached to the *end* of an already existing word or main part of it.

For example, if you add the suffix *-ment* (meaning "an action, process, or result") to the word *manage,* you have formed a different word: *management.* That's not all you've changed. The word *manage* is a verb, but adding *-ment* to it changes it to a noun.

For the moment, however, let's concentrate on the fact that you can use suffixes to enlarge your vocabulary in the same way that you can use prefixes to do this. For example: *back + ward = backward; courage + ous = courageous; press + ure = pressure.* In some cases the spelling of an already existing word or the suffix may have to be changed slightly when adding a suffix: *plenty + full = plentiful.* If ever you have any doubts about changes in spelling, look up the proposed new word in a dictionary.

Now, if you've made the mental switch from "front" (prefixes) to "rear" (suffixes), let's move on to Exercise 2 and put all of this information into practice.

## EXERCISE 2

This exercise has ten new suffixes, each with a brief description that indicates common meanings. For pronunciations, refer to the pronunciations of words with these suffixes in this exercise.

-ancy: quality or state
-arium: place, model, or device associated with or exposed to
-cy: condition or rank
-ent: causing an action or being determined by something else
-ial: characterized by or relating to
-ible: capable of, suitable for, worthy of, or liable to
-ive: performing or tending toward an action
-or: agent, device, condition, or way
-ule: small one
-worthy: warranting or being of sufficient worth

### STEP 1

Follow the same procedure used in Exercise 1. We'll give you ten basic words, and your assignment will be to attach a suffix to each of the basic words to form new words. Again, use each suffix only once in the test, even though it may work with more than one word.

If any of the basic words is not familiar to you, check the column 2 definitions of the next test for clues to its meaning, or check a dictionary for further information.

When you've finished combining basic words and suffixes, write each newly formed word in column 1 of the test across from the appropriate matching definition in column 2. We'll take you through the steps of forming the first new word in the test.

First, notice the definition of test item 1, which refers to a *state* or feeling of annoyance or of feeling *piqued*.

Next, review the list of basic words preceding the test; one word (*pique*) is obviously related to the word *piqued*.

Then, review the list of suffixes preceding the test (definitions were given at the beginning of this exercise); one suffix (*-ancy*) means a "quality or state."

Finally, put the two together (basic word + suffix), and you have a new word, *piquancy,* that fits the column 2 definition.

After you've formed all the words for the test in this way, check the answer section after the test for pronunciations and parts of speech.

Here are the ten suffixes and basic words that you'll need to form new words to match the column 2 definitions.

| | |
|---|---|
| bankrupt, *adj.* | -ancy |
| coalesce, *vb.* | -arium |
| collect, *vb.* | -cy |
| credit, *n.* | -ent |
| demean, *vb.* | -ial |
| demonstrate, *vb.* | -ible |
| node, *n.* | -ive |
| pique, *vb.* | -or |
| planet, *n.* | -ule |
| resident, *n.* | -worthy |

1. <u>piquancy</u> — a state or feeling of annoyance or wounded pride; feeling piqued

2. _____ — characterized by or relating to a residence

3. _____ — a model of the solar system; a device projecting planets and other bodies onto a dome; the building or place housing such things

4. _____ — the way in which one behaves or conducts or demeans oneself

5. _____ — a small mass, node, knot, or growth

6. _____ — having a credit rating of sufficient worth

7. _____ — an item prized by others and suitable for or worthy of collection

8. _____ — tending to prove or demonstrate openly

9. _____ — a condition of being financially ruined, or bankrupt; unable to meet all debts

10. _____ — causing the action of coalescing, or of different things coming together to form one whole

ANSWERS: 1. piquancy, *n.* (PĒ kənt sē)
2. residential, *adj.* (rez′ ə DEN shəl)
3. planetarium, *n.* (plan′ ə TER ē əm)
4. demeanor, *n.* (di MĒ nər)

5.  nodule, *n.* (NÄJ ül')
6.  creditworthy, *adj.* (KRED it wər' thē)
7.  collectible, *n.* (kə LEK tə bəl)
8.  demonstrative, *adj.* (di MÄN strə tiv)
9.  bankruptcy, *n.* (BANGK rəpt sē)
10. coalescent, *adj.* (kō' ə LES sənt)

## STEP 2

In this step we'll use the same suffixes but switch to a different group of words. If you've forgotten the definitions of any suffixes, return to the beginning of this exercise and reread them.

Next, read the definitions in column 2 of the test and create a new word—basic word + suffix—to match each definition. Remember to use each suffix only once in the test. Then write the newly formed word in column 1 of the test across from the most appropriate definition in column 2.

We'll again go through the steps for forming the first new word of the test.

First, check the definition of test item 1, which refers to *causing* light or *luminescence*.

Next, review the list of basic words preceding the test; the closely related word *luminesce* is on that list.

Then, review the list of suffixes preceding the test (definitions were given at the beginning of this exercise); one suffix (*-ent*) means "causing an action."

Finally, put the two together (basic word + suffix), and you have a new word, *luminescent,* that fits the column 2 definition.

See if you can form new words to fit the remaining nine definitions in column 2. Then check the answer section following the test for pronunciations and parts of speech.

Here are the ten basic words and suffixes that you'll need to form new words for the test.

| | |
|---|---|
| accelerate, *vb*. | -ancy |
| buoy, *vb*. | -arium |
| congest, *vb*. | –cy |
| digest, *vb*. | –ent |
| glob, *n*. | –ial |
| influence, *vb*. | -ible |
| luminesce, *vb*. | -ive |
| solar, *adj*. | -or |
| solvent, *adj*. | -ule |
| trust, *n*. | -worthy |

1. <u>luminescent</u>      causing light, or luminescence, that doesn't derive energy from the body emitting it, as in a fluorescent lamp

2. _____      a place, such as a glassed-in porch, exposed to solar rays

3. _____      characterized by or relating to influence or considerable importance

4. _____      warranting trust or being reliable

5. _____      a small, round mass, drop, or glob

6. _____      a device for increasing speed or accelerating

7. _____ the quality or state of being buoyant or able to float

8. _____ the condition of being solvent or able to meet financial obligations

9. _____ tending to cause congestion by overfilling or overcrowding

10. _____ capable of being easily digested or absorbed and used

ANSWERS: 1. luminescent, *adj.* (lü′ mə NES ənt)

2. solarium, *n.* (sō LAR ē əm)
3. influential, *adj.* (in′ flü′ EN shəl)
4. trustworthy, *adj.* (TRƏST wər′ thē)
5. globule, *n.* (GLÄB yül′)
6. accelerator, *n.* (ik SEL ə rā′ tər)
7. buoyancy, *n.* (BȮI ən sē)
8. solvency, *n.* (SÄL vən sē)
9. congestive, *adj.* (kən JEST iv)
10. digestible, *adj.* (dī JES tə bəl)

## STEP 3

Let's close this final word-forming exercise with a true-false test. The words in this test are drawn from the twenty new words that were created in Exercise 2. To reinforce your understanding of the suffixes and the newly formed words, read each of the following sentences and circle either true or false.

1. If you behave badly, your *demeanor* will be subject to criticism. *True False*

2. A *solarium* is a model of the solar system. *True False*

3. *Piquancy* is a feeling of being annoyed or miffed. *True False*

4. *Demonstrative* people have a tendency to express emotion openly. *True False*

5. Too many people in too small a place causes *congestive* conditions. *True False*

6. A *planetarium* is a place or room designed so that it will be regularly exposed to solar rays. *True False*

7. A *nodule* is a device used to increase speed. *True False*

8. A *collectible* is an object, such as very old glassware, that is often highly prized by those who appreciate such items. *True False*

9. A *globule* is a massive, shapeless accumulation of solid material. *True False*

10. A *luminescent* fixture is one that does not emit heat or light. *True False*

ANSWERS: (1) True (2) False (3) True (4) True (5) True (6) False (7) False (8) True (9) False (10) False

## BONUS WORDS

In this chapter your bonus consists of five prefixes, five suffixes, and ten words that have these attachments.

1. *circum-* around
   *circumvent, vb.* (sər′ kəm VENT) to make a circuit around: *circumvent* the globe

2. *extro-* outward

*extroversion, n.* (ek′ strə VƏR zhən)   the habit of receiving satisfaction primarily from what is outside the self: the *extroversion* of someone who seeks happiness from external sources

3. *intra-* within
*intrapersonal, adj.* (in′ trə PƏR sə nəl) occurring within the individual person or mind: the intrapersonal concerns of the homeless

4. *poly-* having more than one
*polycentric, adj.* (pä′ lē SEN trik)   having many centers or central parts: *polycentric* control in which there are several centers of authority

5. *trans-* across
*transcontinental, adj.* (trans′ kän tə NEN təl)   spanning or crossing a continent: a *transcontinental* advertising campaign

6. *-ic* characterized or caused by
*seismic, adj.* (SIZ mik)   caused by an earthquake or earth vibrations: *seismic* damage from the quake

7. *-ism* practice, condition, or characteristic manner
*colloquialism, n.* (kə LŌ kwē ə liz′ əm) an informal, conversational expression; a local or regional expression: a southern *colloquialism*

8. *-kinesis* motion
*photokinesis, n.* (fō′ tō kə NĒ səs)   movement in response to light: the *photokinesis* demonstrated by students at the science fair

9. *-osis* condition or action
*symbiosis, n.* (sim′ bē Ō səs)   the act of unlike organisms living together in close association, usually in a mutually beneficial relationship: the *symbiosis* between animals and birds when the birds feed on insects that bother the animals

10. *-urgy* technique or process for working with
    *metallurgy, n.* (MET əl ər′ jē) the science
    and technology of working with metals: new tech-
    niques for shaping and forming metals in
    *metallurgy*

## REVIEW TEST

Do you want to try a different type of review test?
We'll give you twenty words from which you can pick
the ten that work best in the following sentences. First,
read the sentences and the twenty words. Then, for
each sentence, write your word choice on the blank
line. Remember that a review test covers all previous
chapters as well as the present chapter.

After you've finished, record the number of correct
and incorrect answers you gave on the lines following
the answer section. If you did better than last time,
good for you! If you didn't, consider repeating exercises with words that are causing problems.

Here are the twenty words you can use to find good
choices for the ten sentences.

| | |
|---|---|
| aficionado | ingenuous |
| amenable | importune |
| censor | integrate |
| censure | intransigent |
| consummate | intrapersonal |
| contentious | quaternary |
| creationism | raison d'être |
| Darwinism | specious |
| habitué | supersede |
| ideology | tertiary |

1. An _____ deeply appreciates and enthusiastically pursues an interest or activity.

2. To examine and remove something objectionable is to _____ it.

3. The word _____ describes something that is third in rank or order.

4. An actor's _____ performance is perfect in every way.

5. The theory of _____ states that the world was created by God as described in Genesis.

6. A person's _____ refers to a body of ideas that reflect the beliefs and desires of one or more people.

7. One's _____ thoughts occur within one's own mind.

8. A coworker who is willing to accept your suggestions is _____ to them.

9. A _____ argument is deceptively attractive and sounds true even while being false.

10. To replace an obsolete item with a more recent one is to _____ the old with the new.

ANSWERS: (1) aficionado (2) censor (3) tertiary (4) consummate (5) creationism (6) ideology (7) intrapersonal (8) amenable (9) specious (10) supersede
*Correct Answers:* _____ *Incorrect Answers:* _____

# 12. Become Familiar with Important Legal Terms

*An Arizona woman once sued God for $100,000 damages after her house was struck by lightning.*

You're thinking that God won that case, aren't you? After all, God doesn't lose cases or anything else. Losing is something reserved for unfortunate mortals like us, right? Wrong—God lost that one.

According to a popular story, an Arizonan once accused God of *negligence* for not wielding enough power over the weather to stop a bolt of lightning from striking her house. The woman apparently didn't receive the $100,000 in *damages,* but she did win the case—for a very simple reason: God didn't show up in court.

We hope that relaying this story doesn't prompt a new wave of lawsuits against God. Our motive in telling you about it is to illustrate the use of a couple common legal terms—*negligence* and *damages.*

Did you notice the use of those two words in the second paragraph? Although the words can be used in other ways, in a legal sense *negligence* refers to a failure to exercise reasonable care, resulting in harm to someone or something. *Damages* refers to money that a court may order a negligent party to pay when the victim suffers a loss or injury because of this negligence.

As you can see, legal terms are not all mysterious, complex words and phrases used only by lawyers and judges with a law degree. Many are words that we hear every day at work or in television programs. We often read them in newspapers, magazines, and books, or they may creep into our conversations at parties, over the dinner table, or in the supermarket.

The law is a very important and inescapable part of everyday life, so it's essential that we include legal terms in our vocabularies. For the exercises in this chapter we've selected some common legal words and phrases in English that everyone should know. We already defined some Latin legal expressions, such as *nolo contendere* and *amicus curiae,* in Chapter 9.

## Legal Words That You Should Know

We'll begin the exercises with common legal words and end them with common legal phrases. The bonus section will also have a collection of legal terms that you should know. However, if you have an avid interest in legal matters and would like to know even more terms, we urge you to purchase a dictionary of legal terms for your home or office.

### EXERCISE 1

To ease into the subject of law and to put us in the right mood, let's begin with some of the more familiar legal words—all nouns, some of which you may already know. As always, you'll find it easier to remember these terms if you practice pronouncing and spelling them before you begin Step 1.

adjudication, *n.* (ə jü di KĀ shən)
affidavit, *n.* (af′ ə DĀ vət)
attestation, *n.* (at′ es′ TĀ shən)
covenant, *n.* (KƏV ə nənt)
exoneration, *n.* (ig zän′ ə RĀ shən)
interrogatories, *n.* (in′ tə RĀG ə tōr′ ēz)
jurisprudence, *n.* (jùr′ əs PRÜD əns)
lien, *n.* (LĒN)
probate, *n.* (PRŌ bāt′)
tort, *n.* (TȮRT)

## STEP 1

How many of the words did you know? In case some are not familiar, here's a brief description and a phrase using each term. As you read the sentences in this next list, slowly pronounce each word again. The more often you say a term, the better your chances are of remembering the correct pronunciation.

1. *Adjudication* is the formal hearing and settling of a case in court: the *adjudication* of a case in favor of the accused.
2. An *affidavit* is a formal written statement that someone swears to, or makes under oath; this must be done before a person who is legally permitted to witness the signing of documents and to administer an oath, such as a notary public or an officer of the court: an *affidavit* of service stating that a legal paper was served on, or delivered to, someone involved in a lawsuit.
3. *Attestation* is the act of being present to witness (to see) a written legal document and signing it

as the witness; this act is meant to confirm that the document and the signatures on it are genuine: an *attestation* of someone's last will and testament.

4. A *covenant* is a written promise or agreement included in a legal document stating that the signers will do or not do something: a *covenant* in a business contract whereby one of the parties signing the contract promises not to operate a business similar to that of the other party.

5. *Exoneration* is the removal of a responsibility, hardship, or blame: the *exoneration,* or clearing, of someone who was previously accused of wrongdoing.

6. *Interrogatories* are formal questions sent by one side in a lawsuit to the other side or to a witness; the receiving party must answer these questions in writing and under oath: the *interrogatories* being sent to the opposition to get important facts from the other side.

7. *Jurisprudence* is the science or study of law, legal systems, and legal philosophy: the vast differences between Chinese and American *jurisprudence.*

8. A *lien* is a legal claim or charge placed against someone's property to make certain that the person will pay a debt or will fulfill another obligation: a mechanic's *lien* giving a worker the legal right to hold property that was worked on until his or her charges are paid.

9. *Probate* is the court procedure of proving that a deceased person's will is genuine and valid and, if it is, distributing the possessions named in it: the *probate* of her uncle's will.

10. A *tort* is a private or civil (noncriminal) wrong, injury, or failure to perform a legal duty, not in-

volving a contract, that causes someone harm: a *tort* in which one person damages the reputation of another by printing harmful gossip about the victim in a newspaper.

## STEP 2

How about it—do you think that adding legal terms to your vocabulary is going to be pleasant or painful? We hope it's the former, because there are more words to come. But first, let's double-check your understanding of the present words. Write each term—*adjudication, affidavit, attestation, covenant, exoneration, interrogatories, jurisprudence, lien, probate, tort*—across from the appropriate definition in the following list.

1. _____   a court procedure of deciding the validity of a will and distributing the deceased person's possessions

2. _____   the science or study of law, legal systems, and legal philosophy

3. _____   a private or civil wrong causing harm

4. _____   the process of formally hearing and settling a court case

5. _____   the act of witnessing and confirming that a legal document and its signatures are genuine

6. _____   a legal claim or charge against someone's prop-

erty to ensure that the person pays a debt

7. _____ a written statement sworn to under oath before someone permitted to administer an oath

8. _____ formal written questions in a court case to be answered in writing under oath

9. _____ a written promise or agreement in a legal document to do or not do something

10. _____ the removal of responsibility or blame

ANSWERS: (1) probate (2) jurisprudence (3) tort (4) adjudication (5) attestation (6) lien (7) affidavit (8) interrogatories (9) covenant (10) exoneration.

## STEP 3

To wind up this exercise, let's strengthen your understanding of the ten words with a multiple-choice quiz. Circle your choice of the most appropriate word—a, b, or c—in the following sentences.

1. He was fascinated with murder mysteries long before he took his first course in criminal *(a) jurisprudence (b) tort (c) adjudication.*

2. The property deed contained a/an *(a) affidavit (b) attestation (c) covenant* stating that a fence around the yard could not be over six feet high.

3. After our neighbor died, his last will and testament had to go through *(a) interrogatories*

*(b) probate (c) attestation* before the estate could be divided.

4. The car has a *(a) lien (b) covenant (c) tort* on it that must be paid off before the car can be sold.

5. The *(a) lien (b) adjudication (c) tort* arose when a store owner failed to take reasonable care of the floors, causing a customer to fall and be injured.

6. Eventually, the case had to be settled in court; however, because of a full court schedule, the *(a) adjudication (b) attestation (c) jurisprudence* didn't take place for another eleven months.

7. His *(a) affidavit (b) covenant (c) attestation* involved witnessing the signing of a construction contract and then signing the document himself as the witness.

8. The *(a) interrogatories (b) affidavits (c) attestations* were presented before the trial to the defendant, who was given fifteen days to answer the questions under oath.

9. Before the *hearing* (preliminary examination of an accused person), a sworn statement known as a/an *(a) attestation (b) affidavit (c) covenant* was drawn up to confirm that notice of the hearing had been delivered to all parties in the lawsuit.

10. He expects to be found not guilty and to receive complete *(a) adjudication (b) jurisprudence (c) exoneration.*

ANSWERS: (1) a (2) c (3) b (4) a (5) c (6) a (7) c (8) a (9) b (10) c

## EXERCISE 2

If the previous ten words were easy to recognize or learn, you may already be attuned to legal terminology. However, the ten legal terms in this exercise—eight nouns and two adjectives—may seem a little more difficult. Nevertheless, they're words that all of us should have in our vocabularies.

You'll want to pay special attention to the pronunciation and spelling of these words. Some, such as *escheat*, are frequently mispronounced and misspelled.

actionable, *adj.* (AK shə nə bəl)
affirmation, *n.* (af' ər MĀ shən)
contravention, *n.* (kän' trə VEN shən)
encroachment, *n.* (in KRŌCH mənt)
encumbrance, *n.* (in KƏM brəns)
escheat, *n.* (is CHĒT)
estoppel, *n.* (e STÄP əl)
garnishment, *n.* (GÄR nish mənt)
laches, *n.* (LACH əz)
testamentary, *adj.* (tes' tə MEN tə rē)

## STEP 1

First we need to learn the definitions, and then we'll practice using the terms. To work on pronunciation and spelling, remember to repeat each term and mentally spell it again as you read these sentences.

1. The adjective *actionable* means giving cause for legal action or providing a legal reason for a lawsuit: the company's *actionable* negligence.
2. The noun *affirmation* refers to a solemn and formal declaration, or assertion, used in place of the traditional sworn statement, or oath; it is used by persons whose religious beliefs prevent them from taking an oath: the *affirmation* of the witness that he would tell the truth.

3. The noun *contravention* refers to something that breaks or violates a legal obligation: *contravention* of the judge's direct order to the jury not to read any newspapers about the trial.

4. The noun *encroachment* refers to the act of trying to claim part of another person's property; this is done by unlawfully extending one's own property onto or into the property of the other person: his *encroachment* onto a neighbor's property when he built a fence three feet over the boundary of his lot on land belonging to his neighbor.

5. The noun *encumbrance* refers to a claim, charge, or other liability (debt) against property that affects title to the property and lowers its value: an *encumbrance* in the form of a mortgage that affected the sale of the property.

6. The noun *escheat* refers to the return of property to the state when no owner or heir can be found: the *escheat* following the death of a property owner who had not named anyone to inherit his property.

7. The noun *estoppel* means the act of stopping someone from saying or proving something because it would contradict something the person had previously stated or indicated as being true: the principle of *estoppel* that was called for when she wanted to attack the accuracy and validity of papers she had previously signed and accepted as correct and valid.

8. The noun *garnishment* refers to a court order or legal procedure that helps a creditor collect an unpaid debt from another person (the debtor); it allows the creditor to require a third party who owes the debtor money to pay part of that money to the creditor instead of the debtor: the *garnish-*

*ment* of an employee's wages to be applied to the employee's past-due bank loan.

9. The noun *laches* refers to an unreasonable delay in pursuing or enforcing a legal claim against a defendant; this delay causes the defendant to be harmed in some way: the *laches* unfairly affecting her ability to prepare an effective defense because so much time had passed that evidence and witnesses were no longer available.

10. The adjective *testamentary* means having to do with a will: the mentally challenged person's lack of *testamentary* capacity, or mental ability, to make a valid will.

## STEP 2

Are the meanings clear? We want to double-check your understanding in this step. As you did in Step 2 of the previous exercise, write each of the ten words—*actionable, affirmation, contravention, encroachment, encumbrance, escheat, estoppel, garnishment, laches, testamentary*—on the blank line across from the brief definition that most closely matches it.

1. _____ the return of property to the state when no owner or heir can be found

2. _____ an unreasonable delay in enforcing a claim causing harm to a defendant

3. _____ a formal declaration used in place of taking an oath

4. _____ the procedure of collecting money a debtor owes you from a third party who owes the debtor money

5. _____ the act of stopping someone from saying or proving something that contradicts the person's earlier statement or act

6. _____ the act of trying to claim another's property by extending one's own property onto that of the other person

7. _____ having to do with a will

8. _____ giving cause or reason for legal action

9. _____ something that breaks or violates a legal obligation

10. _____ a claim, charge, or other liability against property affecting its value and title to the property

ANSWERS: (1) escheat (2) laches (3) affirmation (4) garnishment (5) estoppel (6) encroachment (7) testamentary (8) actionable (9) contravention (10) encumbrance.

## STEP 3

If you're still with us, let's drive the definitions home. Here's a true-false test to reinforce your understanding of the meanings. Read each sentence and circle either true or false

1. Because of *laches,* a defendant might have trouble finding witnesses for his or her defense. *True   False*

2. If *estoppel* is called for, a person cannot deny

the truth of something that he or she previously expressed as correct. *True  False*

3. A *testamentary* matter is one involving the testament, or statement, given under oath by a witness in court. *True  False*

4. If a court has approved the procedure of *garnishment,* you might be able to collect money that a debtor owes you from a third person who owes the debtor money. *True  False*

5. Someone who plants a garden that unlawfully extends onto a neighbor's yard is guilty of *encroachment.* *True  False*

6. Signing a contract and then failing to abide by its terms and conditions is a potentially *actionable* matter. *True  False*

7. An *affirmation* is an oath, or sworn statement, taken by people who hold strict religious beliefs. *True  False*

8. An *encumbrance,* such as a lien against a house, affects its value. *True  False*

9. If you are driving at sixty miles an hour in an area where speed limits of forty miles an hour are in effect, you are exceeding the speed limit in *contravention* of the law. *True  False*

10. *Escheat* would occur if no heir could be found for a deceased person's property and it therefore would have to revert to the state. *True  False*

ANSWERS: (1) True (2) True (3) False (4) True (5) True (6) True (7) False (8) True (9) True (10) True

## Common Legal Phrases You Should Know

Some legal terms are not single words such as those we learned in the previous exercises. Rather, they're phrases of two or more words, such as *nolo conten-dere,* defined in Chapter 9, or *circumstantial evidence,* defined in the next exercise. We've separated these terms from the single-word terms in this chapter merely for convenience. In all other respects the terms in Exercise 3 will be treated the same as the words in the first two exercises.

## EXERCISE 3

Are you ready? Here are ten common expressions pertaining to the law—all nouns. We've given the pronunciation of both parts of each expression, although you'll immediately recognize the simple words, such as *fact* in *evidentiary fact.* But you may not be familiar with the pronunciation of the more challenging part of a term, such as *evidentiary.* So we urge you to practice pronouncing and spelling such words in the following group before beginning Step 1.

circumstantial evidence, *n.* (sər′ kəm STAN shəl E və dəns)

corroborating evidence, *n.* (kə RÄB ə rāt ing E və dəns)

derivative action, *n.* (di RIV ə tiv AK shən)

double jeopardy, *n.* (DƏB əl JEP ər dē)

Draconian law, *n.* (Drā KŌ nē ən LŌ)

eminent domain, *n.* (EM ə nənt dō MĀN)

evidentiary fact, *n.* (ev′ ə DEN shə rē FAKT)

extrinsic evidence, *n.* (ek STRIN zik E və dəns)

proximate cause, *n.* (PRÄK sə mət KŌZ)

vicarious liability, *n.* (vī KER ē əs lī ə BIL ə tē)

## STEP 1

Let's see what the expressions mean. As you read the definitions, repeat each term to keep the pronunciations firmly in mind.

1. *Circumstantial evidence* refers to secondary, or less direct, facts or information that indirectly proves a main fact; such evidence is less important than actual, direct personal knowledge or observation of facts: the *circumstantial evidence* of thorns stuck in an accused person's clothing; this suggested that the person might have been in the area where a crime was committed, because the crime scene consisted of vegetation with thorns.

2. *Corroborating evidence* is additional evidence that serves to strengthen the evidence already given: the *corroborating evidence* of an eyewitness who saw the person accused of a crime leaving the scene at a certain time.

3. *Derivative action* refers to a lawsuit that someone who owns stock in a corporation files against a third party; the person does this when the corporation itself fails to take action against the third party to protect or enforce its rights: stockholder John Smith's *derivative action* against a convention center that he thought had wronged the corporation in which he owns stock.

4. *Double jeopardy* means being tried a second time for the same crime after the first trial has ended, regardless of whether the accused is found guilty or not guilty; this practice is prohibited by the U.S. Constitution: the constitutional provision of *double jeopardy* that made it illegal to hold a second trial for someone who was found not guilty but, later, was discovered to be guilty.

5. *Draconian law* means especially harsh and severe law, much like that promoted by seventh century B.C. politician Draco of Athens: the trend away from *Draconian law* in Western nations, such as in the United States and France.

6. *Eminent domain* is a government's right to take private land for public use by paying for it: the state's use of *eminent domain* to claim and tear down three houses so that a highway could be widened.

7. An *evidentiary fact* is a supporting fact learned directly from testimony or other evidence; it is used in determining the ultimate facts that the court needs to make a decision in a case: the *evidentiary fact* about missing files in the case concerning the disappearance of pension funds.

8. *Extrinsic evidence* refers to facts taken from something outside, rather than contained within (in the words of), a particular document: the *extrinsic evidence* consisting of the circumstances leading to a formal contract but not the words contained in the contract.

9. *Proximate cause* is the real cause of an injury or accident; without this cause, a series of events and the result (the accident or injury) would not have occurred: the *proximate cause* of faulty brakes causing a car to roll down a hill into other cars parked below, pushing each car into the one ahead of it.

10. *Vicarious liability* is indirect legal responsibility: the *vicarious liability* of an employer who is responsible for the acts of his or her employees.

## STEP 2

If you found Step 1 to be exhausting, stop and catch your breath. Or are you eager to press on? Either way, if you made it through those definitions, you're in good shape. You should be all set to watch the next trial of the century over television or to enjoy some old *Perry Mason* reruns.

To be certain you remember the definitions, however, fill in each term—*circumstantial evidence, corroborating evidence, derivative action, double jeopardy, Draconian law, eminent domain, evidentiary fact, extrinsic evidence, proximate cause, vicarious liability*—across from the definition that best fits it in this next test.

1. _____    the real cause of an injury or accident

2. _____    a supporting fact needed to determine the ultimate facts in a court decision

3. _____    indirect legal responsibility

4. _____    additional evidence that strengthens evidence already given

5. _____    facts taken from someone or something outside, rather than within, a document

6. _____    a constitutional provision that prevents someone from being tried twice for the same crime

7. _____    secondary facts or information that indirectly proves a main fact

8. _____    the right of a government to take private property for public use

9. _____    a lawsuit filed by a corpo-

ration stockholder against a third party that has wronged the corporation

10. _____ especially harsh and severe law

ANSWERS: (1) proximate cause (2) evidentiary fact (3) vicarious liability (4) corroborating evidence (5) extrinsic evidence (6) double jeopardy (7) circumstantial evidence (8) eminent domain (9) derivative action (10) Draconian law

## STEP 3

Any problems? Let's find out. Admittedly, this hasn't been the easiest exercise, so the Step 3 test is going to be very important in reinforcing your understanding of the definitions. Fill in the most appropriate term—*circumstantial evidence, corroborating evidence, derivative action, double jeopardy, Draconian law, eminent domain, evidentiary fact, extrinsic evidence, proximate cause, vicarious liability*—in each sentence.

1. In a trial, evidence consisting of a personnel director's statement about an employment application—but not what is actually written in the application—would be considered _____.

2. When the government purchases land from a private owner, whether or not the owner wants to sell it, and uses it to construct a public park, the government is applying the principle of _____.

3. The main cause of an accident, which may or may not be the event occurring just before the accident, is called the _____.

4. A fact learned from testimony or other evidence that supports the ultimate facts used in deciding a court case is called an _____.

5. Assume that you saw the driver of one car clip the fender of another car; you can add weight to the evidence in the accident by presenting _____ in the form of your eyewitness account.

6. Indirect legal responsibility, such as a store owner's being responsible for the actions of the store's salesclerks, is known as _____.

7. A law that imposes an exceptionally harsh penalty for a relatively minor offense is commonly referred to as a _____.

8. If you own stock in a corporation and realize that an outside third party has committed a wrong that the corporation is ignoring, you may be able to do something; for example, you may be able to bring a lawsuit known as a _____ against the third party and for the benefit of the corporation.

9. Assume that a mugging occurred and nearby you later found a scarf similar to one owned by the alleged attacker; also assume that you did not actually see the mugging or see the attacker drop the scarf. The evidence you found would be considered _____.

10. A jury might decide that a man accused of murder is "not guilty," but later it is proven that the person committed the crime; nevertheless, he cannot be tried again because of the constitutional provision against _____.

ANSWERS: (1) extrinsic evidence (2) eminent domain (3) proximate cause (4) evidentiary fact

(5) corroborating evidence (6) vicarious liability (7) Draconian law (8) derivative action (9) circumstantial evidence (10) double jeopardy

## BONUS WORDS

For this chapter's bonus we'll define ten important legal words—all nouns—that are a must for any vocabulary. Some, such as *libel* and *slander,* may seem familiar, but we've included them here because they're often confused.

Remember that bonus words may appear in the review tests at the ends of the chapters.

1. *acquittal* (ə KWIT əl) the decision of a jury or judge that a defendant is not guilty of a crime as charged: the *acquittal* of O. J. Simpson
2. *arraignment* (ə RĀN mənt) the act of bringing a defendant before a judge in a trial court to hear the complaint or charges against this person and to inform him or her of a choice in pleas, such as guilty or not guilty: the *arraignment* of the accused murderer
3. *felony* (FEL ə nē) a serious crime that requires a sentence of one or more years: the *felony* of burglary
4. *forbearance* (fòr BAR əns) the act of holding back, especially in enforcing a right: his *forbearance* in not demanding payment of a past-due loan
5. *hearsay* (HIR sā′) secondhand evidence based on the report of someone else rather than the personal knowledge of a witness, usually not allowed as testimony: the remarks about learning

of his drinking habits from a friend that were declared *hearsay* by the judge

6.  *libel* (LĪ bəl)  a malicious published statement in writing, printing, signs, or pictures that injures a person's character or reputation: a charge of *libel* caused by his statement in a magazine article that her campaign was fueled with illegal drug money

7.  *malfeasance* (mal′ FĒ zəns)  wrongdoing, or the act of doing something unlawful, especially by a public official: a charge of *malfeasance* against the mayor for destroying project bids from others so that his friends would be awarded the city contracts

8.  *misdemeanor* (mis′ di MĒ nər)  a criminal offense less serious than a felony, usually punished by a fine or less than a year in jail: the *misdemeanor* of vandalism

9.  *slander* (SLAN dər)  malicious spoken statements about someone to a third party that tend to damage the subject's character or reputation: a charge of *slander* caused by her comment to the nominating committee that he had stolen funds in his previous position as treasurer

10. *subpoena* (sə PĒ nə)  a formal, written court order to a person that he or she must appear in court at a certain time to testify, or give evidence: the *subpoena* requiring him to testify at 10 A.M. on Monday in the *Madison* case

## REVIEW TEST

Once again, let's find out how well you're remembering new words, not only words from this chapter but from all previous chapters as well. This time we'll use a reverse multiple-choice quiz in which you're given the word, but it's up to you to pick the most appropriate definition. To do this, circle either definition a, b, or c in the following list.

After you've finished, don't forget to record the number of correct and incorrect answers that you gave and to compare your progress with that on previous review tests. If you're not doing well, go back to the chapters causing problems and repeat their exercises.

1. *Word engineering* is jargon for a
    (a) process of deceptively modifying information
    (b) study of language
    (c) form of slang
2. *Ad hominem* means
    (a) pertaining to human beings
    (b) being ordinary or common
    (c) appealing to emotions
3. *Depravation* is
    (a) corruption or perversion
    (b) the act of taking away
    (c) the condition of being deprived of something
4. To *proscribe* is to
    (a) set forth as a guide
    (b) condemn
    (c) write out
5. To be *taciturn* is to be
    (a) untalkative
    (b) technically inclined
    (c) tactful or diplomatic
6. To *warrant* is to
    (a) issue an order
    (b) charge with a crime
    (c) secure or guarantee

7. *Damascus* is
    (a) the capital city of Syria
    (b) a country in the Middle East
    (c) an uninhabited city in Egypt
8. *Attestation* is
    (a) an informal court paper
    (b) a legal claim against someone
    (c) the act of witnessing a legal document
9. *Downmarket* is jargon for a
    (a) declining stock market
    (b) low-income market
    (c) market for parts and accessories
10. *Corroborating evidence* is
    (a) additional evidence
    (b) unreliable evidence
    (c) evidence from outside a document

ANSWERS: (1) a (2) c (3) a (4) b (5) a (6) c (7) a (8) c (9) b (10) a
*Correct Answers:* _____ *Incorrect Answers:* _____

# 13. Learn the New Words of Information Technology

*The first electronic computer was a Godzilla–size monster that weighed thirty tons, had to be housed in a building with fifteen hundred square feet, and needed eighteen thousand vacuum tubes to function.*

Neither Godzilla nor the computer would fit on any desktop we've seen. That may have been a drawback, but at least we know that no one ever tried to tuck it into a briefcase and whisk it away in the night. Nowadays, someone could do exactly that—hide a little notebook computer in a briefcase and walk away with it. This difference in computer size, then and now, says a lot about the distance that electronic technology has traveled in our society.

Those of you who own small computers may be interested to know that your little machines probably have as much or more power than their huge ancestor had when it was built in the mid-1940s. Today, we're much more impressed by the size of that first computer than by its power.

Nowadays, we usually refer to computers in simple terms, such as the "personal computer," or PC, found in homes and offices. But wait till you hear what the builders called the giant forerunner to modern computers: the *E*lectronic *N*umeral *I*ntegrator and *C*alculator (ENIAC). How's that for a mouthful? Although the ENIAC was more calculator than computer, it is generally considered the first electronic *digital* computer.

What about that word *digital*? You may have heard people talk about *digital* computers on many occasions. But do you really know what the word means? If you don't, you'll soon find out—in Exercise 2. It's an example of the type of information-technology words and expressions that we'll be learning in this chapter.

If you *truly* love computers, however, you may already know some of the terms we're going to introduce. But check the list in each exercise before you decide that you've "been there, done that," and move on. We'll start the exercises with information-technology words and expressions and end with important abbreviations.

## Information-Technology Words and Expressions

We hear a lot about *information technology* nowadays. This is a broad term referring to the handling of information electronically. The word *technology* alone refers to the practical use or application of knowledge to a particular area, as in "computer technology."

Information technology includes all the new computer, telephone, and other technologies that involve handling information. These technologies are used to create, send, receive, and store information electronically. The reason we keep mentioning the computer is that it's central to any contemporary information-handling activity.

The first two exercises in this chapter introduce new technology words and expressions that we may hear over television or read in the newspapers. But some of these terms are still not widely understood: They're not all household words. In fact, most are commonly regarded as technical jargon. Remember, we described that kind of language in Chapter 10?

As fast as technology is moving, however, we can soon expect all of the words in this chapter to qualify as standard English. When this happens, you'll find the terms in traditional, general-purpose dictionaries, not just in computer and other specialized dictionaries. But for now let's think of the words and expressions simply as basic information-technology terms that everyone should know. If you're ready, then, let's get technological.

## EXERCISE 1

We'll begin with a collection of ten terms—nouns, verbs, and adjectives—that you'll want to have in the specialized or technical portion of your vocabulary. You presumably already know or can easily guess the pronunciation of some terms, such as *download*. But you may be surprised by the pronunciation of others, such as *telephony* (no, it's not *tel-e-phone-ee*).

binary, *adj.* (BĪ nə rē)
cyberspace, *n.* (sī′ bər SPĀS)
download, *vb.* (DAÚN lōd′)
duplex, *adj.* (DÜ pleks′)
emoticon, *n.* (i MŌ ti con′)
fiber optics, *n.* (FĪ bər äp tiks)
microchip, *n.* (MĪ krō chip′)
multiplexor, *n.* (MƏL tə pleks′ ər)
telephony, *n.* (tə LEF ə nē)
upload, *vb.* (əp′ LŌD)

## STEP 1

Did you practice pronouncing and spelling the words? Say them again as you read these definitions and the brief phrases using the words.

1. The adjective *binary* means having two parts: a *binary* number system that uses only two digits— 10 and 1—suitable for processing by computers.

2. The noun *cyberspace* is a buzzword (see Chapter 10) that refers to a place you can't see—a non-physical environment; it's where computer users go, or travel through, when they're connected to other users and are communicating with them long-distance by computer: a computer user's journey into *cyberspace,* using the telephone lines, satellites, or other services to send and receive electronic information.

3. The verb *download* means to use your computer and the telephone lines to copy electronic files from another, usually larger, host computer system in a different location; you can then save and use the files you copy in your own computer; to *download* information about the stock market from a large central computer.

4. The adjective *duplex* means consisting of a two-way system with the ability to send and receive information at the same time: having a *duplex* system in which two computers can send and receive messages simultaneously.

5. The noun *emoticon* refers to typed symbols, sometimes called "smileys," that computer users insert in their computer messages to show emotion: the *emoticon* typed as *:D* that means "laughing."

6. The noun *fiber optics* refers to a technology that

uses long, tiny glass or plastic fibers, often in a highly transparent cable, to send information on light waves; these waves travel at high speeds over long distances, with little outside interference: the use of *fiber optics* to transmit an entire encyclopedia in a mere second.

7. The noun *microchip,* another name for *integrated circuit,* refers to a miniature electronic circuit produced on a semiconducting material, such as a tiny slice of a substance called "silicon"; the microchip can house millions of electronic components, thereby enabling a device such as a computer to operate: the *microchip* that houses the memory function of a computer.

8. The noun *multiplexor* refers to the equipment that allows a number of signals, whether data or voice, to be sent over the same channel, such as a telephone line, at the same time: the savings in time by using a *multiplexor* in sending computer messages.

9. The noun *telephony* refers to the changing of voice, data, video, or image signals into electrical impulses that can be sent long distances by wire or radio; also, the integration, or union, of the telephone and the computer: the process of *telephony* that makes it possible to send a pen-and-ink drawing across the country over the telephone lines.

10. The verb *upload* means to send a file directly from your computer over the telephone lines to a host system, such as a large central computer, in a different location: to *upload* a report from your home computer to the central computer in your company's headquarters.

## STEP 2

Are you ready to go to dinner with friends and listen to someone talk about the wonders of "fiber optics" or complain about the two hours it took to "download" a useless file from a friend a thousand miles away? Let's find out. To double-check your understanding of the ten terms, fill in each word—*binary, cyberspace, download, duplex, emoticon, fiber optics, microchip, multiplexor, telephony, upload*—across from the appropriate definition in column 2.

1. _____ to copy a file in your computer and send it to a host computer

2. _____ a miniature integrated circuit that houses electronic components

3. _____ the invisible "space" used by interconnected computers communicating with one another

4. _____ to copy a computer file from a host computer and send it to your computer

5. _____ equipment that allows voice and data signals to be sent simultaneously over the same line or channel

6. _____ technology for sending information long distances at very high speeds using light waves

7. _____ consisting of a two-way system for sending and receiving information at the same time

8. _____ the translation of voice and other signals into a form that can travel by wire or radio

9. _____ consisting of two parts, as in a number system with only two digits, 1 and 0

10. _____ a typed symbol used to indicate emotion in computer messages

ANSWERS: (1) upload (2) microchip (3) cyberspace (4) download (5) multiplexor (6) fiber optics (7) duplex (8) telephony (9) binary (10) emoticon

## STEP 3

Let's make sure that the ten information-technology terms—*binary, cyberspace, download, duplex, emoticon, fiber optics, microchip, multiplexor, telephony, upload*—will be fired into your memory forever. Try this fill-in test to reinforce your understanding.

1. To indicate displeasure in a computer message, you could include an _____ , such as the typed symbol :( meaning a frown.

2. Another name for *integrated circuit* is _____.

3. The imaginary space used by interconnected computers in sending and receiving messages to and from one another is called _____.

4. To copy a computer file from your computer and send it to a large central computer in another location is to _____ the information.

5. A two-way system for sending and receiving in-

formation simultaneously is known as a _____ system.

6. The technology of _____ enables one to send information by light waves at very high speeds and over long distances through the use of glass or plastic fiber in a highly transparent cable.

7. A number system that uses only two digits, 0 and 1, is called a _____ system.

8. To copy a computer file from a large central computer in another location and send it to your computer is to _____ the information.

9. The equipment that permits voice or data signals to be sent over the same channel at the same time is called a _____.

10. The process of changing voice and other signals into a form that can travel by wire or radio is called _____.

ANSWERS: (1) emoticon (2) microchip (3) cyberspace (4) upload (5) duplex (6) fiber optics (7) binary (8) download (9) multiplexor (10) telephony

## EXERCISE 2

Have you heard the saying that young people don't just use the *Internet;* they live on it? It's true. A whole new "*digital* generation" is heading for a high-tech future. Members of this generation function in a technological universe that, to them, consists not of stars and planets that light up the night skies; rather, it consists of computers and the new invisible "data highway" that electronically interconnects people and machines across the globe.

Have you also heard others say that they don't want to live each moment of their lives in a technological universe? They're quite happy with the stars and the planets, thank you. But even those people would agree that they at least should be able to recognize and correctly use terms such as *digital* and *Internet,* defined in this exercise.

Whichever universe you prefer—the technological or the natural—we hope that Exercise 1 put you in the right mood to expand the high-tech part of your vocabulary. If it did, here are ten more information-technology terms—nine nouns and an adjective.

digerati, *n.* (dij′ ə RÄ tē)
digital, *adj.* (DIJ ə təl)
encryption, *n.* (in KRIP shən)
hypertext, *n.* (HĪ pər tekst′)
Internet, *n.* (IN tər′ net)
micrographics, *n.* (mī′ krō GRA fiks)
microprocessor, *n.* (mī′ krō PRÄS es ər)
netiquette, *n.* (NET i kət)
protocol, *n.* (PRŌ tə kȯl′)
telecommuting, *n.* (TEL i kə myüt ing)

## STEP 1

You may want to work on the pronunciation and spelling of some of these terms, such as *digerati* and *encryption.* Say each word aloud and mentally spell it as you read the following definitions.

1. The noun *digerati* refers to people who are exceptionally skilled and knowledgeable in matters concerning computers and computer data: the *digerati* who tend to speak in an advanced technical language of their own.

2. The adjective *digital* means operated with or expressed in digits (numbers), such as 0 and 1: *digital* information that can be processed by a computer.

3. The noun *encryption* refers to the changing or scrambling of computer data into a secret coded form; this is done to prevent people who don't have the necessary password from reading it: the *encryption* of confidential personnel files.

4. The noun *hypertext* refers to a computer text retrieval system; it enables users to search for related information in various files without having to close one file before moving on to the next one: the *hypertext* he used to search six nature files to locate various types of information about elephants.

5. The noun *Internet* refers to the world's largest global *electronic network* (system of interconnected computers allowing for information exchange); it consists of millions of computer users and thousands of smaller computer networks: the worldwide *Internet*, which offers a way for computer users to send electronic messages (*E-mail*) by telephone, satellite, or other means.

6. The noun *micrographics* refers to the process of reducing full-size documents to miniature images and storing them on film: the use of *micrographics* to store numerous documents in vastly reduced size on rolls of film (*microfilm*) or sheets of film (*microfiche* or *ultrafiche*).

7. The noun *microprocessor* refers to an integrated circuit, or *microchip* (defined in Exercise 1), that contains the entire central processing unit (see *CPU* in Exercise 3) of a computer: the *microprocessor* consisting of a computer's arithmetic/logic and control units.

8. The noun *netiquette* refers to the accepted standards of behavior used by people sending electronic messages on the *Internet* (see definition 5): the Internet etiquette known as *netiquette*.

9. The noun *protocol* refers to a standard procedure used to regulate the transfer of data between computers; the sending and receiving computers can thereby avoid error by both using the same settings and standards: a communications or file-transfer *protocol* that allows computer messages or other data to be sent back and forth without error.

10. The noun *telecommuting* refers to the practice of working in a home office and communicating with a company office through a computer link: *telecommuting* by using a computer and the telephone lines to send and receive electronic messages at home.

## STEP 2

Are you starting to feel more technologically aware? Or are you one of the *digerati* we just described who thinks that these exercises are a digital piece of cake?

If you don't quite qualify for digerati status, a couple more steps may be in order. With this step you can double-check your understanding of the ten information-technology terms by filling in each word—*digerati, digital, encryption, hypertext, Internet, micrographics, microprocessor, netiquette, protocol, telecommuting*—across from the most appropriate description in column 2.

1. _____ a computer text retrieval system in which you can

|   |   |
|---|---|
|   | open and search several files at the same time |
| 2. _____ | a process of reducing documents to a tiny size and storing them on film |
| 3. _____ | a standard procedure for regulating the transfer of data between computers |
| 4. _____ | the largest computer network consisting of interconnected smaller networks and computer users worldwide |
| 5. _____ | the practice of working at home by computer connected to one's office |
| 6. _____ | Internet etiquette |
| 7. _____ | those who are highly skilled in computer usage |
| 8. _____ | changing computer data into a secret coded form to restrict access to it |
| 9. _____ | a microchip containing a computer's entire central processing unit |
| 10. _____ | consisting of or using digits (numbers) |

ANSWERS: (1) hypertext (2) micrographics (3) protocol (4) Internet (5) telecommuting (6) netiquette (7) digerati (8) encryption (9) microprocessor (10) digital

## STEP 3

Any problems? This true-false test should help you pinpoint any difficulty you're having in remembering some of the more challenging terms, such as *hypertext* and *protocol*. Let's see how you do: Simply read each sentence and circle either true or false.

1. *Encryption* is a computer text retrieval system that requires the use of passwords to retrieve data. *True False*

2. *Micrographics* is a process of converting and reproducing images stored on film to photographic prints. *True False*

3. The *Internet* is an electronic network consisting of thousands of other, smaller networks and millions of computer users around the world. *True False*

4. A computer whiz would likely be considered a member of the *digerati*. *True False*

5. A *microprocessor* is another name for the film medium known as microfiche. *True False*

6. *Protocol* refers to the standards of etiquette used on the Internet. *True False*

7. A *digital* computer processes data in the form of digits (numbers), such as 1 and 0. *True False*

8. *Telecommuting* is the practice of working at home and communicating with one's office by computer using the telephone lines. *True False*

9. *Netiquette* refers to the accepted standards for regulating data transfer between computers. *True False*

10. *Hypertext* is a secret coded system for safeguarding confidential files. *True False*

ANSWERS: (1) False (2) False (3) True (4) True (5) False (6) False (7) True (8) True (9) False (10) False

## Information-Technology Abbreviations

You may have noticed that we live in an abbreviations-happy world. Nowhere is this more obvious than in scientific and technical areas, including information technology. It's shocking but true that there are hundreds of thousands of abbreviations in the English language. Moreover, the number is increasing daily.

The word *abbreviation* is often used as a broad term to refer to any one of three types of shortened words.

1. One type of shortened word omits some of the middle or concluding letters: *mgr./manager; admin./administration.* These abbreviations are used only in note taking or very informal writing but not in speaking. Therefore, you don't have to worry about how they're pronounced.
2. Another type, called an *acronym,* consists of some or all of the initial letters of words in a name. This type of shortened word is itself pronounced like an actual word: *WATS (WĀTS) wide area telephone service.*
3. A third type, called an *initialism,* also consists of some or all of the initial letters of words in a phrase. But this type of shortened word is not itself pronounced like an actual word; rather, each letter is pronounced as a letter, one at a time: *sase (s̄ ā s̄ ē)/self-addressed stamped envelope.*

Many technology acronyms and initialisms, such as *LAN* and *CPU* in the next exercise, are written in all capital letters, without spaces between the letters. But most general initialisms, such as *asap (ā s̄ ā p̄)/as soon as possible,* are written with small letters, although, again, without spaces between the letters.

## EXERCISE 3

This list of ten abbreviations has three acronyms (*ASCII, LAN,* and *WYSIWYG*) pronounced as words. The rest are initialisms and are pronounced letter by letter the same way that you would pronounce letters of the alphabet—*a, b, c, d,* and so on. Before beginning Step 1, practice saying the acronyms and initialisms aloud, and you'll see what we mean.

ASCII (AS kē)
BBS (B̄ B̄ S̄)
CPU (C̄ P̄ Ū)
FAQ (F̄ Ā Q̄)
IRC (Ī R̄ C̄)
LAN (LAN)
LCD (L̄ C̄ D̄)
OCR (Ō C̄ R̄)
WWW (W̄ W̄ W̄)
WYSIWYG (WIZ ē wig′)

## Step 1

Now that we have this acronym-initialism business out of the way, let's find out what these common information-technology abbreviations mean.

1. *ASCII* stands for "*A*merican *S*tandard *C*ode for *I*nformation *I*nterchange"; this code represents letters, numbers, and symbols as *binary* (see Exercise 1) digits that can be used by computers to exchange information: the letter *z* represented by the *ASCII* digits, or binary code, *0101 1010.*

2. *BBS* stands for "*b*ulletin *b*oard *s*ystem," a site, or place, on a computer network for holding information; the system enables participants to

use their computers and the telephone lines for various purposes, such as to leave electronic messages or to *download* (see Exercise 1) information: the *BBS* where he left an electronic message for his friend.

3. *CPU* stands for "central *p*rocessing *u*nit," the brains or heart of a computer; it contains the instructions needed by the machine to carry out various functions, such as the processing and storage of data: the arithmetic calculations by the *CPU*.

4. *FAQ* stands for "*f*requently *a*sked *q*uestions," an introductory list of questions commonly asked by new computer network users, along with the answers: the usefulness of reading a file labeled *FAQ* when researching a new topic by computer on the *Internet* (see Exercise 2).

5. *IRC* stands for "*I*nternet *R*elay *C*hat," an *Internet* (see Exercise 2) service; it enables numerous computer users to chat with one another via their computer keyboards and display screens: the *IRC* discussion held on Tuesday.

6. *LAN* stands for "*l*ocal *a*rea *n*etwork," a group of interconnected computers that provide a private network for information exchange among the users: the company *LAN* consisting of twenty-nine desktop computers and one large central computer, all connected by cable in a star pattern.

7. *LCD* stands for "*l*iquid *c*rystal *d*isplay," a display screen made from liquid crystals; it is found in many calculators, digital clocks, and small computers: the flashing green numbers in the *LCD* showing the time as 9:15 in the morning.

8. *OCR* stands for "*o*ptical *c*haracter *r*ecognition," a technique for detecting light and dark patterns

on a sheet of paper; it is used to recognize and convert handwritten, typed, or printed text to *digital* (see Exercise 2) form so that it can be handled electronically, such as by a computer. OCR also stands for "*o*ptical *c*haracter *r*eader," the device used in the optical character recognition process: the *OCR* used in post offices to read and sort appropriately addressed mail.

9. *WWW* stands for "*W*orld *W*ide *W*eb," a collection of numerous sites, or places, on the *Internet* (see Exercise 2); it offers various text, graphics, sound, and video to computer users who can then "visit" various sites, jumping electronically from one to another: the *WWW* site used by Pizza Hut to advertise its pizzas.

10. *WYSIWYG*, a desktop publishing term, stands for "*W*hat *y*ou *s*ee *i*s *w*hat *y*ou *g*et"; this means that a printed page of information will look the same on paper as it looks on the computer's display screen: the advantages of *WYSIWYG* in setting up a complex document, such as a magazine.

## STEP 2

Does it seem a little strange to be working with letters instead of full words? If it does, try thinking about the abbreviations as actual words. After all, the acronyms are pronounced as words anyway. Also, both the acronyms and initialisms are widely used in place of the words they stand for.

This step and the next one should be relatively easy since the letters of the abbreviations are an obvious clue to their meanings. But we won't take any chances. As usual, you can double-check your understanding in this step. This time, however, we'll list the abbreviations in column 1. Your task, then, will be to fill in the words that those abbreviations stand for in column 2.

1. OCR _____
2. FAQ _____
3. WWW _____
4. ASCII _____
5. CPU _____
6. WYSIWYG _____
7. BBS _____
8. LCD _____
9. IRC _____
10. LAN _____

ANSWERS: (1) optical character recognition/reader (2) frequently asked questions (3) World Wide Web (4) American Standard Code for Information Interchange (5) central processing unit (6) what you see is what you get (7) bulletin board system (8) liquid crystal display (9) Internet relay chat (10) local area network

## STEP 3

If you're certain you remember all of the abbreviations, use this multiple-choice quiz to reinforce your understanding of the meanings.

1. *(a) IRC (b) WWW (c) WYSIWYG* is a desktop publishing term meaning that a printed page will look exactly as the page looks on the computer's display screen.
2. Someone who is using a computer network for the first time should read the network's file of *(a) IRC (b) FAQ (c) BBS* before trying to locate any other information.

3. Stores that use a scanning device to "read" product information on labels and convert the data to *digital* (see Exercise 2) form are applying the technique of *(a) OCR (b) LCD (c) CPU.*

4. In some companies a number of computers are interlinked by cable in a *(a) CPU (b) LAN (c) WWW* so that they can exchange files and communicate with one another.

5. The weblike group of sites, or places, that you can "visit" by computer on the *Internet* (see Exercise 2) are collectively known as the *(a) BBS (b) IRC (c) WWW.*

6. Numerous computer users can have an electronic discussion on the *Internet* (see Exercise 2) by making use of its *(a) IRC (b) LAN (c) WWW* service.

7. *(a) ASCII (b) CPU (c) OCR* is a code in which symbols, such as *, are represented as *binary* (see Exercise 1) digits, such as *0010 1010,* that can be handled by a computer.

8. The brains of a computer, where instructions for data calculation, processing, and storage are carried out, is known as the *(a) LCD (b) LAN (c) CPU.*

9. The display screens found on *digital* (see Exercise 2) clocks, small computers, and electronic calculators is known as an *(a) LCD (b) OCR (c) IRC.*

10. A place on a computer network where you can send and store an electronic message until the intended recipient is ready to retrieve it is called a/an *(a) WWW (b) BBS (c) IRC.*

ANSWERS: (1) c (2) b (3) a (4) b (5) c (6) a (7) a (8) c (9) a (10) b

## BONUS WORDS

Our venture into the world of information technology is drawing to a close. Did we hear a few of you giving a sigh of relief? Some of you, however, are no doubt still in the mood for this chapter's bonus words. Remember, these terms—nine nouns and an adjective—may be used in end-of-chapter review tests. So do take time to read the definitions and brief examples as well as take note of the spelling and pronunciations of each term.

1. *documentation, n.* (dä kyə mən TĀ shən) the instructions and reference information that computer users need to operate a computer program or system: the *documentation* explaining how to use a new word processing program.
2. *freeware, n.* (FRĒ ware') copyrighted computer programs that are available to the public free of charge, often available for copying from bulletin board systems (see *BBS* in Exercise 3): the *freeware* that the owner wrote and distributed without charge simply to make a name for himself.
3. *modem, n.* (MŌ dəm') a device that converts signals produced by one type of device, such as a computer, to a form that can be used by a different type of device, such as a telephone: the *modem* used to connect her computer to others on a network via the telephone lines
4. *networking, n.* (NET wərk' ing) the act of belonging to and participating in a network, such as a computer network, that links people with common interests for various purposes: sharing information, assisting one another, developing professional contacts, and so on: *networking* via the *Internet* (see Exercise 2)

5. *on-line, adj.* (ÒN LĪN) being connected electronically to a system or service or having a computer link to one or more other computers via telephone, cable, radio, satellite, or other means; the opposite of *off-line* (not being connected or having a computer link): the *on-line* Yellow Pages delivered electronically to your computer rather than in the form of a paper telephone book

6. *peripherals, n.* (pə RIF ə rəls) additional or supporting devices in a computer system: his decision to add one *peripheral* right away—a *modem* (see definition 3)

7. *queue, n.* (KYÜ) the assigned sequence, or order, of computer data or programs awaiting processing, one after the other: the *queue* indicating in which order the computer files were to be printed

8. *telecommunications, n.* (tel′ i kə myü′ nə KĀ shəns) the transmission of information—words, sounds, images, and so on—over a distance, such as by telephone, radio, or television broadcast: the importance of *telecommunications* to business in selling its products and services

9 *teleconference, n.* (TEL i kän′ fər əns) a meeting in which the participants, who are in different locations, communicate with equipment, such as the telephone (*audioconference*), computer (*computer conference*), or television (*videoconference*): the *teleconference* that connected employees in three cities by using sound and video equipment

10. *virtual reality, n.* (VƏR chə wəl rē AL ə tē) an artificial, or imaginary, computer-created environment in which a device linking a person

to a computer causes the person to experience sights, sounds, and events just as if they were taking place in the real or naturally occurring world: a system creating *virtual reality* that consisted of stereo headphones, special sensory gloves, eye goggles, and a computer with a virtual reality program

## REVIEW TEST

It's that time again: Here's your Chapter 13 review quiz—a matching test. Find the definition in column 2 that matches each word in column 1. Then, write the appropriate letter from column 2—a, b, c, and so forth—on the small blank line in column 1.

By now you know that these end-of-chapter tests check your retention of words learned in previous exercises and chapters. As always, you can record your score after the answer section and compare your progress with that in previous review tests.

1. lien _____

    a. the habit of finding satisfaction from outside the self

2. monogenesis _____

    b. high-speed technology for sending information long distances by light waves

3. extroversion _____

    c. being greater than national borders or spheres of influence

4. de jure _____

    d. a claim or charge against property

5. surreptitious _____

6. virtual reality _____

7. unorganized _____

8. complementary _____

9. fiber optics _____

10. supranational _____

e. a theory that the origin of all things is a single cell or ancestor

f. existing by right or according to law

g. being secretive or sneaky

h. not having unity or representation

i. serving to complete or strengthen the whole

j. an artificial computer environment that seems real when you have a sensory link to the computer

ANSWERS: (1) d (2) e (3) a (4) f (5) g (6) j (7) h (8) i (9) b (10) c

*Correct Answers:* _____ *Incorrect Answers:* _____

# 14. Use the Basic Terms of Finance Properly

*The company's annual report lists stockholders broken down by age, sex, and marriage*

Hmmm . . . and all this time we were worried about the effects of smoking and drinking.

That "innocent" remark about age, sex, and marriage was taken from a letter enclosed with a copy of a company's annual report to *stockholders.* We all know that the comment wasn't really referring to the ravages of age, sex, and marriage on stockholders. It was actually referring to the number of people owning *shares* of *stock* in the company stated according to age group (21–35, 36–50, and so on), gender (male or female), and marital status (single, married, and so on).

Notice those italicized words: *stockholders, shares,* and *stock.* Even if you've never purchased stocks, you've no doubt heard those terms on television business reports or perhaps have seen them in the business or financial pages of newspapers.

A *stockholder* is a person or organization that owns one or more shares of stock in a corporation. *Stock* refers to the number of *shares,* or equal parts, of ownership. These shares are sold to investors as a means of raising money for the corporation.

To be well informed in today's world, we need to include such financial terms in our vocabularies. For convenience we'll divide the terms we've selected into two groups. The first group has words pertaining to general financial management and investment matters. The second group has words pertaining to the general financial record keeping that people and companies must do to meet state and federal tax laws and other legal requirements. Additional financial terms are collected in the bonus section at the end of the chapter.

## Basic Financial Terms

Is there anyone who doesn't hear or use financial terms? Probably not. It's almost impossible to function in modern society without being aware of financial terminology. Think how many times you may have unknowingly used such language—when you filed your annual income tax return, when you applied for a car or house loan, when you tried to decide where to put your savings so that it would earn the most interest, and on numerous other occasions.

It's not an exaggeration to say that you can't function in the contemporary world without using words pertaining to financial matters; it's also not an exaggeration to say that the more of these terms you know, the better equipped you'll be to understand the financial matters that affect you so that you can avoid costly errors. After all, you want to understand things such as how much interest or finance charges you're paying each month on your credit cards, don't you? Okay, so you don't necessarily *want* to know. But in the end, it will help if you do.

If you agree, let's put on our financial hats and get started.

## EXERCISE 1

For this exercise we've selected a group of important financial terms that should be in everyone's vocabulary. Even if financial terminology is like a foreign language to you, give it a try—if you want to understand what money lenders, financial reporters, and other business experts are saying and if you want to avoid getting lost the next time someone starts talking about his or her finances.

The following basic terms are all nouns. If you're not in the habit of using some of them, such as *debenture* or *fiduciary,* practice spelling and pronouncing them before you move on to Step 1.

acceleration clause (ik sel′ ə RĀ shən KLȮZ)
collateral (kə LA tə rəl)
debenture (di BEN chər)
diversification (də vər′ sə fə KĀ shən)
fiduciary (fə DÜ shē er′ ē)
negotiable instrument (ni GŌ shə bəl IN strə mənt)
par value (PÄR VAL yü)
prime rate (PRĪM RĀT)
promissory note (PRÄ mə sȯr′ ē NŌT)
rollover (RŌL ō vər)

## STEP 1

How about it—do you know any or all of the terms? If you're not a hundred percent certain, read these definitions and brief examples.

1.  An *acceleration clause* is a statement in a loan

agreement that gives the lender the right to make unpaid amount immediately due and payable; the lender is permitted to do this when the borrower fails to meet the terms of the agreement, such as failing to make payments as required: the *acceleration clause* included in his VISA cardmember agreement.

2. *Collateral* is something of value, such as a house, that a borrower offers as security to a lender until the borrower's loan is repaid; if the borrower fails to pay off the debt as required, the lender may then sell the collateral and use the income from it to pay off the rest of the loan: the car he offered as *collateral* when borrowing $3,000 from the finance company.

3. A *debenture* is a written acknowledgment of debt made by the issuer of the debenture, such as a government or corporation; it is backed only by the issuer's good credit reputation instead of by something tangible, such as property: a *debenture* consisting of unsecured *bonds* (certificates of debt in which the issuer promises to pay the buyer a certain amount plus interest on a future date).

4. *Diversification* is the practice of spreading out one's business activities, such as by producing several products so that a loss will be less harmful if a particular product fails; also, the practice of investing in different types of stocks and bonds, in different locations and in different corporations or governmental bodies, to lessen the risk of losing all or most of one's money if a particular investment fails: the policy of *diversification* in investments that he pursues to protect himself against total loss in case one investment is not profitable.

5. A *fiduciary* is a person or organization, such as a bank, that holds property, money, or something else of value for another party; the fiduciary is expected to manage the holding wisely for the other's benefit: the *fiduciary* appointed to manage the money inherited by the children until they reach the age of twenty-one.

6. A *negotiable instrument* is any written document, such as a paycheck, that expresses a financial or other obligation and can be transferred from the receiver to another party by endorsing (signing) it: the *negotiable instrument* in the form of a stock certificate that she endorsed to transfer her ownership to her son.

7. *Par value,* another term for *face value* or *nominal value,* is the amount printed on a stock or bond certificate; the amount is assigned by the issuer and is usually less than the market, or selling, price: the stock certificate that showed a *par value* of $10 per share.

8. The *prime rate,* or *prime interest rate,* is the most favorable interest rate that banks charge their best and most creditworthy customers on bank loans at any given time; other borrowers must usually pay higher rates: the bank's decision to raise its *prime rate,* which caused other banks to raise their rates and, in turn, triggered a nationwide rise in mortgage rates for home buyers.

9. A *promissory note,* often called simply a *note,* is a written promise to pay a certain amount of money either upon the demand of the lender or at a specified future date, with or without interest: the *promissory note* stating the amount of money he was borrowing, the interest he was being charged for the loan, and the due date.

10. *Rollover* is the practice of continually renewing

short-term loans, reinvesting profits from one investment in another, or moving funds from one investment to another: the immediate *rollover* of money from the sale of one company's stock to the purchase of another company's stock without tax penalty.

## STEP 2

We trust that you have now read the ten words, have pronounced them, have mentally spelled them, and have studied their definitions. If so, it's time to double-check your understanding of the meanings. Write each term—*acceleration clause, collateral, debenture, diversification, fiduciary, negotiable instrument, par value, prime rate, promissory note, rollover*—in column 1 across from the most appropriate brief definition in column 2.

1. _____ an unsecured debt acknowledgment made by a government or corporation

2. _____ one holding the property of another and investing it for the other's benefit

3. _____ the face or nominal value stated on a stock or bond certificate

4. _____ a clause in a loan agreement allowing a lender to demand immediate repayment if a debtor fails to meet the loan terms

5. _____ the most favorable interest rate that a bank charges its best customers on loans

6. _____ the practice of continually renewing a short-term loan, reinvesting profits, or moving funds from one investment to another

7. _____ a written promise to pay a certain sum of money on demand or on a certain date

8. _____ a written statement of an obligation that can be transferred by endorsement

9. _____ the practice of spreading out activities and investments to lessen the potential for heavy loss

10. _____ something of value a borrower offers as security to guarantee payment of a loan

ANSWERS: (1) debenture (2) fiduciary (3) par value (4) acceleration clause (5) prime rate (6) rollover (7) promissory note (8) negotiable instrument (9) diversification (10) collateral

## STEP 3

All of you money experts probably sailed through Steps 1 and 2 without blinking. Others, who enjoy spending money but don't always enjoy learning about it, may have blinked a few times. For all blinkers, here's an easy multiple-choice quiz to reinforce your understanding of the terms' meanings. Simply read each sentence and circle either a, b, or c.

1. The *(a) debenture (b) collateral (c) fiduciary* issued and sold by the city government to raise money was backed only by the issuer's good credit standing.

2. The *(a) prime rate (b) collateral (c) par value* was stated on the face of the stock certificate.

3. After he repeatedly failed to make the loan payments, the lender took advantage of the agreement's *(a) collateral (b) promissory note (c) acceleration clause* to demand full and immediate payment of the unpaid balance.

4. To keep her money continually active and producing income, she tended to use the practice of *(a) diversification (b) rollover (c) acceleration*, moving funds from the sale of one investment into the purchase of another.

5. For the bank loan from his credit union, he put up his new Ford Taurus as the *(a) collateral (b) par value (c) rollover*.

6. The Management Division of the First American Bank acted as a *(a) diversification (b) fiduciary (c) rollover* for the widow's investment account.

7. The *(a) acceleration clause (b) debenture (c) promissory note* stated that the unpaid balance on his loan, plus any remaining interest, is due on September 1 next year.

8. In her stock purchases she relied on the practice of *(a) rollover (b) par value (c) diversification* to avoid huge losses in case one investment failed.

9. The terms of his MasterCard said that cardholders would be charged interest at the current *(a) prime rate (b) par value (c) debenture* plus eight additional percentage points.

10. He endorsed the *(a) rollover (b) negotiable instrument (c) collateral* to make it payable to his partner.

ANSWERS: (1) a (2) c (3) c (4) b (5) a (6) b (7) c (8) c (9) a (10) b

## Basic Accounting Terms

We shouldn't overlook another side to the process of making money and managing one's finances. It involves the financial records and statements that are used to keep track of the process. The practices and methods that a person or business needs to record, clarify, analyze, and report its financial data are, together, known as *accounting*. In this part of the chapter, we want to change course from financial management and investments to some of the important terms in financial record keeping and reporting.

## EXERCISE 2

If a friend tells you his company's latest financial report indicates that he has built up a lot of *equity* in his business, will you know what he means? If a banker asks you to list your *assets* and *liabilities* on a loan application, will you know what things to list? If you're not certain, take time to review this next group of financial accounting terms. Each of these basic terms—all nouns—should be in your vocabulary.

assets (AS sets')
audit (Ȯ dət)
depreciation (di prē' shē Ā shən)
equity (EK wə tē)
goodwill (gu̇d' WIL)
journal (JƏR nəl)
ledger (LE jər)

liabilities (lī′ ə BIL ə tēs)
spreadsheet (SPRED shēt′)
write-off (RĪT ȯf′)

## Step 1

In the world of financial accounting, those ten accounting terms are very common. Are they common in your world too? Could you define them on your own? Let's find out. This time we'll use the ten terms in sentences before focusing on the definitions in Step 2.

As you read each word, remember to pronounce it and mentally spell it, especially the latter. Although the pronunciations may not be a mystery to most of you, it's easy to misspell a word such as *liabilities*.

1. After the loan officer showed her where to list her *assets* on the form, she tried to think of everything of value that her secretarial service owned.
2. Since an accounting firm had recommended that he have an annual *audit* of his new consulting business, he alerted the staff that next month someone would be conducting an official examination of the firm's financial records.
3. The *depreciation* of their five-year-old car amounted to more than $1,000 a year; however, since it was used exclusively for business purposes, they were able to report this annual decrease in value as a tax-deductible business expense.
4. After subtracting our loans on the property from its total value, we were surprised to see how much *equity* we had in it.
5. When you consider what a wonderful relationship his business has with its customers, I can see

why he's delighted to list *goodwill* as something of value on his financial statements.

6. The bookkeeper is responsible for listing all original entries pertaining to buying, selling, and other transactions in the appropriate company *journal.*

7. After first listing transactions in the accounting records of original entry, he went to the records of final entry and transferred summaries from each journal to the appropriate company *ledger.*

8. The loan officer asked her to list her *liabilities* on the form, so she then named the debts and other financial obligations of her secretarial service.

9. Long before there were computer accounting programs that provide an electronic *spreadsheet,* he was recording financial data on a large accounting pad that had the same type of multiple rows and columns as the computerized version.

10. Declaring that an item is no longer of value and is therefore cancelled is not an unusual practice in business; many companies, in fact, regularly use the *write-off* to remove from the accounting records items that have lost their usefulness.

## STEP 2

How about it—did the sentences tell you enough to form your own definitions for the ten accounting terms? Or did you already know their meanings? If you have any doubts about any of the terms, you can double-check your understanding in this step.

In column 1, write the best term—*assets, audit, depreciation, equity, goodwill, journal, ledger, liabilities, spreadsheet, write-off*—for each brief definition given in column 2. As you read the definitions, you'll find a few italicized words (see the fourth definition in the list). A word in italics indicates that it is one of the ten terms we're learning in this exercise. Therefore, if you don't know the meaning of an italicized word, wait to complete the item in which it appears until you've finished the rest of the list.

1. _____ a multicolumn accounting worksheet

2. _____ an accounting record for making final entries, or summaries, about business transactions

3. _____ the remaining value, or net worth, of a business after subtracting loans and other claims from the firm's total value

4. _____ the good relationship of a business with its customers, often recorded in the *assets* section of the accounting records

5. _____ debts, claims, and charges against the *assets* of a business

6. _____ the cancellation of *assets* that are no longer of value and their removal from the accounting records; the items themselves

7. _____ property or other things of value owned by a person or business

8. _____ an accounting allowance for a loss in the value of

property, recorded as a business expense

9. _____ an accounting record for making original entries about business transactions

10. _____ an examination by a qualified person to check the accuracy of accounting records

ANSWERS: (1) spreadsheet (2) ledger (3) equity (4) goodwill (5) liabilities (6) write-off (7) assets (8) depreciation (9) journal (10) audit

## Step 3

Is everything clear? Don't worry if you think you should repeat Steps 1 and 2. When you're ready, use the following true-false quiz to reinforce your understanding of the meanings of the ten terms. Circle either true or false at the end of each sentence.

As you read the sentences, notice that words other than the main term of that sentence may be italicized (see *assets* in sentence 2). An italicized word means that it is also among the ten terms we're learning in this exercise.

1. A *write-off* is the cancellation of a business item that has lost its usefulness and value and its removal from the accounting records. *True   False*
2. The *goodwill* of a business, such as its good relations with customers, can be considered a thing of value along with the other company assets. *True   False*
3. *Depreciation* is the process of deciding the re-

maining value of a business by subtracting loans from the total company value. *True    False*

4. An *audit* is an accounting adjustment or allowance made for a loss in the value of property. *True    False*

5. A *spreadsheet* is a multicolumn paper or electronic accounting worksheet used in financial planning. *True    False*

6. *Assets* are physical or nonphysical things of value, such as a computer or a copyright on a book, that are owned by a person or business. *True    False*

7. *Liabilities* are the debts, charges, and claims against a company's *assets*. *True    False*

8. A *ledger* is an accounting record where original entries    are    listed    for    business transactions. *True    False*

9. *Equity* refers to the *assets* of a business before liabilities are deducted. *True    False*

10. A *journal* is an accounting record where final summaries of business transactions are listed. *True    False*

ANSWERS: (1) True (2) True (3) False (4) False (5) True (6) True (7) True (8) False (9) False (10) False

## BONUS WORDS

Can you handle ten more financial terms? We realize that financial terminology may not be among your favorite things. If it isn't, you can congratulate yourself for taking the plunge anyway and adding some important words to your vocabulary. Either way, we urge you not to skip the ten miscellaneous terms—all nouns—in this bonus section since those words may be used in future review tests.

Italicized words in the definitions refer to terms that were defined in the two previous exercises.

1. *attrition* (ə TRI shən) a gradual reduction in the value of stored merchandise (*inventories*) through influences such as spoilage, error, theft, or other loss; a natural reduction in the number and costs of company personnel through retirements, resignations, or deaths: corporate savings as a result of *attrition* amounting to $2 million a year.

2. *cash flow* (KASH FLŌ) the pattern of income and expenses of a person or company and the resulting availability of cash: the improvement in *cash flow* as his income increased while his expenses stayed the same

3. *leveraged buyout* (LEV ər ijd BĪ aut′) the purchase of a controlling interest in a company by using the company's *assets* as *collateral* to borrow the money needed to make the purchase: the *leveraged buyout* of the manufacturing company in which the value of the company's assets were used to finance the purchase

4. *liquidation* (lik′ wə DĀ shən) the process of settling the affairs of a business by paying off its debts, claims, and other obligations, usually with the aim of ending its existence as an operating entity: the planned *liquidation* of the furniture store when the owners decided to retire

5. *margin* (MÄR jən) a partial payment of money or securities, such as stocks, that an investor deposits with a broker as *collateral* in order to borrow from the broker and thus buy additional securities on credit: a required *margin* of 50 per-

cent of the purchase price of the security, with a minimum deposit of $2,000.

6. *money market* (MƏN ē MÄR kət) a market for buying and selling short-term (less than a year), low-risk investments, such as a certificate of deposit (CD): her preference for the *money market* because of the safety and ease of investing that it offers

7. *option* (ÄP shən) an agreement or right to buy or sell certain stocks, bonds, or commodities, such as grain, at a specific price within a specified time: the *option* to buy 100 shares of company stock at $50 per share within three months

8. *overhead* (Ō vər hed′) business operating expenses—including things such as rent, utilities, and taxes but excluding labor and materials—that are not directly tied to a particular unit of production or to the sale of goods and services: the rising cost of *overhead* as the cost of heat and electricity increased

9. *pecuniary interest* (pi KYÜ nē er′ ē IN trəst) a monetary interest: a house builder having a *pecuniary interest* in the outcome of the vote on restricting building permits

10. *residual value* (ri ZIJ ə wəl VAL yü) the remaining value at the end of a process or period: the leased car's *residual* value of $8,000 at the end of the three-year lease

## REVIEW TEST

How's your memory holding up? You'll soon know because this review quiz draws on words not only from this chapter but from Chapters 3 through 13. If you find that you're forgetting words from the earlier chapters, remember that the more times you work with a word, the better your chances are of remembering it. Therefore, we encourage you to repeat earlier exercises. Don't think that doing so is a sign of failure. To the contrary, it's usually a good idea.

But first, try this multiple-choice quiz. Circle the most appropriate answer—a, b, or c—in each item. Then record your score after the answer section and compare it with your score on previous review tests.

1. *Contraband* is
      (a) a band worn by *contra* rebels
      (b) illegally smuggled goods
      (c) military hardware
2. *Deduction* is
      (a) reasoning from the specific to the general
      (b) reasoning from the general to the specific
      (c) reasoning from the concrete to the abstract
3. To *expunge* is to
      (a) delete or destroy
      (b) stir up or arouse
      (c) scheme or plot
4. Something that is *bête noir* is
      (a) strongly acclaimed
      (b) strongly worded
      (c) strongly disliked
5. An *innocuous* color is
      (a) likely to offend
      (b) unlikely to offend
      (c) neither of the above
6. A *boondoggle* is a/an
      (a) impractical activity
      (b) enjoyable activity
      (c) strenuous activity

7. A *triptych* is a
     (a) planned auto route
     (b) series of road maps
     (c) three-panel work of art
8. A *debenture* is a
     (a) guarantee of loan payments
     (b) written acknowledgment of debt
     (c) person who manages another's money
9. *Microchip* is another name for
     (a) integrated circuit
     (b) central processing unit
     (c) micrographics
10. A *biorhythm* is a/an
     (a) device that measures time
     (b) musical pattern
     (c) inborn life cycle

ANSWERS: (1) b (2) b (3) a (4) c (5) b (6) a (7) c (8) b (9) a (10) c

*Correct Answers:* _____ *Incorrect Answers:* _____

# 15. Be Aware of Essential Environmental Terms

*Cleverly adapting to the harsh, dry environment of the desert Southwest, kangaroo rats can live out their entire lives without ever taking a drink of water.*

Just reading that has made us thirsty! But we were relieved to learn that these strange little creatures at least chew on moist roots and desert herbs. Perhaps that's similar to having a cup of ginseng tea instead of a glass of water.

Have you ever seen a kangaroo rat? It's an odd-looking animal—except to another kangaroo rat. Only about three inches long, it has powerful long back legs and short front legs, as well as a long tail that it can use to sit on, just like a real kangaroo.

Although the kangaroo rat is a rodent and is not related to the large Australian kangaroo, it hops around like its namesake. In fact, when two kangaroo rats get in a fight, they leap into the air and slash at each other while off the ground. The kangaroo rat is apparently the Superman of rodents, able to leap large rocks in a single bound.

One of the most noteworthy facts about the tiny creature, however, is not its acrobatic skill. More important, the life of this strange animal is a prime example of a living thing that has successfully adapted to its environment, in this case to a sometimes hostile environment where water is either scarce or nonexistent.

In one respect, we're all somewhat like the kangaroo rat (no offense intended): All living things must either adapt to their environment or die. People, fortunately, have the option of modifying an unsuitable environment to make it more hospitable.

The latter alternative is probably what space explorers will one day do—convert some cold, barren planet into a livable, earthlike environment. In Latin, *terra* means earth, so science fiction writers like to call this conversion process *terraforming*. As yet, though, residents of planet Earth are happily occupied with turning swamps and deserts into Disneylands and condominium developments. Terraforming in a faraway galaxy will have to wait.

## Environmental Words and Expressions

The word *environment* isn't a mystery to most people. But it is an especially broad term, referring to practically "everything" around us. Generally, our personal environment includes things both natural, like trees, and constructed, like a housing complex. It also includes all kinds of social and cultural aspects and influences, such as language, religion, and education. Because the subject is so broad, it would be easier to describe *specific* environments, such as the environment of Gary, Indiana, or the environment of a water lily or polar bear.

Regardless of how you approach the subject, you'll find that certain terms, such as *greenhouse effect* (defined in Exercise 1), keep popping up. We're going to begin with a few of these widely used terms and then look at some of the new environmental-protection language that we're hearing more and more nowadays.

## EXERCISE 1

Most of the ten terms in this exercise are used so often in contemporary life that they're household words—almost. But even though they may seem familiar, many of us still stumble over the definitions. We *sort of* know what people mean when they talk about an *ecosystem* or changing *demographics.* But "sort of" isn't good enough. So let's get a glass of water or find a juicy root to chew on—and begin.

Remember to pronounce and mentally spell the words—all nouns—especially the more difficult ones such as *homeostasis.* Others, such as *rain forest,* should pose no problem.

acid rain (AS əd RĀN)
biodiversity (bī′ ō də VƏR sə tē)
demographics (dem′ ə GRAF iks)
ecology (i KÄL ə jē)
ecosystem (ĒK ō sis′ təm)
ecotype (ĒK ō tīp′)
greenhouse effect (GRĒN haüs′ i FEKT)
homeostasis (hō′ mē ō STĀ səs)
photosynthesis (fō′ tō SIN thə səs)
rain forest (RĀN FÓR əst)

### STEP 1

Use the following definitions and brief examples of the ten nouns to prepare yourself for the quizzes in Steps 2 and 3.

1. *Acid rain* is precipitation (mist, rain, sleet, hail, and snow) containing acid pollutants—usually substances called "sulfuric" or "nitric acid"—principally coming from automobiles and factories: the *acid rain* that harms or even kills plants, fish, and other life where it falls.

2. *Biodiversity* refers to a given area's abundance and number of *species* (a class or group of living things, such as dogs or fish, that resemble one another and can produce offspring only with others of the same group): the extensive *biodiversity* of the Florida Everglades.

3. *Demographics* refers to the statistical characteristics of human populations, such as age and income: the advertiser's interest in the *demographics* of the New England consumer market.

4. *Ecology,* a branch of *biology* (the study of living things), refers to the study of the interrelationships among living things and their environment: the need to consider *ecology* in developing conservation policies.

5. An *ecosystem* is a particular community, regardless of size, of living things and their environment that function together as a unit: the *ecosystem* of the pond at the bottom of the hill.

6. An *ecotype* is a local population that has adapted to a particular place: an *ecotype* with slightly different physical characteristics and living habits compared to that of other members of the same species.

7. The *greenhouse effect* refers to the heating of the earth's atmosphere caused by sunlight coming in to the earth while the resulting heat is being kept from leaving because it is absorbed by gases created in activities such as burning fuel; the term comes from the similar effect in a greenhouse,

which lets light in but keeps the resulting heat from escaping: the *greenhouse effect* that may be contributing to rising temperatures around the world.

8. *Homeostasis* refers to the ability of a living thing to maintain a constant internal, or inner body, environment independent of the environment outside the body: through *homeostasis,* a person's ability to keep his or her inner body within a certain necessary temperature range even though the temperature outside the body is different.

9. *Photosynthesis* is a complex process by which green plants and certain other living things change light energy into chemical energy by producing sugar (or other energy compounds) and oxygen from water and a gas called "carbon dioxide": because of *photosynthesis,* the benefits of having houseplants that release oxygen into a room.

10. A *rain forest* is a large, dense forest receiving very heavy rainfall—about one hundred inches a year—and providing a home for a great many plants and animals: the South American *rain forests,* which are believed to contain half of all the earth's living species.

## STEP 2

Did those definitions help you feel more environmentally aware? Some of the terms, such as *rain forest,* point to topics that are fascinating as well as crucial to our survival on earth. Therefore, you may want to visit your local library and read more about such subjects in an encyclopedia or other reference work.

For now, however, let's double-check the definitions. In column 1, fill in each term—*acid rain, biodi-*

*versity, demographics, ecology, ecosystem, ecotype, greenhouse effect, homeostasis, photosynthesis, rain forest*—across from the appropriate brief definition in column 2.

1. _____    the ability of a living thing to keep a constant internal environment

2. _____    a large, dense forest receiving heavy rainfall and supporting abundant life

3. _____    a local population that has adapted to a particular place

4. _____    the abundance and number of species in a given area

5. _____    the process by which plants change light to chemical energy and give off oxygen

6. _____    the study of interrelationships among living things and their environment

7. _____    precipitation with an abnormal amount of destructive acid pollutants

8. _____    the statistical characteristics of human populations

9. _____    a particular community of living things and their environment functioning as a unit

10. _____    the heating of the atmosphere caused by gases that prevent heat from escaping

ANSWERS: (1) homeostasis (2) rain forest (3) eco-type (4) biodiversity (5) photosynthesis (6) ecology (7) acid rain (8) demographics (9) ecosystem (10) green-house effect

## STEP 3

While everything is fresh in your mind, take this next multiple-choice test to reinforce your understanding of those definitions. In each item of the next list, pick the best example or definition to fit the term mentioned on the first line. Circle your choice of either a, b, or c.

1. A *rain forest* may have rainfall up to
   (a) ten inches a week
   (b) a hundred inches a month
   (c) a hundred inches a year
2. Under the *greenhouse effect,* heat is held in by
   (a) cloud covers
   (b) gases
   (c) light energy
3. Through *homeostasis* we can keep a constant
   (a) internal environment
   (b) external environment
   (c) both of the above
4. Through *photosynthesis* plants release
   (a) water
   (b) carbon dioxide
   (c) oxygen
5. *Biodiversity* refers to the
   (a) statistical characteristics of population
   (b) abundance and number of species in an area
   (c) ability of living things to reproduce

6. Pollutants in *acid rain* include a substance called
   (a) carbohydrates
   (b) carbon dioxide
   (c) sulfuric acid
7. Ecology is the study of how living things
   (a) interact with their environment
   (b) respond to pollutants in the environment
   (c) absorb light energy and release oxygen
8. An *ecotype* is a local
   (a) population that has adapted to its environment
   (b) species that has interbred with different species
   (c) environment with many types of species
9. An *ecosystem* consists of the environment and
   (a) a small community of living things
   (b) a large community of living things
   (c) any size community of living things
10. *Demographics* commonly refers to factors such as
    (a) income
    (b) biodiversity
    (c) pollution

ANSWERS: (1) c (2) b (3) a (4) c (5) b (6) c (7) a (8) a (9) c (10) a

## Environmental-Protection Terms

*Environmental protection,* like the *environment,* is another broad term. It covers all the ideas, research, regulatory policies, efforts, and problems of controlling air and water pollution, radiation and pesticides, waste disposal, and many other factors. In fact, the term pertains to anything that affects the environment and, in turn, our own health and safety.

Take the matter of trash. This is a familiar problem, and for anyone who hates to take out the trash, it's a big nuisance. But there's more to the subject than that. Imagine saving all your daily or weekly trash collection for an entire year. On the last day you would probably have a stack of at least a hundred large bags full of trash. When you realize how much trash just one person or family collects, it's easy to see that, in general, Americans generate millions of tons of trash every year.

The most popular solution to the problem of disposing of waste is *recycling*. This term refers to the separation, collection, processing, marketing, and reuse of materials that would otherwise be thrown away. Environmental advocates of recycling promote what they call the three R's (no, not "reading, 'riting, and 'rithmetic"):

*Reduce* the amount of material you use and discard.

*Reuse* containers and products whenever possible, rather than buy new each time.

*Recycle* your trash and buy recycled products whenever they are available.

The next group of words is directly related to matters of environmental protection. It includes terms you must know to be able to understand and respond intelligently to the many serious environmental problems we're creating with some of our personal and industrial activities. As these activities put more and more stress on the natural environment, we'll no doubt hear terms such as *emissions* and *source reduction* (defined in Exercise 2) used with increasing frequency.

## EXERCISE 2

We all need to be aware of a variety of matters related to environmental protection and conservation, not just the problem of waste disposal. This exercise therefore covers terms that pertain to everything from cutting down trees to discharging dangerous gases from the cars we drive. If you're ready, then, let's get *green* (the current code word for anything involving environmental concerns).

biodegradable, *adj.* (bī′ ō di GRĀ də bəl)
clear-cutting, *n.* (KLIR kət′ ing)
composting, *n.* (KÄM pōst′ ing)
deforestation, *n.* (dē′ fȯr ə STĀ shən)
effluent, *n.* (EF lü ənt)
emissions, *n.* (ə MISH əns)
reclamation, *n.* (rek′ lə MĀ shən)
source reduction, *n.* (SŌRS ri DƏK shən)
threshold effect, *n.* (THRESH ōld′ i FEKT)
waste stream, *n.* (WĀST STRĒM)

## STEP 1

Here are the definitions. As you read them, pay special attention to the spelling and pronunciation of the more difficult terms, such as *effluent*.

1. The adjective *biodegradable* means capable of being broken down into natural substances by bacterial or other agents: the *biodegradable* paper cartons that will eventually decay in the earth.

2. The noun *clear-cutting* refers to a method of logging, or harvesting timber, in which all trees, regardless of size or age, are cut down at one time:

the danger of extensive soil erosion from *clear-cutting*.

3. The noun *composting* refers to the process of decomposition, or decay, of a mixture of matter derived from living organisms, such as plants or animals, into a soil-like material: the *composting* of leftover food, leaves, grass clippings, and animal manure to make a fertilizer for the garden.

4. The noun *deforestation* refers to the practice of clearing forest land to make room for a different type of land use: the *deforestation* of the fifty-acre timber tract so that the owner could increase the amount of pasture he needed for his livestock.

5. The noun *effluent* refers to a discharge of sewage or liquid waste into the environment from industrial processes or human activity: the *effluent* from the paper mill.

6. The noun *emissions* refers to the discharge of gas or sometimes liquid waste into the environment, especially from cars and other vehicles: the regulation of allowable *emissions* from cars, trucks, and buses to control urban air pollution.

7. The noun *reclamation* refers to the process of filling, grading, replanting, or in some other way reclaiming land that was disturbed by a natural disaster, such as a fire: the *reclamation* of cropland destroyed by the flood.

8. The noun *source reduction* refers to the act of reducing consumer purchase of things that can't be recycled or reused—plastics, dangerous materials, and other items—by reducing the use of such materials at the source, where the goods are manufactured: the government's policy of promoting source *reduction,* ultimately aimed at re-

ducing the amount and *toxic* (poisonous) nature of waste that is created.

9. The noun *threshold effect* refers to the harmful or deadly result of a small change in environmental conditions that pushes a living thing beyond what it can tolerate: the *threshold effect* that was reached in a stream when overhanging shade trees were removed, causing water temperatures to rise to a level that in turn caused some of the stream-dwelling life to vanish.

10. The noun *waste stream* refers to the ongoing flow of *all* solid waste in the country, excluding liquid and gaseous waste, especially that produced by homes and businesses: the millions of tons of solid waste moving continually in the national *waste stream* each year.

## STEP 2

How about a matching test to double-check the meanings of the ten terms? Match terms in column 1 with definitions in column 2, writing your choice of a, b, c, and so forth on the short line after each term.

1. deforestation _____

2. reclamation _____

3. threshold effect _____

4. biodegradable _____

a. the process of decay of matter from living organisms

b. a timber-harvest method in which all trees are cut at once

c. a discharge of sewage or liquid waste from human or industrial activity

d. the ongoing flow of all solid wastes in the country

5. source reduction ___

  e. the process of reclaiming land disturbed by a natural disaster

6. composting ___

  f. the harmful effect on life from a small change in environmental conditions

7. effluent ___

  g. a discharge of gas or liquid waste, especially from vehicles

8. waste stream ___

  h. capable of being broken down into natural substances by bacterial or other agents

9. clear-cutting ___

  i. reducing consumer use of nonrenewable products by reducing use at the source, or at the production level

10. emissions ___

  j. the practice of clearing forest land to make it suitable for another use

ANSWERS: (1) j (2) e (3) f (4) h (5) i (6) a (7) c (8) d (9) b (10) g

## STEP 3

Now we should be ready to reinforce those meanings. Let's use a fill-in-the-blank quiz for this step. Pick the most suitable term—*biodegradable, clear-cutting, composting, deforestation, effluent, emissions, reclamation, source reduction, threshold effect, waste stream*—for each of the following sentences.

1. As a result of extensive _____, there are now town houses and shopping centers built

where magnificent pine and spruce once blanketed the hillsides.

2. On some days, when traffic is heavy, the car _____ make the air almost unbreathable.

3. They could see the _____ at work when a large decrease in rainfall caused the disappearance of certain plant and animal life that could not tolerate the prolonged drought.

4. The advantage of _____ is that it stops the use and spread of nonrenewable products at the source, where they're produced, rather than put the responsibility in the hands of the buyer.

5. The _____ project was started after forest fires had destroyed twenty thousand acres, when the legislature decided it was important to renew the land.

6. She wished that all carry-out containers used by restaurants would be _____ so that they would eventually decompose naturally in the earth when thrown away.

7. Recycling is an appealing alternative to other waste-disposal methods, especially when you think about the millions of tons of garbage continually moving in our country's _____ _____.

8. During the rainy season the residents were troubled by repeated mud slides caused by the practice of _____, which left no trees to hold the soil.

9. People in the small town complained bitterly about the foul odor coming from the _____ that polluted the creek running through a residential area.

10. All of the neighbors practice _____,

letting the leaves, grass clippings, and even table scraps decay into an excellent soil conditioner and garden fertilizer.

ANSWERS: (1) deforestation (2) emissions (3) threshold effect (4) source reduction (5) reclamation (6) biodegradable (7) waste stream (8) clear-cutting (9) effluent (10) composting

## BONUS WORDS

We're not quite through with environmental terms. If you take time to add the following group of words to the others we just learned, you'll have a useful initial collection to help you understand and discuss environmental topics with confidence.

However, we hope that the terms you're learning for this topic—and all the others in this book—are only the beginning. Vocabulary building should be an ongoing process, not a one-time effort. But enough of the pep talk: Here are your ten bonus words—a variety of nouns and an adjective.

1. *chlorophyll, n.* (KLŌR ə fil′) the light-absorbing green-colored substance in leaves and any other green parts of most plants that is necessary for *photosynthesis* (see Exercise 1) to occur: the *chlorophyll* in the plant that traps energy from sunlight
2. *exfoliation, n.* (eks fō′ lē Ā shən)    the peeling or removal of a loose layer of rock in the form of scales or flakes; the stripping or removal of leaves from a tree or other plant: the *exfoliation* of the large rocks exposed to continual wind, rain, and other harsh effects of weather

3. *kinesis, n.* (kə NĒ səs)    the unintentional movement of an animal in response to an environmental condition or action, with the extent, nature, and rate of the movement dependent on the strength of the condition or action but not on its physical direction: the *kinesis* indicated by the more rapid panting of the prairie animals as the heat from the summer sun increased dramatically in the afternoon hours on the treeless plain

4. *leaching, n.* (LĒCH ing)    the filtering and draining of dissolved substances through the upper soil and rock layers into the deeper layers, with the downward movement occurring as the top layers become nearly saturated by precipitation or other water: the *leaching* of fertilizer dissolved in water down the plant's stem to its roots

5. *osmosis, n.* (äz MŌ səs)    the process in which water or other liquid in a solution moves through a thin, tissuelike covering (*membrane*) of a plant or animal until there is a generally equal amount or concentration of solution on both sides of the membrane: through *osmosis,* the movement of fresh water through the walls of a plant's roots to mix with the higher concentration of solution inside the roots

6. *pH factor, n.* (PĒ ĀCH FAK tər)    a measure of the acid or *alkali* (mineral salt) content of a solution, with a pH factor, or value, of 7 indicating a neutral solution, below 7 indicating acidity, and above 7 indicating alkalinity: vinegar's *pH factor* of 3 and ocean water's value of 8

7. *pollination, n.* (päl' ə NĀ shən)    the process of plant fertilization necessary for the production (birth) of a new plant, occurring with the transfer of *pollen grains,* substances usually seen as a yellowish powder, from one flowering plant to an-

other: the *pollination* that occurs in nature when wind, birds, insects, bats, and water carry pollen to flowering plants

8. *propagation, n.* (präp′ ə GĀ shən) the creation, reproduction, or birth of a plant or animal, especially the intentional multiplication or increase in numbers as a result of human activities: the *propagation* of plants carried out in a nursery to increase the inventory of new plants for sale

9. *riparian, adj.* (rə PER ē ən) pertaining to features or land use along the banks of rivers, streams, or lakes: the *riparian* vegetation along Arizona's Oak Creek

10. *watershed, n.* (WȮ tər shed′) the total land surface from which a river or other system collects its water; the total land area catching precipitation and other water that drains into a specific river or other system: the huge *watershed* of the Mississippi River

## REVIEW TEST

Now that we're all environmental experts, let's pause for a moment to see if we still remember the words we studied in other chapters. This review quiz covers terms from Chapters 3 through 14 as well as words from the current chapter. We've already done matching, fill-in-the-blank, and multiple-choice tests in this chapter. So let's end our environmental journey with a true-false test.

Read each of the following sentences and circle either true or false. Then check the answer section and record your score beneath it.

1. A *copreneur* refers to a married couple who set up and run their own business as partners. *True False*

2. The *Bering Strait* is a famous waterway passage that dissects the Antarctic Circle west of Alaska. *True False*

3. Hieroglyphs are replicas of Egyptian art painted on special paper made from a plant that grows in the Nile valley. *True False*

4. An *evidentiary fact* is a supporting fact that helps to determine the final facts a court needs to decide a case. *True False*

5. To *machinate* is to carry out one's duties in a robotlike manner. *True False*

6. The *prime rate* is the interest rate that banks charge their credit card customers. *True False*

7. An *intransigent* person is someone who is prone to drift from job to job. *True False*

8. *Biodiversity* refers to the abundance and number of species in a given area. *True False*

9. *Denotation* refers to the primary dictionary definition of a word. *True False*

10. The abbreviation *OCR* stands for "optical computer reader." *True False*

ANSWERS: (1) True (2) False (3) False (4) True (5) False (6) False (7) False (8) True (9) True (10) False

*Correct Answers:* _____ *Incorrect Answers:* _____

# 16. Add the Key Words of Health and Nutrition

> Blood vessels *is a general term for an internal network of arteries, veins, and caterpillars.*

How many of you have arteries, veins, and *caterpillars* carrying blood throughout your body? If you raised your hand, we sincerely hope that you're not planning to become a doctor. The rest of us have an internal network of arteries, veins, and *capillaries,* all of which are various types of blood vessels.

For those who haven't studied medicine, terms like *capillaries* are hard to spell, pronounce, and remember. Yet most of us want to know as many of such terms as possible because we're concerned with health and nutrition—at least to the extent that what we know or don't know will significantly affect our well-being.

You may have noticed that people talk more openly nowadays about health problems and solutions. They also talk more about prevention. Therefore, if you don't know what terms such as *free radicals* (Exercise 1) or *antioxidant* (Exercise 2) mean, you'll have trouble understanding current public discussions about health and nutrition. You also may miss some valuable information, even tips that could save you from serious or deadly health problems.

This chapter has a collection of basic health terms, both traditional and new, that you should know to be well informed. First, we'll look at common health terms, and second, we'll learn some key terms of nutrition. As always, the bonus section will have additional useful terms to add to your vocabulary.

To everyone in favor of good health and a good life, then, this chapter is for *you.*

## Words of Health

*Health* is another one of those awesome terms, like the *environment* in the previous chapter, that covers a lot of territory. It refers to the overall condition of a living thing at any given time. For a topic that broad, the most we can do in this chapter is select a group of terms that are clearly important for any vocabulary. But never fear: Plenty of medical dictionaries and other health books are available for anyone who wants to dig deeper and learn more words.

## EXERCISE 1

This group of health terms—eight nouns and two adjectives—includes some fairly general words, such as *disorder,* and some more technical terms, such as *chelation therapy.* You'll want to pay special attention to the spelling and pronunciation of the technical language. It's not uncommon to find such terms misspelled or mispronounced.

chelation therapy, *n.* (kē LĀ shən THER ə pē)
disorder, *n.* (dis′ ŌR dər)
free radicals, *n.* (FRĒ RAD i kəls)

generic, *adj.* (jə NER ik)
pandemic disease, *n.* (pan DEM ik di ZĒZ)
placebo, *n.* (plə SĒ bō′)
retrovirus, *n.* (ret′ rō VĪ rəs)
syndrome, *n.* (SIN drōm)
therapeutic, *adj.* (ther′ ə PYÜ tik)
trauma, *n.* (TRAÙ mə)

# Step 1

Let's find out what the ten health terms mean. Since most of us aren't medical experts, we'll keep the definitions as nontechnical as possible and, as usual, will use each term in a brief example following the definition.

1. The noun *chelation therapy* refers to the introduction of an agent into the body—by pills or through the veins (*intravenously*)—that attaches itself to harmful metals and minerals and helps to dissolve them so that they can be washed out of the body in the urine: the *chelation therapy* that her doctor prescribed to help unclog blood vessels in her legs.

2. The noun *disorder* refers to an abnormal mental or physical condition or disturbance of one of the functions of health: the substance-use *disorder* in which his heavy daily consumption of alcohol interfered with his job performance.

3. The noun *free radicals* refers to very small, dangerous particles in the body that cause substantial damage, such as by destroying essential proteins or by attacking and killing healthy body *cells* (the smallest units of living matter that can function

on their own): the *free radicals* that many doctors believe contribute to aging and the development of major diseases.

4. The adjective *generic* means being general or relating to an entire group or class; not having the brand name or trademark of a particular manufacturer: *generic* drugs, which are often less expensive than those produced under a specific brand name.

5. The noun *pandemic disease* refers to a general or widespread disease: the *pandemic disease* of cholera, which commonly afflicts large populations in Asia, causing acute diarrhea, vomiting, and severe loss of body fluids.

6. The noun *placebo* refers to a harmless substance prescribed by a doctor that contains no medication although the patient believes or suspects that it does; sometimes given to selected members of a group in an experiment to test and compare the reactions of those who receive a medication with those who receive a placebo: the *placebo* given to satisfy a demanding patient, who then appeared to feel better because he thought he had just received a real drug.

7. The noun *retrovirus* refers to a dangerous, sometimes tumor-producing, *virus* (a parasite that can cause infection and can reproduce only in living cells); a *retro*virus is able to reverse the normal process of *genetic* (inherited) development: the *retrovirus* HIV (human immunodeficiency virus).

8. The noun *syndrome* refers to a group of signs and symptoms that appear together with reasonable consistency and, collectively, indicate a disease or other abnormal condition: the fever, vomiting, rash, and other signs and symptoms indicating toxic shock *syndrome*.

9.  The adjective *therapeutic* means having healing powers: the *therapeutic* effect of regular exercise.
10. The noun *trauma* refers to a serious injury or shock to the body or some part of it: the *trauma* to her head caused by the car accident.

## STEP 2

How many terms did you recognize? If you're one of an increasing number of health-conscious people, you may have heard or read all of them before this. Either way, take time to double-check the meanings in this next matching test. Find a definition in column 2 to match each term in column 1. Write your choice of a, b, c, and so forth on the short line after each term.

1. retrovirus ____

a. a serious injury or shock to the body

2. therapeutic ____

b. a harmless substance given to a patient instead of an actual drug

3. pandemic disease ____

c. general; pertaining to an entire group or class

4. syndrome ____

d. the process of removing harmful metals and minerals from the body

5. disorder ____

e. having healing powers

6. trauma ____

f. a virus that can reverse normal genetic development

7. free radicals ____

g. a widespread disease

8. chelation therapy ____

h. a group of symptoms that indicate a disease or other abnormal condition

9. generic ____

    i. an abnormal mental or physical condition

10. placebo ____

    j. dangerous particles that cause damage in the body

ANSWERS: (1) f (2) e (3) g (4) h (5) i (6) a (7) j (8) d (9) c (10) b

## STEP 3

To plant those definitions firmly in your mind—and give you a chance to practice spelling the words—take this fill-in test. Write the most appropriate term—*chelation therapy, disorder, free radicals, generic, pandemic disease, placebo, retrovirus, syndrome, therapeutic, trauma*—in each sentence.

1. Attention deficit _____ is an abnormal mental condition found in very young children that causes them to have trouble sitting still and concentrating.

2. The most persistently damaging villains in our bodies are the _____ that latch onto and damage everything they touch, changing and destroying healthy cells, among other things.

3. They were saddened to learn that she had perhaps the most feared _____ of the decade—HIV.

4. Although rare in the United States, the plague is a _____ in some less developed countries; there, fleas that have bitten infected rodents and then bite humans are in abundance and rapidly spread the disease over large areas.

5. In many nursing homes, administrators have

found that the presence of animals has a soothing and _____ effect on the patients.

6. Computer operators who use repeated motions at the keyboard may be subject to carpal tunnel _____, a serious problem producing signs and symptoms of numbness, weakness, and pain in the hand and wrist areas.

7. The company wanted to test the new drug before putting it on the market, so it conducted an experiment it which half of a group were given the actual drug and the other half were given a _____ containing a harmless substance.

8. The fall from his horse caused considerable _____ to his right leg and arm as well as large cuts and bruises all along his right side.

9. She was surprised that the _____ painkiller had exactly the same ingredients as that of a well-known pharmaceutical company while it cost nearly 40 percent less.

10. After the executive started having memory lapses, his doctor suspected that he may have absorbed lead into his brain from repeated use of a hair coloring; fortunately, _____ successfully removed the lead from his body, and his brain function returned to normal.

ANSWERS: (1) disorder (2) free radicals (3) retrovirus (4) pandemic disease (5) therapeutic (6) syndrome (7) placebo (8) trauma (9) generic (10) chelation therapy

## EXERCISE 2

If topics such as "viruses" or "widespread disease" make you a little queasy, this exercise should settle your stomach. The terms we'll learn here are mostly about good things, especially things such as the beneficial nutrients that you can take *before* you get sick to prevent problems from ever occurring.

This group—all nouns—also has a few terms, such as *proanthocyanidin,* that may seem a little scary. But hang on: They're really not as difficult to deal with as they look.

adaptogen (ə DAP tō jən)
amino acid (ə MĒ nō' A səd)
antinutrient (an' tē NÜ trē ənt)
antioxidant (an' tē ÄK sə dənt)
bioflavonoid (bī' ō FLĀ və noid')
herbal extract (ƏR bəl EK strakt')
phytochemical (fī' tō KEM ə kəl)
proanthocyanidin (prō an' thō sī' AN ə dən)
supplementation (səp' lə mən' TĀ shən)
triglycerides (trī' GLIS ə rids')

## STEP 1

Do you need some time to respell and repronounce those words, especially the ones that are a big mouthful? Don't rush. When you're ready, just take a swig of your favorite health tonic and start reading the following definitions and brief examples.

1. An *adaptogen* is the root or extract of a rare *herb* (a plant used in medicine and cooking) that has the ability to return the body to good health by dealing with negative stress factors before they

have a chance to damage healthy cells; it does this work by stimulating the body's own renewal abilities and by helping cells to shield themselves from attack: the *adaptogen* known as the common dandelion, which has a much higher Vitamin A content than carrots.

2. An *amino acid* is one of about eighty *organic* (relating to living things) acids that represent the key components of *protein* (a substance found in the cells of all animals and plants); amino acids are often described as the "building blocks" of protein: the *amino acid* lysine, which is essential for growth and is also used in the repair of living tissue, such as a cold sore.

3. An *antinutrient* refers to any bacteria, pesticide, industrial *toxin* (poison), or other harmful substance that puts stress on the body's *immune* (self-protective and self-healing) system: the *antinutrient* polyunsaturated fat, a type of fat found in margarine and many vegetable oils that tends to weaken the body's ability to protect itself from *free radicals* (see Exercise 1) and other harmful invaders.

4. An *antioxidant* is any agent or substance, such as a vitamin, that prevents harmful *oxidation*—the process of a substance combining with oxygen and causing deterioration, as in butter spoiling or liver tissue becoming cancerous: the *antioxidant* Vitamin E, believed to slow the oxidation process that clogs arteries, leading to heart disease and stroke.

5. A *bioflavonoid* is a substance found in plants that in humans helps to maintain the strength of *capillary* (blood vessel) walls: the *bioflavonoid* hesperidin, found in most citrus fruits.

6. An herbal extract is an herb that has been ex-

tracted, or removed, so that the active ingredients are suspended in a liquid, such as in water or alcohol: the *herbal extract* valerian, commonly used as a sleep aid.

7. A *phytochemical* is any one of the natural, plant-based chemical nutrients common in a variety of fruits, vegetables, and grains and believed to be essential for good health: the *phytochemical* lycopene, found in tomatoes.

8. *Proanthocyanidin* is the name of a special group of *bioflavonoids* (see definition 5), often taken from grape seeds or the bark of pine trees; it is used as a powerful *antioxidant* (see definition 4) as well as a weapon against harmful *free radicals* (see Exercise 1): the *proanthocyanidin* sold under the registered trademark name *Pycnogenol.*

9. *Supplementation* is the act of adding vitamins, minerals, and other such nutritional support to one's regular food diet: her *supplementation* of the foods she ate with a multiple-vitamin tablet.

10. *Triglycerides,* a combination of a sweet substance called "glycerol" and one to three acids, are the main class of fats in the body, comprising about 95 percent of all the fats we eat; they bond with proteins in the body and are stored as a fat reserve until needed for fuel (energy): a high level of *triglycerides* stored in the bloodstream and causing weight gain.

## STEP 2

If you're exhausted after trying to spell and pronounce, let alone remember, terms such as *triglycerides,* take a short break. When you're ready, find the right term—*adaptogen, amino acid, antinutrient, antioxidant, bioflavonoid, herbal extract, phytochemical, proanthocyanidin, supplementation, triglycerides*—to match the definitions in column 2 of this next test. Write your choice in column 1.

1. _____    a group of bioflavonoids used as an antioxidant and a weapon against free radicals

2. _____    the main class of fats in the body

3. _____    an agent or substance that prevents harmful oxidation in the body

4. _____    any organic acid that is a key component of protein

5. _____    the act of adding vitamins and other such nutrients to one's regular diet

6. _____    an essential plant-based chemical nutrient common in fruits, vegetables, and grains

7. _____    a plant substance that can be used to strengthen capillaries

8. _____    an herbal root or extract that helps to restore health by stimulating the body's own renewal process

9. _____    any harmful substance that puts stress on the body's immune system

10. _____    an herb with its active ingredients suspended in water or alcohol

ANSWERS: (1) proanthocyanidin (2) triglycerides (3) antioxidant (4) amino acid (5) supplementation (6) phytochemical (7) bioflavonoid (8) adaptogen (9) anti-nutrient (10) herbal extract

## STEP 3

Is it getting easier? If the definitions of health and nutrition terms still seem like a giant muddle, keep telling yourself one thing: You'll finally know what all those magazine articles and nutrition ads are talking about as the writers casually drop terms such as *antioxidant* and *adaptogen* in the readers' laps.

Now, to reinforce those superlong words, try this true-false test. Simply read each sentence and circle your choice of true or false after each one.

1. *Triglycerides* consist of a sweet substance called "glycerol" and one, two, or three acids. *True False*
2. *Proanthocyanidin* refers to a special group of amino acids found in grape seeds and pine bark. *True False*
3. *Supplementation* is the act of adding vegetables, fruits, and grains to one's regular meals. *True False*
4. An *herbal extract* is an herb with the water and alcohol removed. *True False*
5. A *phytochemical* is a plant-based chemical found in fruits, vegetables, and grains and believed to be essential for good health. *True False*
6. An *antioxidant* is an agent used to add oxygen to substances in the body. *True False*
7. A *bioflavonoid* is a plant substance that helps maintain the strength of capillary walls. *True False*

8. An *amino acid* is one of a group of organic acids that are commonly called the building blocks of protein. *True False*
9. An *antinutrient* is a harmful substance that puts stress on the body's immune system. *True False*
10. An *adaptogen* is a rare herb that restores good health by activating the body's own renewal abilities. *True False*

ANSWERS: (1) True (2) False (3) False (4) False (5) True (6) False (7) True (8) True (9) True (10) True

## BONUS WORDS

The following are the last of the new words to be defined in the book. Should we celebrate? Before sending out the party invitations, perhaps we should wait until we've completed the final tests in the next chapter. In that case, let's proceed as usual, studying the next ten terms—all nouns—as more important words to add to your vocabulary.

1. *aerobics* (a' RŌ biks) a system of physical conditioning that emphasizes vigorous, continuing exercise to increase one's breathing and heart rate: the class in *aerobics* that she attended four days a week
2. *biopsy* (BĪ äp' sē) the removal and examination of a tissue sample from a living body to use in identifying disease, injury, or other problem: the *biopsy* that enabled the doctors to determine that the lump in her breast wasn't cancerous
3. *carcinogen* (kär SIN ə jən) a cancer-caus-

ing substance or agent: the *carcinogen* found in pesticides

4. *chemotherapy* (kē′ mō THER ə pē) a form of treatment in which a chemical substance is given to a patient to attack a disease: the *chemotherapy* used to treat his liver cancer

5. *Heimlich maneuver* (HĪM lik′ mə NŪ vər) named after its creator, surgeon Henry Heimlich, an emergency technique used on choking victims in which a thrust is applied just below the rib cage to force air out of the lungs and thereby eject any object lodged in the throat: his fast action in applying the *Heimlich maneuver* to save his uncle who had stopped breathing when a piece of carrot blocked his air passage.

6. *homeopathy* (hō′ mē ÄP ə thē) an alternative form of medical practice based on the belief that a substance causing certain symptoms in a healthy person will cure a sick person who has the same symptoms if the substance is given in extremely small doses: the use of *homeopathy* to treat *chronic* (ongoing) illness such as arthritis or allergies

7. *naturopathy* (nā′ chə RÄP ə thē) an alternative system of healing that (a) emphasizes steps to prevent disease, (b) recommends natural (nondrug) remedies that assist the body's own natural healing powers, and (c) considers the whole person (physical, emotional, mental, and spiritual) in selecting a form of treatment: the use of natural remedies such as herbs and sunlight in *naturopathy*

8. *phobia* (FŌ bē ə) a persistent, abnormal, unreasonable, or illogical fear of a certain thing or situation: her *phobia* about being the first person in a line, causing her extreme stress and anxiety.

9. *plasma* (PLAZ mə) the liquid part of blood and *lymph* (a colorless fluid that comes from body tissues) in which cells are suspended: the *plasma* that hospitals collect and store for use in surgery

10. *prosthesis* (präs THĒ səs) an artificial (human-made) replacement for a missing or an improperly working body part, such as an arm or a tooth: the *prosthesis* he needed for a defective heart valve.

## REVIEW TEST

One more time: Here are ten multiple-choice questions to test how much you've retained from past exercises throughout the book. This is the last short review test before the collection of final review tests in Chapter 17.

You know what to do—read each sentence and circle your choice of a, b, or c. Then check the answer section and record your score beneath it.

1. He used $20,000 worth of stocks and bonds that he held as *(a) goodwill (b) collateral (c) liabilities* to secure the loan he received to open a gift store.

2. As the hikers passed the large flakes of rock, they stopped to examine these signs of *(a) exfoliation (b) source reduction (c) osmosis* caused by the region's continually severe weather.

3. The attorney had five key points that he wanted the witness to respond to in writing, so he included them in the *(a) interrogatories (b) affidavit (c) subpoena.*

4. Since he had a number of questions about the

procedure in exploring different topics on the Internet, he began his computer session by checking the file of *(a) IRCs (b) WWWs (c) FAQs.*

5. The computer technique of *(a) infomercial (b) morphing (c) broad-brush* is used in commercials to make one object appear to change into another.

6. The correct term for a white, powdered substance used in place of sugar is *(a) saccharin (b) saccharine (c) saccharene.*

7. Their lavish lifestyle included endless expensive parties in one of their *(a) luxurious (b) luxuriant (c) luxurient* condos.

8. Once the disease has progressed to a certain point, it is generally *(a) illimitable (b) ephemeral (c) irreversible,* and efforts to cure it are changed to efforts simply to control it.

9. She always had an unselfish concern for others, but lately, this *(a) altruism (b) asceticism (c) narcissism* has been replaced with very selfish personal concerns.

10. In the interests of good customer relations, he seemed to feel that he should *(a) vitiate (b) accede (c) attenuate* to their demands, but I would have said no.

ANSWERS: (1) collateral (2) exfoliation (3) interrogatories (4) FAQs (5) morphing (6) saccharin (7) luxurious (8) irreversible (9) altruism (10) accede
*Correct Answers:* _____ *Incorrect Answers:* _____

# 17. Take a Final Review Test

*The end is the very best beginning you'll ever find.*

That may sound like a riddle, but it isn't. It's actually a popular sentiment expressed by many people throughout the ages. It was also said by the same English teacher that, in Chapter 2, suggested looking over the next hill and around the next bend when pursuing a goal. Since that early suggestion turned out to be sound advice, we no doubt should pay serious attention to this final suggestion as well.

What does it mean that the end is the best beginning? You probably already know the answer. It means that by the time you reach the end of a goal or project, everything you've learned puts you in a much better position to begin other new ventures or just to begin each new day better equipped to be successful.

The fact that you've come this far in your vocabulary-building work means that you're better qualified to handle the coming challenges in your life and enjoy a far greater measure of success than was possible before you began. Therefore, the end of this book should really signify a new beginning for you. From now on you'll have a more powerful stock of words to draw on in dealing with the personal, social, and professional challenges that life brings.

However, although you've finished all the regular exercises in the book, we're not quite at the end. This chapter has your final review test—actually, a series of ten-item review tests. This is your last chance to test how much you've retained from the exercises in Chapters 3 through 16.

You may find that you're not remembering what all the new words mean. Your score following each answer section in this chapter will suggest how much you've retained. If you find that you're not scoring well above 50 on the tests (refer to the grading chart in Chapter 2), go back and repeat the problem exercises. In the index you can find the page where particular words were first introduced.

Don't worry if you need to repeat exercises. By now you know that practice—over and over—is an effective tool in vocabulary building. As we've said before, the more you work with a word, the better your chances of remembering it.

But first, let's see how you do. Here are your *final* review tests: Good luck!

## FINAL TEST 1

This fill-in test will review the use of nouns that we learned in Chapters 3 and 4. Those two chapters focused on words that name people, places, and physical or nonphysical things.

Notice that a group of twenty nouns precedes the ten test items. Your task is to pick a word from this group that accurately completes each of the ten sentences in the test and to fill in that word on the blank line.

After you've chosen ten words for the test, compare your selections with the answer section and record your score below it.

| | |
|---|---|
| allusion | mosaic |
| analogy | Napoleon |
| archetype | Neapolitan |
| assimilation | Newton, Sir Isaac |
| collusion | nuance |
| Edison, Thomas | Riviera |
| extrapolation | Saudi |
| Fertile Crescent | Saudi Arabian |
| insinuation | syllabus |
| Levant | Wilson, Samuel |

1. Writers, speakers, and teachers frequently prepare a summary outline of their paper, speech, or course of study. A common name for this type of summary outline is _____.

2. Often called the greatest inventor in the world, this man—who lived from 1837 to 1931—invented the phonograph, the lightbulb, and more than a thousand other items. His name is

   _____.

3. People and companies have many types of relationships and work together in many ways. Usually, such cooperation is beneficial to all. But sometimes they secretly agree to cooperate for an illegal or deceitful purpose. This type of undesirable, and usually unethical or illegal, action is called _____.

4. We use names that describe people who live in a specific city or country. For example, someone who lives in Los Angeles is known as a *Los An-*

*gelean.* Someone who lives in Australia is known as an *Australian.* What would we call someone who lives in Saudi Arabia: _____?

5. A large semicircle of fertile land skirts the edge of the great Syrian desert from the Persian Gulf to the southeastern coast of the Mediterranean Sea. What is the name of this rich area of land: _____?

6. An English mathematician and physicist, who lived from 1642 to 1727, is credited with inventing differential calculus. Supposedly inspired by a falling apple, he also developed the theory of universal gravitation. His name is

_____.

7. A popular surface decoration is made by inserting or setting into a surface small pieces of variously colored material to form a picture or pattern. For example, ceramic tile might be set into the surface of a coffee table to form the image of a deer. The word that identifies this type of surface decoration is _____.

8. Recalling the explanation given in test item 4 for naming residents of cities and countries, what is the correct name for someone who lives in Naples, Italy: _____?

9. Sometimes we make statements that compare two things that are similar in some respect, although not necessarily in all ways. For example, we might refer to a politician who makes vicious comments about an opponent as an attack dog. This type of comparison is called an

_____.

10. In addition to the harmful action described in test item 3, another type of action may also have harmful results for some. When people skillfully make a subtle or indirect comment that suggests

something unfavorable about another, they have made an _____.

ANSWERS: (1) syllabus (2) Thomas Edison (3) collusion (4) Saudi (5) Fertile Crescent (6) Sir Isaac Newton (7) mosaic (8) Neapolitan (9) analogy (10) insinuation

*Correct Answers:* _____ *Incorrect Answers:* _____


## FINAL TEST 2

The second quiz will test your retention of words that enrich and strengthen your vocabulary by adding life, clarity, and color to it. In Chapter 5, for example, we learned action words, especially active verbs, that add life and energy to your messages. In Chapter 6 we learned words that add clarity and color—adjectives that describe.

For this test we'll list twenty words that you learned in Chapters 5 and 6. Then, in column 1 of the test, we'll provide words that are similar to some in the list of twenty. Your assignment is to pick a word from the group of twenty that could logically be substituted for each word(s) in column 1 of the test.

For example, the first word in column 1 is *intervene*. Your task is to look through the group of twenty words preceding the test to find one that has a similar meaning and to write your selection on the blank line across from *intervene*.

Here are the twenty words from which you can select substitutes to write in column 2 of the test.

| | |
|---|---|
| arcane, *adj.* | decennial, *adj.* |
| conciliate, *vb.* | deprecate, *vb.* |
| construe, *vb.* | diurnal, *adj.* |

| | |
|---|---|
| efficacious, *adj.* | reprove, *vb.* |
| ephemeral, *adj.* | supersede, *vb.* |
| eschew, *vb.* | tenacious, *adj.* |
| immutable, *adj.* | tertiary, *adj.* |
| intercede, *vb.* | triennial, *adj.* |
| omnipotent, *adj.* | usurp, *vb.* |
| protract, *vb.* | vitiate, *vb.* |

1. intervene _____
2. explain _____
3. scold _____
4. seize _____
5. third _____
6. brief _____
7. ten-year _____
8. replace _____
9. belittle _____
10. daily _____

ANSWERS: (1) intercede (2) construe (3) reprove (4) usurp (5) tertiary (6) ephemeral (7) decennial (8) supersede (9) deprecate (10) diurnal
*Correct Answers:* _____ *Incorrect Answers:* _____

## FINAL TEST 3

Test 3 will quiz you on your ability to tell apart words that are easily confused because they seem similar in some ways. In Chapter 7, for example, we learned words that are easily confused because they have the same beginning or ending. In Chapter 8 we learned words that are often confused because they are generally pronounced the same (*homophones*) or are spelled the same (*homographs*).

To find out if you can successfully tell these words

apart, we'll give you a definition, and your assignment is to supply a word that matches it. Pick the correct word for each definition from the group of easily confused pairs preceding the test. Then write your choice on the blank line in column 2 across from the definition.

Here are the pairs from which you can choose words to match the definitions. Keep in mind that the differences in meaning between words in a pair may be slight or substantial. Also, notice that in two cases—*resoluble* and *recession*—the words in the pair are spelled the same but are pronounced differently. For those words, write only the pronunciation on the line in column 2 of the test.

|  |  |
|---|---|
| adherence, *n.* | explicit, *adj.* |
| adherents, *n.* | implicit, *adj.* |
|  |  |
| adverse, *adj.* | extended, *adj.* |
| averse, *adj.* | extensive, *adj.* |
|  |  |
| complementary, *adj.* | resoluble, *adj.* (rē SÄL yə bəl) |
| complimentary, *adj.* | resoluble, *adj.* (ri ZÄL yə bəl) |
|  |  |
| connotation, *n.* | recession, *n.* (rē SESH ən) |
| denotation, *n.* | recession, *n.* (ri SESH ən) |
|  |  |
| disorganized, *adj.* | veracious, *adj.* |
| unorganized, *adj.* | voracious, *adj.* |

1. being large, vast, or broad      _____
2. being clearly defined or          _____
   expressed

3. transferring back to a former owner    _____

4. being honest or accurate    _____

5. serving to complete or add to    _____

6. being strongly opposed to    _____

7. capable of being dissolved again    _____

8. not having a leader or unity    _____

9. sticking to or being devoted to    _____

10. a suggested meaning beyond the dictionary definition    _____

ANSWERS: (1) extensive (2) explicit (3) rē SESH ən (4) veracious (5) complementary (6) averse (7) rē SÄL yə bəl (8) unorganized (9) adherence (10) connotation

*Correct Answers:* _____ *Incorrect Answers:* _____


# FINAL TEST 4

This multiple-choice quiz will test you on language you shouldn't use with everyone, such as foreign words, jargon, and idioms; the words you should avoid entirely, such as slang, discriminatory language, and clichés. We learned such words and expressions in Chapter 9 and 10.

This time we want you to complete the phrase on line 1 of the test by picking the appropriate response from the three choices that follow. First, read the top line and notice the italicized word—a word you learned in Chapter 9 or 10. Then select the phrase that best completes the top line, circling your choice of a, b, or c.

1. An *ingenue* would most likely enjoy
   (a) home and family
   (b) a business career
   (c) nice clothes and dinner parties
2. *Ageism* is a
   (a) type of advertising aimed at the elderly
   (b) form of discrimination against a certain age group
   (c) form of discrimination against the elderly
3. The Chinese word *Tao* refers to a
   (a) state of sadness over the state of the world
   (b) guiding principle of all reality
   (c) deep appreciation of art and music
4. A person or company with a *flatliner* has a/an
   (a) unsuccessful product
   (b) memorable line in an ad
   (c) dull response to someone or something
5. A *pro forma* agreement is made or done
   (a) unofficially
   (b) on standardized forms
   (c) as a formality
6. A more acceptable expression for *jaundiced eye* is
   (a) yellow journalism
   (b) prejudiced view
   (c) colorful outlook
7. A legal plea of *nolo contendere* is a statement of
   (a) complete guilt with a request for mercy
   (b) partial guilt with no special requests
   (c) no contest, without claiming guilt or innocence
8. A *checkered career* usually means one with
   (a) more failures than successes

(b) more successes than failures

(c) nothing but failures

9. The noun *bête noir* means

(a) someone or something strongly disliked

(b) full, unrestricted power to act

(c) an unlikely solution to a problem

10. A *factoid* is assumed to be true because

(a) it is factual

(b) it appears in print

(c) neither of the above

ANSWERS: (1) a (2) b (3) b (4) a (5) c (6) b (7) c (8) a (9) a (10) b

*Correct Answers:* _____ *Incorrect Answers:* _____

# FINAL TEST 5

This fifth quiz is a two-part test that deals with word forming, the subject of Chapter 11. There we learned how to attach prefixes and suffixes to already existing words to form new words. The following paragraphs describe what to do in Parts 1 and 2 of the test. After you've finished each part, check the answer section and record your score as usual.

## PART 1

To test your word-forming skills, we'll first provide a list of prefixes and suffixes. Your assignment is as follows: For this first part of the test, pick five prefixes from the list to attach to the beginnings of five words **given in** the test. Then pick five suffixes to attach to **the ends** of five words given in the test. Keep in mind that it may be necessary to drop or change letters in a word when adding a suffix.

Sometimes the same prefix or suffix can be used with different words. But in this test you should use a particular prefix or suffix only once.

When you're ready, write the prefixes and suffixes on the first blank line, and write the new words you've created on the second blank line. For example:

*pre-* + arrange = *prearrange*
dark + *ness* = *darkness*

To begin, here is a collection of prefixes and suffixes.

| *Prefixes* | *Suffixes* |
|---|---|
| ante- | -arium |
| counter- | -cide |
| extra- | -cy |
| geo- | -ent |
| hydro- | -ible |
| intra- | -ion |
| mono- | -ive |
| neo- | -ment |
| supra- | -or |
| trans- | -ule |

1. _____ + balance = _____

2. _____ + conservative = _____

3. _____ + electric = _____

4. _____ + diluvian = _____

5. _____ + magnetic = _____

6. demean + _____ = _____

7. collect + _____ = _____

8. solvent + _____ = _____

9. planet + _____ = _____

10. node + _____ = _____

ANSWERS: (1) counter-/counterbalance (2) neo-/neoconservative (3) hydro-/hydroelectric (4) ante-/antediluvian (5) geo-/geomagnetic (6) -or/demeanor (7) -ible/collectible (8) -cy/solvency (9) -arium/planetarium (10) -ule/nodule

*Correct Answers:* _____ *Incorrect Answers:* _____

## PART 2

The second part of the test gives you a chance to check your understanding of the new words you just formed. Each of the words appeared in one of the exercises of Chapter 11. To test your understanding of the meanings, match the new words listed in column 1 with the definitions in column 2. Small letters precede the column 2 definitions so that you can write the appropriate letter—a, b, c, and so forth—on the short line after each new word in column 1.

Notice that there are eleven definitions in column 2 but only ten new words in column 1. One definition, therefore, will not be used.

1. antediluvian _____

    a. the way in which one behaves or conducts or demeans oneself

2. counterbalance _____

    b. an item prized by others and suitable for or worthy of collection

3. geomagnetic _____

    c. a former liberal, or new conservative, who supports intellectual and political conservatism

4. hydroelectric _____

    d. a model of the solar system; a device projecting planets and other bodies onto a dome; the building housing such things

5. neoconservative _____    e. the quality of being suggestive or tending to call to mind

6. demeanor _____    f. generating electricity by converting the energy of running water

7. collectible _____    g. existing before the biblical diluvial deluge (the great flood)

8. solvency _____    h. relating to the attractive force, or magnetism, of the earth

9. planetarium _____    i. a small mass, node, knot, or growth

10. nodule _____    j. to offset or balance with an equal or contrary force

   k. the condition of being solvent or able to meet financial obligations

ANSWERS: (1) g (2) j (3) h (4) f (5) c (6) a (7) b (8) k (9) d (10) i

*Correct Answers:* _____ *Incorrect Answers:* _____

# FINAL TEST 6

Law is the subject of the sixth test. Here we'll be checking your retention of the legal terms learned in Chapter 12.

This is a standard multiple-choice type of test used throughout the book. Your task is to pick the most appropriate term—a, b, or c—for each sentence.

Circle your choices and compare them with the answers below the test. Don't forget to record the number of correct and incorrect answers on the last line.

1. She credits old *Perry Mason* movies for her interest in criminal *(a) escheat (b) jurisprudence (c) probate.*

2. The damaging, malicious comments he made about his neighbor at the fund-raiser on Friday are grounds for charges of *(a) slander (b) libel (c) malfeasance.*

3. The court order providing for *(a) adjudication (b) garnishment (c) contravention* of her wages forced her employer to begin paying her weekly check to the bank where her loan was past due.

4. The *(a) corroborating evidence (b) circumstantial evidence (c) extrinsic evidence* that he provided was exactly the additional information the attorney had hoped to receive to strengthen his case.

5. During the *(a) acquittal (b) interrogatories (c) arraignment* the accused listened passively to the charges against him.

6. Because of the U.S. Constitution's provision that prohibits *(a) double jeopardy (b) proximate cause (c) vicarious liability,* the verdict of "not guilty" means that there won't be a second trial.

7. The formal written statement made under oath was a/an *(a) attestation (b) subpoena (c) affidavit* confirming that the legal paper was delivered to the defendant in the lawsuit.

8. When someone dies, a conventional last will and testament has to go through *(a) adjudication (b) probate (c) affirmation* before the person's estate can be settled.

9. The government's right to take private land for public use by providing just compensation is con-

firmed under the principle of *(a) eminent domain*
*(b) Draconian law (c) forbearance.*
10. The public official who was caught in the act of
    tampering with contract awards was promptly
    charged with *(a) encroachment (b) laches (c)*
    *malfeasance.*

ANSWERS: (1) b (2) a (3) b (4) a (5) c (6) a (7)
c (8) b (9) a (10) c
*Correct Answers:* _____ *Incorrect Answers:* _____

## FINAL TEST 7

Test 7 will examine your retention of the information-
technology words and abbreviations learned in Chapter 13.

This is a true-false test, similar to those used in the
previous chapters. Read each sentence carefully and
circle your choice of true or false. Then check the
answer section and record your score beneath it.

1. The technology of *fiber optics* refers to a high-
   speed process in which information can travel
   long distances over sound waves.  *True   False*
2. The term *microchip* is another name for "integrated circuit."  *True   False*
3. The word *upload* means to use a computer and
   the telephone lines to copy electronic files from
   another computer system into your own system.
   *True   False*
4. *Emoticons,* also called "smileys," are typed symbols that computer users insert in their messages
   to indicate emotion, such as winking or laughing.  *True   False*
5. *Encryption* refers to the changing or scrambling

of computer data into a secret coded form to prevent people who don't have the necessary password from reading it. *True   False*

6. *Micrographics* is the process of reducing full-size documents to miniature images and storing them on film. *True   False*

7. *ASCII* stands for "Associated Standard Code for Internet Interchange," a code that represents letters, numbers, and symbols as digits that can be used by computers. *True   False*

8. A *queue* is an assigned sequence, or order, of computer data or programs awaiting processing, one after the other. *True   False*

9. *Hypertext* is a computer text retrieval system in which you can open and search several files at the same time, without having to close one when you move on to another. *True   False*

10. *OCR* stands for "optical character recognition," a process used to recognize and convert digital information into standard, human-readable text. *True   False*

ANSWERS: (1) False (2) True (3) False (4) True (5) True (6) True (7) False (8) True (9) True (10) False

*Correct Answers:* _____ *Incorrect Answers:* _____

## FINAL TEST 8

This eighth quiz will test you on the financial terms we learned in Chapter 14, including basic financial terms and those used in accounting and other financial record keeping.

For this test we'll provide a list of twenty terms. Your assignment is to pick those that best fit the definitions provided in the test. Fill in your choices in column 2 across from the matching definition.

Here is your collection of financial terms for Test 8.

| | |
|---|---|
| acceleration clause | liquidation |
| assets | margin |
| audit | negotiable instrument |
| debenture | option |
| equity | par value |
| goodwill | prime rate |
| journal | promissory note |
| ledger | rollover |
| leveraged buyout | spreadsheet |
| liabilities | write-off |

1. another name for face value or nominal value as printed on a stock or bond certificate _____

2. the cancellation of assets that are no longer of value and their removal from the accounting records _____

3. the practice of continually renewing short-term loans, reinvesting profits, or moving funds from one investment to another _____

4. an accounting record for making final entries, or summaries, about business transactions _____

5. a written promise to pay a certain sum of money on demand or on a certain date _____

6. an agreement or right to buy or sell certain stocks, bonds, or commodities at a specific price within a specified time  _____

7. debts, claims, and charges against the assets of a business  _____

8. a written acknowledgment of debt, such as unsecured bonds, made by the issuer  _____

9. the remaining value, or net worth, of a business after subtracting loans and other claims from the firm's total value  _____

10. property or other things of value owned by a person or business  _____

ANSWERS: (1) par value (2) write-off (3) rollover (4) ledger (5) promissory note (6) option (7) liabilities (8) debenture (9) equity (10) assets
*Correct Answers:* _____ *Incorrect Answers:* _____

# FINAL TEST 9

This test reviews environmental words and expressions and environmental protection terms. We learned both types of words in Chapter 15.

Test 9 is a fill-in-the-blank quiz. We'll provide a collection of terms from which you can choose. Your task is to pick appropriate terms for the ten sentences in the test.

After you've written your choices on the blank lines

in the test, check the answer section and record your score as usual.

Here are the terms for you to use in the test.

acid rain               exfoliation
biodegradable           greenhouse effect
biodiversity            homeostasis
clear-cutting           leaching
deforestation           osmosis
demographics            pH factor
ecosystem               rain forest
ecotype                 reclamation
effluent                source reduction
emissions               threshold effect

1. For many years scientists have been talking about the effects of sunlight coming in and heating the earth while the heat is being absorbed by gases that prevent it from escaping. These gases are caused by human activity, such as burning fuel. Some say that temperatures are rising around the world because of this process, called the

   _____.

2. Floods and fires are two of nature's most devastating occurrences. They claim tens of thousands of acres of land each year. Fortunately, it is often possible to replant, refill, or in some other way reclaim the lost land. This process of restoring what was lost is called

   _____.

3. Changes in environmental conditions affect plants and animals as well as humans. If rainfall diminishes or ceases, for example, those living things that can't adjust to the change will suffer or die. When a small change pushes a living thing

beyond what it can tolerate, the result is called the _____.

4. Sometimes an animal or plant population changes to survive in a particular place. It adapts to the different environment. For example, it may grow taller or shorter. It may require more or less water. Or it may adapt to local conditions in another way. This type of local population that adapts to the change is called an _____.

5. Scientists have a way of measuring the acid or salt (alkali) content of a solution. Depending on the content, they assign a value of 7 (neutral) or something less (tending to have acidity) or more (tending to have alkalinity). This value is known as the _____.

6. As we reach the limits of where and how to dispose of waste material, environmentalists look for new ways to reduce the amount of trash. One strategy involves reducing the use of materials that can't be reused. Many believe that the place to put this policy into practice is at the production level, where the goods are manufactured. This policy of going to the source to reduce materials that can't be reused is called _____.

7. When you water and fertilize a plant until the top layers of soil are saturated, the dissolved substances filter down into the deeper layers of rock and soil. This filtering or draining process is called _____.

8. Environmentalists like products that, when thrown away or buried in a landfill, can decompose or break down into natural substances. This is good for the earth and in part helps to solve the problem of increasing amounts of garbage.

Products that are naturally broken down by bacteria or other agents are _____.

9. You may have noticed a farmer clearing trees and shrubs from a forested area and later planting crops where once the trees stood. This process of clearing forest land to make room for a different type of land use is called _____.

10. Rain, sleet, snow, and other forms of precipitation have been found to have high sulfuric and nitric acid content. These substances, which principally come from automobiles and factories, cause the precipitation to be so polluted that it sometimes kills fish, plants, and other life where it falls. The popular name for such polluted rainfall is _____.

ANSWERS: (1) greenhouse effect (2) reclamation (3) threshold effect (4) ecotype (5) pH factor (6) source reduction (7) leaching (8) biodegradable (9) deforestation (10) acid rain

*Correct Answers:* _____ *Incorrect Answers:* _____

# FINAL TEST 10

This is the last test of the book—a multiple-choice quiz. In this case we'll check your retention of key words in health and nutrition, the subject of Chapter 16.

Your assignment is to complete the opening line of each test item. In that opening line, the italicized word is one of the terms we learned in Chapter 16. Circle your choice of a, b, or c in each item.

To complete the test, check the answer section and

record the number of your correct and incorrect answers.

1. *Chelation therapy* involves the
   - (a) effect of natural healing techniques
   - (b) removal of harmful metals from the body
   - (c) process of stimulating the body's immune system
2. *Bioflavonoids* are naturally occurring substances in
   - (a) plants
   - (b) animals
   - (c) humans
3. *Triglycerides* primarily consist of
   - (a) glycerol and water
   - (b) glycerol and acids
   - (c) glycerol and alcohol
4. An *antioxidant* prevents the occurrence of
   - (a) pollutants
   - (b) viruses
   - (c) oxidation
5. A *retrovirus* will commonly reverse normal
   - (a) genetic development
   - (b) chemotherapeutic development
   - (c) carcinogenic development
6. An *adaptogen* tends to stimulate the
   - (a) oxidation process
   - (b) growth of fat cells
   - (c) body's renewal ability
7. *Proanthocyanidin* refers to a/an
   - (a) special group of bioflavonoids
   - (b) powerful chemical agent
   - (c) experimental cancer drug
8. *Free radicals* are believed to
   - (a) attack toxins in the body

(b) destroy healthy cells
(c) prevent harmful oxidation

9. A *pandemic disease* is a
   (a) disease with plaguelike symptoms
   (b) disease caused by a virus
   (c) widespread disease

10. Compared to brand names, *generic* drugs tend to be
    (a) less expensive
    (b) more expensive
    (c) the same price

ANSWERS: (1) b (2) a (3) b (4) c (5) a (6) c (7) a (8) b (9) c (10) a

*Correct Answers:* _____ *Incorrect Answers:* _____

## REVIEW

Can you believe it? You've finished a very serious program of vocabulary building. We hope, though, that it wasn't all work. We also hope it stimulated some interest in the subjects that were covered—enough so that you're tempted to go to the library and read more about your favorite topics. Finally, we hope that your dictionary is now one of your favorite and most valued books and that it shows a suitable amount of wear and tear.

If you've decided that you need to review some of the earlier exercises, we'll see you there. But if you scored so high on the tests that you're ready to move on, we'll say good-bye and wish you great success in your next venture.

Before you leave, though, pause with us a moment to reflect again on the opening quote: "The end is the very best beginning you'll ever find." In that sense, this really isn't the end; it's the beginning. Wherever you travel from here, you'll be armed with a much more powerful vocabulary—and a good friend. That's what words are—your friends. We hope you'll enjoy them each day of the rest of your life.

# Index

The index consists of words that are defined in Chapters 3 through 16. The page number following each word is the place where the word is first introduced.